Recent Titles in
Contributions in Political Science

Neocolonialism American Style, 1960–2000
William H. Blanchard

Government Structures in the U.S.A. and the Sovereign States of the Former U.S.S.R.:
Power Allocation Among Central, Regional, and Local Governments
James E. Hickey, Jr. and Alexej Ugrinsky, editors

Roman Catholicism and Political Form
Carl Schmitt
Translated and annotated by G. L. Ulmen

International Theory: To the Brink and Beyond
Andrew P. Dunne

To Sheathe the Sword: Civil-Military Relations in the Quest for Democracy
John P. Lovell and David E. Albright, editors

President Reagan and the World
Eric J. Schmertz, Natalie Datlof, and Alexej Ugrinsky, editors

Ronald Reagan's America
Eric J. Schmertz, Natalie Datlof, and Alexej Ugrinsky, editors

Germany for the Germans? The Political Effects of International Migration
Wesley D. Chapin

Out of Russian Orbit: Hungary Gravitates to the West
Andrew Felkay

Ideas of Social Order in the Ancient World
Vilho Harle

Voting Rights and Redistricting in the United States
Mark E. Rush, editor

Democratization in Late Twentieth-Century Africa: Coping with Uncertainty
Jean-Germain Gros, editor

EISENHOWER'S EXECUTIVE OFFICE

Alfred Dick Sander

Contributions in Political Science, Number 386

GREENWOOD PRESS
Westport, Connecticut • London

Library of Congress Cataloging-in-Publication Data

Sander, Alfred Dick.
    Eisenhower's executive office / Alfred Dick Sander.
       p.   cm.—(Contributions in political science, ISSN 0147–1066
 ; no. 386)
    Includes bibliographical references and index.
    ISBN 0–313–30922–1 (alk. paper)
    1. United States.   Executive Office of the President.
2. Presidents—United States—Staff.   3. United States—Politics and
government—1953–1961.   I. Title.   II. Series.
JK552.S35   1999
352.23'7'0973—dc21   98–28289

British Library Cataloguing in Publication Data is available.

Copyright © 1999 by Alfred Dick Sander

Library of Congress Catalog Card Number: 98–28289
ISBN: 0–313–30922–1
ISSN: 0147–1066

First published in 1999

Greenwood Press, 88 Post Road West, Westport, CT 06881
An imprint of Greenwood Publishing Group, Inc.

Printed in the United States of America

The paper used in this book complies with the
Permanent Paper Standard issued by the National
Information Standards Organization (Z39.48–1984).

10 9 8 7 6 5 4 3 2 1

To Barnesie, Sam and
The Ricker

Contents

Introduction

By 1952 Dwight Eisenhower was confident of his ability to organize and direct the affairs of man. His army training together with his successful command of the most complex military operation in history had convinced him of the value of organization.[1] After over half a century of experience with group mechanisms, large and small, he thought himself well equipped to bring the organization of the presidency to new heights.

Although almost all of his experience had been as a military officer, his years in Washington had brought him into frequent contact with the Executive Office of the President. It was inevitable that he would compare what he found there with what he considered sound organization. He was not being immodest when he wrote that with his "training in problems involving organization it was inconceivable to me that the work of the White House could not be better systematized than had been the case during the years I observed it."[2] Eisenhower felt so strongly about his talents as an organizer and the inadequacy of the Executive Office under Harry Truman that he made it an issue in the presidential campaign of 1952. He promised that if he were elected he would improve the organization and effectiveness of the National Security Council and the Bureau of the Budget.[3]

For the first time a presidential candidate had made the organization of the presidency an issue in his campaign. Eisenhower's determination to honor this commitment provides the rationale for this book. It affords an opportunity to develop a case study of how much or how little a president committed to the reorganization of the Executive Office could accomplish within the constraints of the federal environment. What follows is an organizational history of the Executive Office of the President from 1953 through 1960 that assesses the effectiveness of Eisenhower's management of his office.

THE EXECUTIVE OFFICE IN 1953

When Eisenhower came into office the budget bureau told the new president that

while the Executive Office of the President has existed since 1789 when President Washington first assumed office, action taken in 1939 first gave institutional recognition to the staff units in the office and augmented them. . . . A conscious attempt has been made to develop procedures among the agencies and the presidential staff units so that the President can control "choke points" which supply him, through his staff, with intelligence concerning agency proposals and activities and with controls which he may exercise.[4]

The Executive Office came into existence on 1 July 1939 when Congress approved Reorganization Plan No. 1.[5] This plan, which transferred the Bureau of the Budget and the National Resources Planning Board to this newly created office, had been sent to Congress earlier that spring by Franklin Roosevelt at the urging of Louis Brownlow. The proposal was made possible by the Reorganization Act that gave the president the authority to submit reorganization plans that would have the force of law if both houses of Congress did not reject them within sixty days. Roosevelt had approved the Reorganization bill on 3 April 1939.[6] This law extended to the president the power and funds to appoint six personal administrative assistants. The act thus marked the beginning of a significant White House staff.

The Executive Office of the President (EOP) was first defined in Executive Order No. 8248 which Roosevelt signed on 8 September 1939, a few days after the German invasion of Poland initiated World War II. FDR's purpose in signing the order was to maintain presidential control of the economic mobilization agencies that would be created as the United States responded to the war. From the president's point of view the most important part of the EOP was the Office of Emergency Management which served as the organizational home of the myriad agencies created during the war.[7] These mobilization organizations, whose establishment caused a rapid expansion of the EOP, were never intended to be permanent. When the last of the agencies, the Philippine Alien Property Administration, was abolished on 15 June 1951 the Office of Emergency Management became inactive.[8]

The establishment of the Executive Office of the President began the institutionalization of the president's staff. While Roosevelt was focused on the immediate problem of the mobilization agencies, his adviser, Louis Brownlow,
saw the executive order as a device to define the EOP. In addition to the Office
of Emergency Management the order established the Bureau of the Budget,
the National Resources Planning Board, an Office of Government Reports, a
Liaison Office for Personnel Management, and a White House Office. Since
then the Bureau of the Budget (now the Office of Management and Budget)
has become the president's right arm. But the remainder of Roosevelt's executive office has had a more transitory existence. Congress abolished the National
Resources Planning Board in 1943, while the Office of Government Reports
disappeared in 1946.[9] Then the Eisenhower administration abolished the Liaison Office for Personnel Management by Executive Order 10452 of 1 May
1953.[10] As a result the budget bureau and the White House Office are all that
still remain of Roosevelt's original EOP.

With the end of war the Truman administration gradually eliminated the
wartime agencies. The most important of these, the Office of War Mobilization and Reconversion (OWMR), had become virtually a part of the White
House staff by 1946. The head of the OWMR, John R. Steelman, became *the*
Assistant to the President and brought key members of his staff to the White
House with him.[11] Steelman and his assistants became an important component of the White House staff that Truman had begun to assemble.

THE BUREAU OF THE BUDGET

When Eisenhower became president, the Executive Office of the President
consisted of the White House Office, the Bureau of the Budget, the Council of
Economic Advisers, the National Security Council, and the National Security
Resources Board. The Bureau of the Budget had been established in 1921 for
the express purpose of coordinating departmental budget requests before they
were submitted to Congress. The bureau examiners worked directly with the
various departments, checking their figures, the programs they represented,
and the efficiency of their administration. In 1939, when the bureau was transferred from the Treasury Department to the Executive Office of the President,
its functions were broadened to include administrative management and economic analysis. During the Truman years the bureau added the important legislative clearance function. A bureau office began reviewing and controlling all
of the legislative requests coming from the executive branch, supplying congressional committees with information and helping to develop the State of

the Union Message. In many ways the bureau became virtually an adjunct to the White House staff.[12]

The end of the OWMR allowed the Bureau of the Budget to regain its position as the dominant element in the Executive Office. Its influence was further enhanced during the first years of the Truman administration as most of the experienced members of Roosevelt's staff departed and the new president needed time to assemble a White House staff of his own. James E. Webb, Truman's first budget director, increased the bureau's power by infiltrating the growing White House staff with his own men and by ensuring a high quality of staff work from his agency. Because of Webb's efforts Truman's concept of the bureau's proper function was broadened and he began to see it as a neutral force whose judgment could enhance the quality of his administration. Many consider the Webb years as the golden age of the Bureau of the Budget.[13]

During Truman's administration the first Hoover Commission examined the budget bureau as well as most of the rest of the executive branch. The task force that looked specifically at the bureau was headed by well-known accountants from some of the large firms. They were traditionalists who believed that these new functions diverted the bureau from its primary mission of administering the budget. Their critical analysis of the budget bureau shocked many of its members. Their recommendations prompted Frederick Lawton, a careerist who served as Truman's last budget director, to reorganize the bureau in 1952. The thrust of the changes made was to base the bureau's activities on the examiners' function and include within these groups that worked directly with the departments and agencies administrative and fiscal analysts, management specialists, and economists.[14] This new organizational structure of the bureau was in place when Eisenhower became president.

THE COUNCIL OF ECONOMIC ADVISERS

An unforeseen result of the Employment Act of 1946 was the establishment of the Council of Economic Advisers (CEA) within the Executive Office of the President. Harry Truman favored the statute (which some intended to commit the federal government to the concept of full employment) but he did not welcome the prospect of being "advised" by professional economists. However, politically he had no choice but to sign it. Truman, without any clear concept of the role the economic council would play in his administration, allowed his appointments to it to be guided by pressure from a variety of sponsors. The first CEA chairman, Edwin Nourse, was a professional economist who wanted to make the council a nonpartisan mechanism for bringing the best professional judgment to bear on the economic problems of the country. The other two members, Leon Keyserling and John Clark, owed their appointments to the sponsorship of two powerful Democratic senators. While Keyserling and Clark had professional training as economists, they were both intense partisans who saw the council as a political instrument that should be used in vigorous support of the president's program.[15]

The history of the Council of Economic Advisers is a striking demonstration of the truism that although Congress can create an advisory body for the president, it cannot force him to take the advice it offers. Nourse tried for over two years to engage Truman in an intellectual discussion of economic issues. But the president avoided these technical discussions, possibly because he was relatively ignorant of the terms and techniques used by economists and was not anxious to display this lack of background. It seems clear that Truman did not consider the council a significant part of his staff and liked to get his advice from businessmen, politicians, and lawyers. When Nourse finally resigned in frustration Truman named Keyserling as chair by default. Truman still did not welcome advice from the council, but under Keyserling's direction it became an active agent in support of the president's program. However, Keyserling's partisanship was so strident that Congress sought to destroy the council by denying it any funds after March 1953.

THE NATIONAL SECURITY COUNCIL

The National Security Council and the National Security Resources Board were established by the National Security Act of 1947. The primary purpose of the legislation was to unify the armed forces. Its passage came only after a bitter struggle by the U.S. Navy against it. The navy secretary, James Forrestal, and his friend, Ferdinand Eberstadt, had proposed the establishment of a national security council and a board to plan for mobilization as a stratagem to avoid unification. In the chaos of the legislative process the plot failed, and these coordinating devices were created along with a Department of Defense. Again Truman, who favored unification, had to accept two new staff groups he did not want in order to achieve his larger objective.[16] In 1949, in an effort to tidy up the organization charts, the Hoover Commission recommended and Congress approved a statute formally placing the National Security Council (NSC) and the National Security Resources Board (NSRB) within the Executive Office of the President.

Ironically Forrestal became the first head of the Defense Department he had sought to abort. However, he accepted his new assignment with enthusiasm and decided that he could use the NSC as a device to control the development and conduct of foreign policy. Since the president and his staff were aware of

Forrestal's plan to seize control of both the NSC and NSRB, they maneuvered against it. To make sure the NSC was not used to subvert his presidential powers Truman (on the advice of the budget bureau) rarely attended its meetings before the Korean War and, to foil Forrestal, arranged for the secretary of state to preside in his absence. The White House also made sure that the executive secretary of the NSC knew he was the president's man rather than Forrestal's and that the council did not have their meetings at the Pentagon. Prior to the Korean war the NSC was able to marginally improve the coordination of political-military affairs, but because of the bureaucratic infighting and lack of presidential interest, it had not developed into the deliberative body that many had hoped it would become.[17]

THE NATIONAL SECURITY RESOURCES BOARD

The NSRB was a unique experiment in the American government experience. Its seven-year existence was turbulent in part because of inherent flaws in its organization and mission. Clearly it was awkward to have a presidential staff unit (the board) that was also a subcommittee of the Cabinet (it consisted of seven of the nine Cabinet officers) meeting under the chairmanship of a presidential appointee. Its mission was to engage in peacetime mobilization planning, but there was no clear understanding of what this was or whether it should be a military or civilian responsibility. Add to this mix a struggle for control of the NSRB by Forrestal and Eberstadt on one side and the White House aided by the budget bureau on the other, and it became a recipe for disaster. It is not surprising that the NSRB had a series of chairmen and was never able to determine what its mission should be.

The ambitious and politically adept Stuart Symington became chairman of the NSRB shortly before the outbreak of the Korean War. He sought to have his agency designated to direct the mobilization for war. The main obstacle he faced was the belief of the president and the budget bureau that the NSRB should be a staff planning unit with no operating responsibility or authority. Until China entered the war it was expected that the war would be brief and that the mobilization would be limited. Since no one knew what a "limited" mobilization entailed, the issue of what role the NSRB should play was not joined initially. The work that the NSRB had done previous to the war was used as the basis of the Defense Production Act that was passed in September 1950. The bureau advised the president to retain all of the new mobilization power granted by this act and to use Symington simply to help him coordinate the activities of the regular departments in carrying them out. This was the situation when the involvement of China made it an entirely new war.

Concern in Washington rapidly escalated to panic, and on 15 December 1950 Truman declared a national emergency. The president asked the budget bureau to study the mobilization problem and make recommendations. The bureau suggested some conservative adjustments in the existing mobilization arrangements that were quite different from the sweeping changes that were made. The new organization that was established was the result of a breakdown in communications between the bureau and the president and the demands of Charles E. Wilson. Truman was determined to have his mobilization effort headed by the stately and dignified Wilson. And Wilson, who had an unhappy tenure in Washington during World War II, was determined not to become involved in mobilization again unless he became a "Deputy President." The result was the Office of Defense Mobilization (ODM), a much more elaborate mechanism for economic mobilization than the Korean emergency required.[18]

THE TRANSITION PERIOD

In the fall of 1952 the budget bureau began making plans for the change of administrations. It was known that General Eisenhower was concerned about the Executive Office because he had made the Bureau of the Budget and the National Security Council the subject of specific remarks during the campaign.[19] In October Elmer Staats, a longtime member of the bureau and then its deputy director, chaired a meeting to consider what actions the bureau should recommend that the new president take in respect to the Executive Office. It was obvious that the future of the Council of Economic Advisers had to be addressed because the appropriations for Fiscal Year 1953 contained no monies for the CEA for the fourth quarter which then began on 1 March 1953. The three-man structure of the council was a problem because it made it difficult for the council to assume leadership and take initiative in the government-wide economic problems. Many in the bureau were inclined to support the recommendation of the Hoover Commission that the CEA be replaced by a single economics adviser for the president.[20]

The bureau organizational analysts had for some time been aware of weaknesses in the structure of the National Security Council. While the NSC was recognized as a tremendous step forward over the situation that had existed in diplomatic-political coordination during the Roosevelt administration, it was clear that it had not yet achieved working procedures that would permit it to meet all of the criteria set for its performance. Its practices sometimes produced situations in which several different interpretations of what the policy was could be extracted from the same paper.[21] The Staats group thought the NSC organization encouraged logrolling that resulted in "lowest-common-denominator" advice to the president.[22]

Others in the bureau wanted to see a complete and searching reexamination of the whole Executive Office concept. They believed the Brownlow group had been guided by "certain naive concepts of public administration borrowed from the scientific management movement in United States industry." The resulting organizational elements of the EOP had come into existence on a piecemeal basis and were ill-adapted to helping a president develop national policies and programs. They believed the conceptual framework of the Executive Office should not view the president primarily as a business manager but as political leader of the nation who is also head of one of the two major political parties.[23]

Very soon after the election Eisenhower announced that Joseph Dodge would become his budget director. Dodge, who had considerable government experience and knew how to make things happen in Washington, immediately began meeting with bureau officials and making his own assessment of what had to be done.[24] In respect to the Executive Office he identified the most immediate problems as (1) should the NSRB continue and if so in what form; (2) what should be done with the various agencies reporting to the Office of Defense Mobilization; and (3) what to do about the economic council.[25] It was clear that the new administration intended to design its own Executive Office and that some of changes would come quickly.

As Eisenhower prepared to assume the responsibilities of the presidency, he also received advice from the firm of Coates and McCormick. It had made a study of the executive branch in an effort to isolate for the president-elect the organizational problem areas he would need to remedy. Among its conclusions was the clear need for reorganizing the Executive Office. They found that the present organization of the EOP had been shaped by political considerations and a series of diverse plans that had been revised to meet various emergencies. The report claimed that "faulty administration, both in important matters and in minor ones, has often been demonstrated" by units in the executive office.[26]

Coates and McCormick also identified what they termed fundamental organizational weaknesses. These included the absence of any systematic machinery for determining policy or coordinating it afterwards. They did not feel the Cabinet had ever worked properly nor had its real functions ever been determined. The Bureau of the Budget had not been effective in controlling expenditures because it had been too concerned with detail and not enough with fiscal policy. And finally the National Security Council needed to be reorganized if it was to be effective in formulating policy and coordinating activities in the area of national security and foreign policy.[27]

To consider these and other proposals to improve the functioning of the executive branch the president-elect established a "Special Committee on Government Organization" to develop recommendations for immediate improvements in organization and management. It was chaired by Nelson Rockefeller and included Eisenhower's brother Milton and Arthur Flemming, both of whom had had wide experience in the executive branch. The fact that Eisenhower asked his brother, whom he considered his most intimate adviser, to serve on this committee is indicative of the importance he assigned to this subject. Of overarching importance was the belief that the entry of the new Republican administration provided a unique opportunity to improve the federal government after years of Democratic misrule.[28]

NOTES

1. Dwight D. Eisenhower, *The White House Years: Mandate for Change, 1953–56* (Garden City, N.Y., 1963), pp. 114–115.

2. Ibid., p. 87.

3. "Federal Organization and Management Problems," 14 November 1952, E2–24/52.1, Series 52.6, RG 51, National Archives (henceforth NA).

4. "The Presidential Job in Organizing and Managing the Executive Branch," Series 52.6, E2–50/52.2, RG 51, NA.

5. For a history of the development of the Executive Office through 1952 see my *A Staff for the President: The Executive Office, 1921–1952* (Westport, Conn., 1989).

6. Richard Polenberg, *Reorganizing Roosevelt's Government: The Controversy Over Executive Reorganization, 1936–1939* (Cambridge, Mass., 1966), p. 187.

7. Ibid., pp. 33–40.

8. PACGO Memo, "Presidential Level Organization," 25 October 1960, 52.6, E2–50/57.2, RG 51, NA.

9. Sander, *A Staff for the President*, pp. 35–60.

10. PACGO Memo, "Presidential Level Organization."

11. Sander, p. 100.

12. Ibid.

13. Ibid., pp. 152–169.

14. Ibid.

15. Ibid., pp. 106–115, 131–142.

16. Ibid., pp. 201–232.

17. Ibid., pp. 233–269.

18. Ibid., pp. 337–353.

19. "Federal Organization and Management Problems," 14 November 1952, E2–24/52.1, Series 52.6, RG 51, NA.

20. Ibid.

21. Appendix B, NSC, E2–50/52.1, Series 52.6, RG 51, NA.

22. Ed Strait to Files, 30 October 1952, E2–50/52.1, Series 52.6, RG 51, NA.

23. "Reorganization of Central Mobilization Management Agencies," M7–51, Series 52.6, RG 51, NA.

24. Carl M. Brauer, *Presidential Transitions: Eisenhower through Reagan* (New York, 1986), p. 17.

25. "Most Immediate Organizational Problems, Executive Office," BOB 1952, Series OF 72–B, NA. Official Files (hereforth OF), Dwight D. Eisenhower (henceforth DDEL).

26. Memorandum II, 4 November 1952, Executive Office Reorganization (1), Whitman Name File, DDEL.

27. Ibid.

28. Committee Organization, 12 January 1953, Administration No. 3, PACGO, DDEL.

1

The White House Office

The White House Office (WHO) was created in 1939 as a unit within the Executive Office of the President. Since then it has become a significant part of the institutionalized presidency, but the only thing "institutional" about the WHO has been its name. Its organizational structure has been the most fluid part of the Executive Office because each succeeding president has devised his own scheme for organizing and staffing it. As a result the WHO has always been the most personal element in the Executive Office of the President.

Before the twentieth century, presidents had to pay for part of their staffs from their own pockets. To reduce their costs they began the practice of detailing personnel from the departments to work in the White House. This practice continues today. Gradually Congress authorized clerks, typists, messengers, and military aides but, until Hoover's time, only two professionals: a secretary and an administrative assistant. Roosevelt added a correspondence secretary, a press secretary, and a special counsel. In 1939, Congress, as part of the Reorganization Act of that year provided the president with six more administrative assistants without any specific assignments. This was substantially the extent of the White House Office when Eisenhower became president.[1]

Roosevelt's White House was not a model of efficiency. Truman complained that it took him two months just to clean up the collection of unattended business that he found when he assumed the presidency. Truman was proud of the progress he made and by 1951 was bragging that he had installed "the best administrative setup the White House had ever enjoyed."[2] Some felt there was still room for improvement. When Republican analysts were sent to observe WHO operations as part of the transition to the new administration, they found that policy planning was not systematic, the staff members frequently failed to work as a team, and the White House had no coordination machinery such as a staff secretariat.[3]

CHIEF OF STAFF

John Steelman wanted to be chief of Truman's staff. For that reason, when he was offered a position in the White House, Steelman had insisted that his title be "*The* Assistant to the President." Truman went along with the title when he got the position authorized, but he did not agree with the function that Steelman had in mind for himself. In fact, as Truman's staff structure evolved, the president began acting as his own chief of staff and was determined to remain in that role. He presided over his own staff meetings. Six mornings a week the president himself met with the senior members of the staff to assign tasks and to lay out the day's appointments.[4]

One of Eisenhower's first administrative concerns as president-elect was to devise a White House structure that would best suit his management style. He was not new to the Washington scene, but it had been a shock to him "to find the lack of coordination in the White House." Eisenhower was sure he did not want to continue the model that Truman had gradually and painfully developed as he had coped with the demands of the office.[5]

Eisenhower believed that the creation of an effective personal staff was one of the most important things a president could do to assure an efficient national government.[6] He thought it obvious that the White House staff had to be coordinated within itself by a responsible head. With definite ideas acquired through his years of military experience about how staffs should be constructed and perform, it was probably inevitable that Eisenhower should base his White House organization on the army prototype.[7] The result was Eisenhower's major organizational innovation of the presidency: the establishment of a White House chief of staff.[8]

The idea that the White House needed a chief of staff was not original with Eisenhower. In the 1920s C. E. McGuire had discussed its possibilities in an article in the *Harvard Graduate's Magazine*. Since then most of the major studies that had been made of the federal organization had proposed the establishment of a central administrative official who would be the president's principal assistant. Most recently, in 1949, the first Hoover Commission had called for an expanded White House Office to include a staff secretary and a special assistant for national security.[9]

Eisenhower had decided he wanted a chief of staff even before he was elected, and naturally thought of appointing a military officer such as Walter Bedell Smith or Alfred M. Gruenther. But he soon recognized that this would convince many that the military was now going to dominate the federal government.[10]

After the election, Henry Cabot Lodge was offered an appointment as either the principal assistant to the president or as Ambassador to the United Nations. When Lodge chose the latter post Eisenhower for a time toyed with the idea of asking Herbert Brownell to head the White House staff but eventually he decided that he preferred Brownell to be his attorney general. It was then that he asked Sherman Adams, his friend and former campaign manager, to be his chief of staff.[11] Initially Adams seemed reluctant to take the job. After he finally accepted the post Eisenhower told him that he intended to accord Cabinet rank to the position.[12]

To carry out his plan Eisenhower took Steelman's old title, "The Assistant to the President," and assigned it to Adams. Eisenhower effectively created a White House chief of staff by simply making it clear that Adams would be his principal assistant.

During World War II Eisenhower's then chief of staff, Walter Bedell Smith, had to carry out many difficult decisions. He felt that he had spent much of his army career as "Ike's prat boy, doing his dirty work."[13] Though in many ways an unpleasant role, it was one at which Smith excelled. It is not surprising that Eisenhower sought someone with a personality similar to Smith's to preside over his White House staff. One of those who worked with Adams characterized him as "a rather high-strung man with a short fuse, very conscious of his power and authority, and a bit of a martinet, and every now and then given to an outburst." He jealously guarded his position as the president's principal assistant and in many ways served as chief of the Executive Office as well as the White House staffs.[14] Clearly Eisenhower had not misjudged his man and soon the Adams style set the tone of the new White House.[15]

Eisenhower was aware that Adams "had no time for flattery or cajolery, or even pleasantries over the telephone" but he also saw him grow in the job that he created as he went along.[16] One reason Adams developed a reputation for incivility was the strain due to the enormous amount of work his new position required. Adams was not involved in policy-making, but he served as the coordinator of all of the president's domestic concerns. These included appointments, schedules, patronage, personnel, press, speechwriting, Cabinet liaison, and congressional relations. It was his task to make sure that the policy advice the president was sent from many sources was properly staffed out before it reached the Oval Office and that there were no end runs. Once Eisenhower

made a decision it was Adams's job to make sure that it was accurately communi-
cated back down the line. Although he was the most powerful person on the
White House staff, Adams was not Eisenhower's sole channel for information
and policy recommendations nor did he have the authority to restrict the access of most top administration officials who wanted to see the president.[17]

The staff that Adams headed grew substantially over the next eight years.
During the Eisenhower's tenure the number of professionals in the White
House Office increased almost 300 percent. These people were in turn supported by a large secretarial contingent. As a result, the total number employed
at the White House increased from 250 to over 400 from 1952 to 1960. There
were several reasons for this. One was Eisenhower's desire to increase the efficiency of the government by improving the coordination of policy. But the
principal reason was the president's desire to have his own expert advisers in
fields ranging from basic science to air traffic control.[18]

Like most presidents, Eisenhower tended to select his White House staff
from among those who had worked closely with him during the campaign.
Eisenhower deliberately chose his staff from this group because he believed
that their long experience of working together would make it much easier for
them to develop into a real team. Within a few weeks the new president was
pleased that his new staff was "rounding into shape rapidly."[19]

People who excel as operatives during political campaigns frequently do not
make good staffers in the White House because the talents required in the two
positions are so different. Unfortunately, presidents usually discover this truth
by trial and error. Apparently Eisenhower did not feel that this truism applied
to his staff. Twenty-two of the original thirty-two members of the Eisenhower
WHO had worked in his campaign, many on the campaign train. Of the others, five had worked for the general during his army years and two had been
members of his staff at Columbia. Remarkably a dozen of them remained on
his staff throughout his presidency.[20]

ECONOMIC ASSISTANT

One of those who successfully made the transition from speechwriter on the
campaign train to key White House staffer was Gabriel Hauge. Born in Minnesota, son of a minister, Hauge received a Ph.D. in economics from Harvard
in 1947 and went to work in the New York State Department of Banking.
There he came to the attention of Governor Thomas E. Dewey. Later, while
Hauge was working as an editor for *Business Week* magazine, Dewey got him
involved in the presidential campaign as Research Director for Citizens for
Eisenhower. When his candidate was nominated, Hauge became the general's

full-time economics speechwriter. He had a good deal of personal contact with Eisenhower while traveling on the campaign train as his duties broadened to general speechwriter and other tasks. From then on those who had been "on the train" would have a special relationship to the candidate.[21]

Dewey recommended that Eisenhower appoint Hauge as his adviser on economic matters in the White House. Such a position had not existed before and, while Eisenhower was particularly interested in economics, he doubted that he needed a personal adviser in that field. He also feared that a presidential adviser in economics would get in the way of his relationship with the Council of Economic Advisers, which was then in a state of disarray. But Adams persuaded Eisenhower to hire Hauge for his general versatility in addition to his economic expertise.[22] In 1953 he was appointed to the White Office as one of the six statutorily authorized administrative assistants.

Although he was only thirty-eight years of age when he joined the president's staff, Hauge soon became a key player. One of his jobs was to review the recommendations of the Tariff Commission and prepare position papers for the president's consideration. Sherman Adams recalls that none of these were ever changed before the president signed them.[23] But his role was more than economic advisor. He served also as "utility man, troubleshooter, economic watchdog and implementer."[24] One of his coworkers valued Hauge as "as sound, able and likable a fellow as I ever knew."[25] A member of the Council of Economic Advisers considered Hauge a fine economist who had "a keen appreciation of political power and people's motivations."[26]

In May 1955 Hauge received an offer to become the dean of the Harvard Business School. Eisenhower told him that "it would be a most bitter blow if you left me at this time" and pleaded with Hauge to stay with him through his first term. He confided to him that he did not intend to seek the nomination for a second term barring some emergency in "our national or international affairs."[27] Hauge stayed, and in 1956 was rewarded by being elevated to "Special Assistant for Economic Affairs." He finally did leave the White House in 1958 to join Manufacturers Hanover Trust. In his memoirs Eisenhower identified Hauge as one of the seven men he knew who had the necessary qualities to be president of the United States.[28]

Don Paarlberg, an agricultural economist on leave from Purdue University, replaced Hauge as the White House economic adviser. He had arrived in Washington at the beginning of administration as a political appointee in the Department of Agriculture. He was an effective professional, but since he had not been "on the train," he did not have the close personal relationship with the president that Hauge had enjoyed.[29] Paarlberg limited his speechwriting efforts to agricultural topics and continued to counsel the president on recommendations of the Tariff Commission. His aim was to maintain a low profile and keep troublesome matters off the president's desk. Paarlberg was forceful in urging Eisenhower to submit a balanced budget to Congress near the end of his administration.[30]

LEGISLATIVE LIAISON

Another Eisenhower White House staff innovation was the formal establishment of a congressional liaison office. Of course presidents had always tried to influence Congress, but in 1953 for the first time there was an organization in the White House charged with regular formalized contact with Congress. Franklin Roosevelt and his agents had exerted great pressure to get Congress to follow the White House lead, but Congress had resented this presidential interference in legislative matters. As a member of the Senate during those years Harry Truman shared the congressional attitude. When he became president Truman overreacted. He adopted such a soft approach toward Congress that his influence was minimal. By 1949 Truman had, however, instituted weekly meetings with the "Big Four" of Congress: the vice president, the speaker, and the majority leaders of both houses. He did not begin this practice until the 81st Congress when Democrats occupied these offices.[31]

Early on Eisenhower had decided he wanted a congressional liaison office in his White House, and he was sure he knew who its head should be: Jerry Persons. Major General Wilton B. (Jerry) Persons was one of the president's oldest army friends. Persons had spent fifteen years of his military career assigned to the Pentagon as the army's congressional lobbyist. Before he retired after World War II he had become a lobbyist for the entire Department of Defense. When Eisenhower returned to active duty in 1951 to establish the North Atlantic Treaty Organizsation (NATO) Persons again put on his uniform, this time to serve as Ike's special advisor. Active in the 1952 presidential campaign, Persons had traveled "on the train" to provide liaison between congressional Republicans and the candidate. Eisenhower believed Persons was probably acquainted with more members of Congress than anyone else in Washington.[32]

Eisenhower gave Persons the other five administrative assistant slots the White House staff was authorized. He soon assembled a staff for his legislative liaison office rich in congressional experience. Besides Bryce Harlow, who had worked for the House Armed Services Committee and doubled as one of the president's chief speechwriters, Persons's staff included at various times Gerald Morgan, onetime legislative counsel for the House; Jack Martin, Senator Robert A. Taft's longtime legislative assistant; Jack Z. Anderson, a former member of Congress; Edward McCabe, the erstwhile chief clerk of the House Labor

Committee; Earl Chesney; and General Gruenther's brother Homer. The staff met daily to discuss strategy and on Tuesdays joined the president when he met with the Republican congressional leaders. These meetings served as the foundation of Eisenhower's legislative leadership.[33]

TRADITIONAL STAFF APPOINTMENTS

A White House chief of staff, an assistant for economic matters, and a legislative liaison office were innovations that Eisenhower had committed himself to before he was inaugurated. By December 1952 he also had decided whom he wanted to name to the traditional parts of the White House staff: the appointments secretary, special counsel, and press secretary. Like the others, these positions also went to members of the Eisenhower campaign train support staff. James Hagerty, a respected newspaperman who had once advised Dewey on matters of the press and had served Eisenhower in that capacity during the campaign, now assumed that role in the White House. Thomas Stephens, another former Dewey aide, had become Eisenhower's appointments man on the train. Although Stephens was originally slated to become the White House special counsel, Eisenhower got him to continue as appointments secretary. In this position he became the person who "somehow is supposed to be able to leave everybody happy who wants to see the President and can't, and to induce those people who do get in to see the President, to hold to the schedule. All of this takes all the Irish wit and humor that came with Stephens when he left County Cork at a very early age and came to this country."[34]

SPECIAL COUNSEL

Truman used his special counsel in various roles depending on the incumbents' skills and interests. When he inherited Sam Rosenman from Roosevelt, Rosenman continued his job as speechwriter but he also became a vital factor in educating the new president and developing much of the Fair Deal program. His successor, Clark Clifford, focused on foreign and military affairs while becoming Truman's political confidant and the dominant member of the White House staff. When he left Charles Murphy took over Clifford's staff leadership role while continuing to serve as Truman's legislative technician.

Eisenhower tended to limit his special counsel to legal and legislative matters. The appointment initially went to a Harold Stassen supporter and New Jersey lawyer, Bernard Shanley. He became close to Eisenhower while working on the campaign train and then did legal work for the president-elect. He came to Washington reluctantly as Adams's deputy and agreed to work as special counsel only until they found someone else but stayed in the job four years.[35] Gerald D. Morgan, a lawyer with Capitol Hill experience, then replaced him. Near the end of the administration Eisenhower named David Kendall, a Michigan lawyer, to the post.[36] Roger Jones, head of the budget bureau's legislative reference unit, worked closely with Shanley for several years. He characterized him as

a successful lawyer, successful not so much in terms of personal outstanding intellect as in terms of capacity to instill confidence and loyalty in others. . . . basically a politician in many of his reactions to things, but he had enough respect for the intellectual honesty of the people and for the institutional product so that he would submerge the political kind of thing.

Jones thought that Morgan had a better mind but had none of Shanley's self-assurance. Morgan worked harder but Shanley got on better with the president.[37]

During the early part of the administration Eisenhower took relatively little interest in congressional matters. Shanley said that

it was a process of learning to a great extent on the President's part. I could not get him to take strong affirmative action on legislation except to veto and the prerogatives that he held as President with Congress. He felt very strongly in his school-book days that, he learned in civics in high school, that there were three branches of government and he had no right to interfere with the legislative branch.[38]

Roger Jones had a similar recollection—that at first Eisenhower looked on his job as ministerial rather than executive, "but after we began to explain to him things like the legislative veto and the conflict with the Bricker Amendment, he fast became a great constitutionalist in his own right."[39]

Shanley got into the legislative area accidentally. When he became Special Counsel he intended to confine himself to legal work, but Adams had such a heavy load that he asked Shanley to handle the administration's legislative program. A few days later Roger Jones of the budget bureau's legislative reference stopped by his office to get acquainted, and Shanley confessed to him that he was completely lost and did not know how to get started. He did not know how to put a program together. Fortunately, he did know what Eisenhower

thought because we had spent so much time together. I never had any problems worrying about whether he would approve or disapprove because I knew he would back me up, number one, even if I was wrong, and, of course, I was wrong a number of times. And when I was he always supported me. But I pretty well knew the policies. And if I had any doubt, Sherman and I were together all day long, and there wasn't an important meeting at the White House that he and I weren't there.[40]

So Roger Jones provided the experience and continuity and Shanley put the Eisenhower spin on the departmental legislative proposals. Shanley discovered that the budget bureau was made up of "very, very smart people, and they soon realized that the programs Mr. Truman had advocated were not going to be the programs that the Eisenhower administration was going to propose." As time went on Shanley found that most of his job "became almost like sitting like a judge involved with the departments and agencies of the government to determine specific policies on questions and, when we did, we stuck to them. And we didn't have people running up to the Hill cutting the legs off the administration."[41]

The process of building Eisenhower's legislative program consisted of asking the departments what they wanted for the coming year and having them make presentations to Adams and Shanley in the Cabinet room with Jones and others from the budget bureau's legislative reference staff present to pick up on "technical problems." According to Shanley, he and Adams would cut the "fat" from the departmental proposals on the spot or send them back to the departments to be reworked. After passing this hurdle the proposals went to Eisenhower sitting with his Cabinet. If they survived this stage they were presented to the Republican legislative leaders.[42]

PACGO

One of the first actions that Eisenhower took when he assumed the presidency was to convert the group that had been giving him organizational advice in the preinaugural period into an official unit in the Executive Office of the President. By Executive Order 10432 of 24 January 1953 he created the President's Advisory Committee on Government Organization (PACGO). The members continued to be Nelson Rockefeller, Arthur Flemming, and Milton Eisenhower. Some suspected that a major reason for the establishment PACGO was to get Milton to spend more time in Washington.

Arthur Flemming had first come to Washington in 1927 right out of college. He spent his first night in town in Milton's apartment. The two became close over the years while working in various parts of the federal government. Their common interests were enhanced when each eventually became a college president. During the war Flemming was a member of the Civil Service Commission and was the government's representative on the War Manpower Commission. Later he served as a member of the Hoover Commission and in Truman's Office of Defense Mobilization.[43]

When Eisenhower asked Flemming to become a member of PACGO he explained to him the relationship he wanted to have with the group. The president said that he would from time to time want to try out ideas on the committee; that he also expected us to try out ideas on him. He urged us at that time to make immediate contact with the members of his cabinet and talk with them about their ideas, and see what we could do about coming up with plans designed to implement their ideas.

Flemming found the work of PACGO was greatly facilitated by Milton's membership. Many times the committee would discuss an idea and Milton would volunteer to try it out on his brother when he saw him that evening and report back to the group.[44]

The purpose of this group then was to provide Eisenhower with a continuing consultative body that would meet with him periodically to consider the major policy implications of various possible changes in the organization of the executive branch. It also considered and advised the president on reorganization proposals emanating from other sources. Service on the committee was a part-time responsibility because Rockefeller and Flemming had full-time positions in the administration and Milton Eisenhower was a university president. Rockefeller served as chairman until he left in 1958 to become governor of New York.[45] He was replaced by Don K. Price, and Flemming became chairman.

The committee had a small staff headed by Arthur A. Kimball but relied on the budget bureau for research and analysis of proposals.[46] Many in the bureau considered the mere existence of PACGO evidence of the president's lack of confidence in their organizational experts. In 1959 William Finan, the head of the bureau's management group, recommended that the PACGO staff be liquidated and that he assume the responsibility for supporting the committee's work. He thought this would result in the expenditure of less effort on the part of his staff than it then spent in supporting the committee.[47] By this time the enmity between the two staffs was intense.

STAFF SECRETARY

Eisenhower's passion for order and organization prompted him to adopt several recommendations that the first Hoover Commission had made in 1949 but that Truman had rejected. In making their recommendations the commission had pointed out that "there is no one place in the President's Office to which the President can look for a current summary of the principal issues with which he may have to deal in the near future." As a remedy they suggested the establishment of a staff secretary's office. The Hoover Commission ideas were taken up by PACGO. It recommended, in early January 1953, that a White House staff secretariat be established to work under Adams's general supervision.[48]

Others proposed a similar remedy. In 1952 W. Y. Elliott, a Harvard political scientist then working for Truman's Office of Defense Mobilization, deplored the "mishmash" in the organization of the Executive Office. He called for the establishment of a "chief secretary" who would be "empowered by the President to act as the coordinating center for information and for follow-up on Presidential policies and orders."[49]

As president, Eisenhower found that people came to him with many good ideas and suggestions but as an individual he was unable to sort them out, see that they were directed to the proper department, and then followed up.[50] He was also troubled by the problem of keeping track of commitments he made during interviews and decided that a member of his staff should sit in on all except very few of these conferences.[51] These were the kinds of functions that could be done by a central secretariat in the White House.

During the spring of 1953 Eisenhower asked Carter Burgess to study the White House operations and make recommendations for improvement. He was an organizational expert the president had known during his army days who was now assistant secretary of defense for manpower. One of Burgess's recommendations was to establish a staff secretariat.[52] The idea was a familiar one to a person with the president's military background, since it had been a common practice in the army for a secretary to the general staff to record decisions and keep track of the actions taken to implement them.

In July Eisenhower told his military aide, Army Brigadier General Paul T. Carroll, that he was now his acting staff secretary.[53] Carroll had worked for Eisenhower for a long time as his aide at the Pentagon and at NATO headquarters. In the president's eyes Carroll could never be simply the White House staff secretary because he viewed him as a general assistant. Carroll quietly assumed his additional responsibilities in July 1953 when he circulated a note to the staff announcing that the "functions previously performed by Dr. Hauge in preparing the agenda have been passed to the recently created White House staff secretariat."[54]

The staff secretariat was composed of generalists whose job it was to look at every paper that went through the Oval Office. This White House nerve center was a small, low profile unit that controlled the flow of correspondence to ensure that everyone who could contribute to a task had an opportunity to do so.[55] Eisenhower tried to make sure that the staff secretary was always in the Oval Office when decisions were being made and orders given so that there would be an official record of presidential actions.

In the Truman White House the political and the national security staffs rarely interacted. Truman got his daily intelligence briefing from the executive secretary of the National Security Council, but the council's staff members did

not attend White House meetings. Possibly because of Eisenhower's long association with Carroll he did not make that same distinction between domestic
and international matters. In fact one of staff secretary Carroll's major functions was the daily intelligence briefing of the president. National security assistants attended Adams's staff meetings and Adams, Persons, and Harlow
frequently attended NSC meetings.[56]

It was a real blow to Eisenhower when General Carroll died suddenly in
1954. Seeking a replacement, Adams sought the advice of Generals Persons
and Robert Cutler. He was amazed when both men recommended a young
army engineering colonel named Andrew Jackson Goodpaster. After being
wounded during World War II, Goodpaster was assigned to a planning job in
the Pentagon where he happened to be associated with Cutler. Persons knew
that Goodpaster had worked well with Eisenhower later when he was assigned
to NATO. The president was enthusiastic when Goodpaster's name was proposed and the appointment was quickly made.[57]

Goodpaster flourished in his new position, and the president continually
increased his responsibilities. On occasion the president even used him as a private agent to visit military commanders in the field to obtain their views on foreign policy problems. Typically, Eisenhower then filtered these through
Goodpaster's own observations before making a decision. At times he also
served as a personal courier for presidential messages to the field. As a result of
these activities the staff secretary became one of the president's major foreign
policy advisers. Although Eisenhower tried to keep Goodpaster out of policy
matters, the colonel was inevitably drawn into that area. As a result he had to
work hard to maintain his good relations with the national security assistant.[58]

Goodpaster tremendously impressed Roger Jones, who through the years
worked with many White House staff aides. Jones characterized him as

thoughtful, provocative, one hundred percent loyal, more capacity to see over the hori-
zon than almost anybody else on that staff. . . . With a circle of friends and acquain-
tances in the military that meant that on two minutes' notice on almost any subject he
could get what the President wanted. . . . Proud of the fact that he could meet the civilians on their own ground. . . . A greater capacity than others to synthesize as opposed to
compromise on issues. . . . Very aware of the prerogatives of his office and insisted on
maintaining that insofar as he was the prime contact with the Pentagon, both military
and civilian.[59]

There is little doubt that the staff secretariat greatly improved the paper flow
in the White House and made the presidential staff a more effective operation
than it had ever been before. Every item for action that came to the desk of
Eisenhower, Adams, or Persons had a "Covering Brief." This was a one-page

paper that stated the problem, discussed its dimensions, recommended a solution, indicated the probable result if the recommendation was implemented, and named the person who had concurred in the recommendation. Before the item reached the desk on any of these principals the staff secretariat would have asked: (a) Is it necessary? (b) Is it responsive? (c) Is it ready for action? (d) Is it timely? (e) Is it consistent? and (f) How will it be followed up? Efforts were made to get the originators of material coming to the White House to ask the same questions before forwarding their papers.[60]

CABINET SECRETARY

Most twentieth-century American presidents come into office full of determination to use their Cabinets in both an advisory and an administrative capacity. Even FDR, who was known for his chaotic administrative practices, had, at least in theory, tried to govern through his Cabinet. He was not successful. Harold Ickes, who sat through Roosevelt's Cabinet meetings for twelve years, thought them a "sheer waste of time" because there was no agenda and important matters were never brought up because of a fear of leaks.[61]

Harry Truman thought Roosevelt was a poor administrator partially because he did not work through his Cabinet. He was determined not to make the same mistake. Harold Smith, Truman's first budget director, warned him: "You will find that as time goes on members of your Cabinet will actually be in political opposition to you, either overtly or otherwise, and neither their judgments nor their facts can be altogether trusted . . . because their judgments are colored by personal ambitions and their operating experiences in only a segment of the Government."[62] Truman continued to work at making his Cabinet feel that they were part of his team, but he eventually lost his illusions about the role of the Cabinet in government administration.[63]

As Eisenhower prepared to assume the presidency the budget bureau told him of their firm view,

which was supported by the Hoover Commission conclusions and even more strongly by the private opinions of ex-President Hoover as well as President Truman, that the Cabinet is necessarily a non-operating agency. It performs its best service for the president as a sounding board and discussion place for certain broad governmental policies. . . . All the Presidents for the last 25 years have handled the matter of Cabinet agenda in a very informal way so that it would not be looked upon as a decision point for many governmental matters. This is so not only because of the President's position but because the views of many of the Cabinet members may or may not be of particular importance on the matter in question.

The bureau staff said they were particularly opposed to the notion of a Cabinet secretariat. They cautioned that if the president wanted to use his Cabinet in a way that required staff work he should make sure that the work was done by his own staff and was subject to his own direction.[64]

Eisenhower's interest in management and a desire to build an effective team such as he enjoyed at Supreme Headquarters, Allied Expeditionary Forces and as NATO commander inclined him toward a formal Cabinet structure. However, warnings from the budget bureau and others gave him pause. But his brother Milton and Arthur Flemming had attended Cabinet meetings presided over by Presidents Roosevelt and Truman. They were particularly appalled by those conducted by FDR and thought the meetings could be much more productive. The two men presented their ideas to the president who said he had been thinking along the same lines. By the summer of 1954 Eisenhower was convinced that he had to follow his original instincts. He had been bothered by instances in which he had been faced with making decisions in Cabinet meetings without the matters being properly staffed.[65]

On 19 October 1954 Eisenhower appointed Maxwell Rabb to the new position of secretary of the Cabinet. Rabb was an old Washington hand who had served as Senator Lodge's administrative assistant on the Hill. His new job was to do what he could to improve the effectiveness of Cabinet operations. As the only Jew in the White House, Rabb was also expected to handle relations with minorities.[66] Roger Jones recalled:

Max Rabb was at first like a big puppy dog who never grew up to his feet in some respects. Max was just terribly enthusiastic about everything that came along and never inclined to challenge anything until after he saw what the results of the initial enthusiasm were. This was interesting, but it was about as strange a reaction as you could have in terms of working for Eisenhower. He used to create some amusement with all of us.[67]

Jones of course represented the view of the sophisticates in the budget bureau.

Rabb soon installed a system in which his office prepared the agenda for Cabinet meetings and screened any formal presentations that were to be made. The Cabinet secretariat distributed information papers and drafts to Cabinet members and their assistants. Members of the Cabinet were advised to read the material before the meeting in which they were to be discussed and be prepared to give the president advice on the subjects raised. The secretariat maintained records of minutes and Cabinet actions. After the meetings Rabb would meet with assistant secretaries to make sure they knew what had happened at the Cabinet, what decisions had been made, and the background of those decisions. About every three months Rabb's office would prepare a "Cabinet Action Status Report" that summarized the various assignments given to the departments and described the degree to which the decisions had been implemented.[68]

It all sounded very structured, and of course meetings of the Cabinet could be made *too* efficient. If everything had to be on the agenda and no one could speak without approval they would be ineffective. But Ike had a deft touch in conducting such meetings, for he was a master of consultative management. He told the Cabinet that he did not want them to assemble as representatives of their departments but as advisers to him. In introducing an item he would say that he put it on the agenda because he wanted to hear them discuss it. He would then give his own views but in such a way as to let them know that his mind was still open. This approach resulted in vigorous debates and wide participation. Sometimes the president would make an immediate decision while at other times he would sleep on it and put his decisions in the meeting's minutes. In either case he would give the reasons why he made them.[69]

Eisenhower enlarged the Cabinet meetings to include Lodge, Adams, the budget director, the chairman of the economic advisers, and the director of defense mobilization. These weekly meetings (he averaged 34 a year) were advisory rather than policy-making, and they took much of the president's time. He continued them because he knew that asking advice was an effective way of winning support and establishing a team spirit. He also knew his orders would be more likely to be followed if his department heads got them from him personally.[70] It was a system especially suited to the way Eisenhower liked to get his information. Many Cabinets were made up of individuals who did not work well together but Eisenhower was blessed with a relatively homogeneous group.

By 1959, however, Eisenhower realized that building a team spirit was easier with army officers than with politicians. By then most of the initial members of his Cabinet, those that he respected most, had disappeared and the meetings had become more boring. They also became less frequent, more general, and more vague.[71] Probably it was the inevitable result of a long time in office. Still Eisenhower's Cabinet secretariat was the most ambitious effort a president has ever made to integrate executive department heads into his administration's operations. While his Cabinet meetings were civil affairs, Eisenhower was not totally successful in forcing decisions to be made through his system.[72]

The 1953 Carter Burgess review of the White House staff work resulted in the establishment of the staff secretariat. His next review in 1954 led to the creation of the secretary to the Cabinet. In early 1956, shortly after he had decided to run again for the presidency, Eisenhower invited Burgess to make yet another study of how his White House staff organization was working and to make recommendations for improvements. On 23 April 1956 Burgess briefed the president in the Oval Office on the results of his most recent study.[73]

Burgess found that the staff secretary had done much to introduce sound staff procedures into the White House Office operations but that it could be improved. The secretariat had been hampered by lack of personnel, the fact that not all staff functions had been channeled through it, and by Eisenhower's tendency to assign jobs to Goodpaster that were "not of a secretariat nature." For it to function with maximum efficiency, Burgess felt that the staff secretariat "should be the one place in the White House through which assignments are channeled, where suspense logs and progress reports are kept, where papers are checked for adherence to approved staff procedures, through which official Presidential papers are funneled, and where Presidential decisions are recorded and disseminated."[74]

To further improve the operation of the staff secretariat Burgess recommended that Eisenhower take the following actions:

1. liberate the staff secretary from all duties outside his staff functions and give him full responsibility for the management and coordination of all staff work in the White House;
2. provide an assistant for administration to the staff secretary to take care of all of the WHO housekeeping services;
3. set up a small, competent research unit in the secretariat to summarize lengthy reports, congressional actions, and public opinion and to prepare briefing material;
4. locate the staff secretary's office next to the Oval Office.[75]

Eisenhower said he preferred that the research unit be set up on an experimental basis to let him examine the product before making it permanent. The president volunteered two areas of his own activities that he thought could be improved. He decided that after each of his telephone calls he would call in his secretary and summarize for her the main points of the conversation. He also directed that his personal letters to friends and department heads be routed through the staff secretary for recording and dispatch.[76]

In analyzing the ongoing White House operations, Burgess identified four functional entities within the staff. The action and coordination group he called the permanent "fire brigade" of the White House. Working under constant stress, they sought to respond to agency officials who needed help with their problems with Congress, the public, the press, and other agencies. This group tried to coordinate and integrate agency views into a broad government approach. In contrast to this action group there were the thinkers in the planning and policy area. The Eisenhower White House was the first to assign staff to working on long-range policies for the solution of major problems that cut across departmental responsibilities. Most of the long-range planners carried the title of special assistant. The third functional area—the one that Burgess called the projects group—worked on specific problems that required temporary White House attention. Finally there was the administrative area that included the staff and Cabinet secretariats.[77]

Although, for purposes of analysis, Burgess identified functional areas among the staff, this was a theoretical rather than an actual or formal distinction. In practice the staff operated almost independently on their individual assignments and reported either to the president, Governor Adams, or General Persons. This flat organization developed because the highly capable people that Eisenhower wanted for his staff could be more easily recruited if each was told that he was to be an immediate assistant to the president. Some might have hesitated to join the staff in a more subordinate capacity. The downside of this practice was that responsibility for similar major functions was spread through several offices. As a result it was difficult for the agencies to know who in the White House was doing what. Clearly Burgess thought the White House should be organized on a more functional pattern although he recognized that this might create problems of reassignment and future recruitment.[78] At the time Eisenhower strongly endorsed centralizing the staff work along the lines Burgess proposed.[79] In practice it proved difficult to make these changes.

COUNCIL ON FOREIGN ECONOMIC POLICY

One reason there was significant growth in the size of the White House staff during the Eisenhower years was the president's propensity to add specialists to his personal staff as a solution to problems as they arose. An example of this was the establishment of the Council on Foreign Economic Policy (CFEP). In this instance the problem to be solved was coordinating foreign economic assistance programs. By 1954 foreign economic policy involved many agencies including the state, treasury, agriculture, and commerce departments, the Foreign Operations Administration, the Export-Import Bank, and the National Security Council. Shortly after Joseph Dodge resigned as Eisenhower's first director of the budget, the president asked him to come back to Washington to study this coordination problem and recommend a solution.[80]

Dodge spent several months examining the problem and talking to the various agency heads, but he could not find a satisfactory mechanism to deal with this problem. He discovered that the authorities and activities in the foreign economic area were widely dispersed among various departments and agencies and that most of these assignments had resulted from legislation. In desperation he finally recommended what he termed a "lousy" solution.[81]

Dodge proposed that the president take a two-step approach. The first was to create an organizational device to make the then current arrangements work better, and then later, devise a plan for a more streamlined and permanent solution. As Dodge described it:

To be able to move on the present situation, we had to come up with an answer that I, more than anyone else, disliked. That was the creation of the Council [on Foreign Economic Policy]. It is in effect, a permanent Cabinet-level committee for the consideration of the highly technical and complicated problems of this area. It has these advantages at least—it provides a central place to which everyone can turn; it avoids the necessity of creating innumerable ad hoc level committees, and it gives the President a usable defense mechanism to ensure that policy matters have been considered by the right people at the right level.[82]

Eisenhower accepted Dodge's recommendation when he established the Council on Foreign Economic Policy on 11 December 1954. Its purpose was to coordinate the policy and provide for the simplification of the various coordinating mechanisms that dealt with foreign economic policy. The council's membership included the secretaries of state, treasury, commerce, and agriculture and the director of foreign operations administration. Ex officio members from the White House staff were the special ssistant for national security affairs, the administrative assistant for economic affairs (Hauge), and a member of the Council of Economic Advisers. Initially the council was chaired by Dodge, who was named to the White House staff as another special assistant. When Dodge left in July 1956, he was replaced by Clarence Randall who stayed in the job through Eisenhower's second term. Randall was authorized to invite the heads of other departments to CFEP meetings when matters of direct concern to them were under consideration. As a result he issued an open invitation to the secretaries of defense, interior, and labor and to the directors of the Bureau of the Budget and the Office of Civil and Defense Mobilization since they usually had an interest in the problems considered by the council.[83]

In setting up the CFEP there was always a danger that it would transgress in the foreign policy area of the National Security Council. To reduce this possibility, the charter of the CFEP said that the NSC would be the superior agency in those instances when the two councils had a common interest. To coordinate the process the special assistants in charge of each council attended each other's meetings and were given advance copies of each other's working papers. About a quarter of the items considered by the CFEP were of interest to the NSC.[84]

In retrospect Dodge felt that the council had served a useful purpose but was less than a perfect solution to the problem. He pointed out that "its Chairman serves without authority, its agreements are voluntary, its members can hide behind their shields of diverse statutory responsibilities, and the Council can not and does not supervise the implementation of its decisions or agreements." As time went on its situation became worse because there were new agencies involved and even greater dispersion of authority and sources of economic assistance without significant improvement in administration, planning, methods, or implementation.[85] Eisenhower never got around to the second stage that Dodge had originally recommended: to devise "a plan for a more streamlined and permanent solution." Apparently no one was ever able to think of one. The area of foreign trade policy has continued to be one that succeeding presidents have tried to deal with in a variety of ways. The council was abolished by Kennedy but functionally reappeared under Ford's Economic Policy Board.[86]

The Eisenhower White House spawned a whole new category of high-level presidential aide titled "Special Assistant to the President." These staff members were considered of a higher rank than the statutorily authorized assistants. For example, Gabriel Hauge, who was initially appointed as an assistant was promoted to special assistant after five years on the job. Truman had eighteen personal staff members when he left the White House while Eisenhower had fifty, many of them in the special assistant category.

When Sputnik went into orbit in 1957 Dr. James Killian was appointed special assistant for science and technology to assess the nation's scientific readiness and advise the president accordingly. From the beginning of the administration Harold Stassen served as special assistant for disarmament. Nelson Rockefeller held a variety of job titles around the White House over the years; in 1955 his title was special assistant for international understanding and cooperation. Other special assistants were retired Major General John Bragdon, who was Eisenhower's coordinator for public works planning; Myer Kestnbaum, who dealt with the recommendations of the Second Hoover Commission; and Lieutenant General Elwood Quesada, who oversaw the national involvement in airports and air traffic.[87]

Since each special assistant was supported by his own subordinate staff, a good deal of the growth of the White House staff during the Eisenhower years was due to the creation of this new strata of presidential aide. For example, Kestnbaum had the primary responsibility for making recommendations to the president with respect to the acceptance or modification of the Hoover Commission's recommendations. To do this he had to consult with and seek the views of all the appropriate agencies and work with PACGO on organizational proposals. There was also a policy committee established to consult with

Kestnbaum in developing proposals to the president for action based upon recommendations of the Hoover Commission. It was chaired by the budget director and included the attorney general, the secretary of commerce, Arthur Flemming, Reuben Robertson, and Dodge.[88]

PERSONNEL MANAGEMENT

The establishment of the Civil Service Commission in the nineteenth century to insulate federal employment from partisan considerations had limited the president's appointment power. The chief executives since that time have not had as much control over personnel as they felt they needed. Roosevelt's attempt to limit some of the commission's authority was one of the reasons why the original effort to establish the Executive Office of the President was rejected by Congress in 1937. As a result of this tension, the creation of the liaison officer for personnel management in 1939 as a unit in the executive office was but an anemic version of what Roosevelt desired. But it was as much as he could do in the absence of congressional support.[89]

Eisenhower abolished the Liaison Office and assigned some additional functions relating to personnel management to the chairman of the Civil Service Commission by Executive Order 10452 of 1 May 1953. This turned out to be less than a satisfactory solution to the problem, so in typical fashion, Eisenhower in 1957 created a special assistant to the president for personnel management.[90] The idea for the position came from PACGO. Rocco Siciliano, who had been the assistant secretary of labor since 1953, was named to the post in July 1957. He was given the responsibility, by Executive Order 10729, to establish personnel management policies and standards for the executive branch and to keep the president informed about how well these were carried out. To do this he was told to work with the budget bureau, the Civil Service Commission, and the departments in developing and improving personnel and pay policies.[91] Siciliano's operation continued through the remainder of the Eisenhower administration, but so did the friction between the White House and the Civil Service Commission.[92] John Kennedy abolished the position.

SUMMARY

Roger Jones admired Eisenhower's White House staff but he did not think they were as effective as Truman's WHO. He attributed this to Truman's hands-on approach of acting as his own chief of staff, giving out assignments, sitting down with all the principals and discussing problems as a group. Jones thought this way of dealing with the staff tended to bring out their best performance. He recalled that "it was seldom that you got all the Eisenhower staff around the cabinet table to chew over an issue that didn't affect them in some way in the area in which they were operating." As a result Eisenhower's staff was, like a millitary staff, much more compartmentalized.[93]

Jones's view might have been colored by the fact that he did not think some of Eisenhower's traits were well suited for the presidency. He found the president to have a very short span of attention on anything like departmental infighting that he was not interested in or did not understand or want to understand and to be unwilling to admit that if he said "Stop!" it was not going to stop. He thought the president's lack of a good sense of how long it would take to do something showed that he did not follow through carefully.[94]

However, Eisenhower brought the White House Office to a new level of power in the American political system. The structured staff system he installed did not become operational and infringe on the work of the departments because Eisenhower knew how to control it. The larger staff did, however, provide the capability to run the departments from the White House, and in less skilled hands, during the Richard Nixon administration, the temptation proved to be too much to withstand. The long-range significance of the Eisenhower White House was not in its hierarchical structure, because that was soon jettisoned by Kennedy, but in the substantially increased appropriations he received from Congress for the White House Office.[95] This created a new floor of resources that succeeding presidents would use in a variety of ways in their pursuit of power.

NOTES

1. Alfred Dick Sander, *A Staff for the President: The Executive Office, 1921–1952* (Westport, Conn., 1989), pp. 52–53.

2. Gordon Gray Memo of Conversation with Truman, 16 October 1951, Truman—PSB 1951, Gray Papers, DDEL.

3. Memorandum II, 4 November 1952, Executive Office Reorganization (1), Whitman Name File, DDEL.

4. Sander, *A Staff for the President*, pp. 81, 90.

5. Monday, 28 September 1953, ACW Diary August–October 53(3), Whitman File, DDEL.

6. Dwight D. Eisenhower, *The White House Years: Mandate for Change, 1953–56* (Garden City, N.Y., 1963), p. 88.

7. Stephen Hess, *Organizing the Presidency* (Washington, D.C., 1988), p. 63.

8. John W. Sloan, "The Management and Decision-Making Style of President Eisenhower," *Presidential Studies Quarterly* 20, no. 2 (spring 1990): 289–290.

9. Philip G. Henderson, *Managing the Presidency: The Eisenhower Legacy—From Kennedy to Reagan* (Boulder, Colo., 1988), pp. 17–18.

10. Eisenhower, *The White House Years*, pp. 88–89.

11. Stephen E. Ambrose, *Eisenhower: The President* (New York, 1984), p. 22.

12. Eisenhower, *The White House Years*, p. 89.

13. H. R. Haldeman, *The Haldeman Diaries: Inside the Nixon White House* (New York, 1994), p. 311.

14. Neil Jacoby Oral History, DDEL.

15. Hess, *Organizing the Presidency* p. 65.

16. Diary entry, 18 January 1954, DDE Personal Diary January–November 54, DDE Diary Series, DDEL.

17. Sloan, "Management and Decision-Making Style," pp. 298–99; Henderson, *Managing the Presidency*, p. 25.

18. Sloan, "Management and Decision-Making Style," p. 300; Hess, *Organizing the Presidency*, p. 70.

19. Robert H. Ferrell, ed., *The Eisenhower Diaries* (New York, 1981), p. 227.

20. Hess, *Organizing the Presidency*, p. 63.

21. Gabriel Hauge Oral History, Columbia University, pp. 54–55; Raymond J. Saulnier Oral History, DDEL, p. 54; Sherman Adams in Kenneth W. Thompson, ed., *Portraits of American Presidents Volume III, The Eisenhower Presidency* (Lanham, Md., 1984), p. 186.

22. Carl M. Brauer, *Presidential Transitions: Eisenhower through Reagan* (New York, 1986), p. 14.

23. Thompson, ed., *Portraits*, p. 186.

24. Hauge Oral History, p. 55.

25. Robert Cutler, *No Time for Rest* (Boston, 1956), p. 282.

26. Neil Jacoby Oral History, pp. 27–28, DDEL.

27. 25 May 1955, Ann C. Whitman Diary, May 1955 (1), Whitman File, DDEL.

28. Eisenhower, *Waging Peace, 1956–61*, note p. 7. Hauge became a president in 1969, but it was of Manufacturers Hanover. He became chairman of their board in 1971. See *Who's Who in America, 1972*.

29. Raymond J. Saulnier Oral History, DDEL.

30. Paarlberg to author, 7 March 1995.

31. Sander, pp. 89–90.

32. Eisenhower, *The White House Years*, p. 116; Joseph G. Bock, *The White House Staff and the National Security Assistant: Friendship and Friction at the Water's Edge* (Westport, Conn., 1987), p. 33.

33. Bock, *National Security Assistant*, p. 33; Henderson, *Managing the Presidency*, pp. 27–28.

34. Hauge speech to National Planning Association, 13 December 1955, Burns Papers, DDEL, *The White House Years*, p. 118.

35. Bernard M. Shanley Oral History, DDEL.

36. Patrick Anderson, *The Presidents' Men* (Garden City, N.Y., 1969), p. 160.

37. Roger Jones Oral History, DDEL.

38. Shanley Oral History, DDEL.

39. Jones Oral History, DDEL.

40. Shanley Oral History, DDEL.

41. Ibid.

42. Ibid.

43. Flemming Oral History, DDEL.

44. Ibid.

45. PACGO Fact Paper, Administration No. 3, PACGO, DDEL.

46. Maurice Stans to Gale McGhee, 26 July 1960, 52.2, B1–1, RG 51, NA; PACGO Fact Paper, Administration No. 3, PACGO, DDEL.

47. OMO Discussion Notes, 20 February 1959, Series 52.2, B1–13/2, RG 51, NA.

48. Special Committee on Government Organization, 3 January 1952, Executive Office Reorganization (2), Whitman Name Series, DDEL.

49. W. Y. Elliott to G. F. Stauffacher, "Organization of an Institutional Staff for the President in the Executive Office," 19 November 1952, NSC Organization and Functions (4), WHO, Project Clean Up, DDEL.

50. 28 September 1953, ACW Diary, August-October 1953(3), Whitman File, DDEL.

51. Arthur Minnich Memo for the Record, 4 August 1954, ACW Diary August 1954(4), Whitman File, DDEL.

52. Bradley H. Patterson, Jr., in Thompson, ed., *Portraits,* pp. 123–124.

53. John Prados, *Keepers of the Keys: A History of the National Security Council from Truman to Bush* (New York, 1991), pp. 65–66.

54. Patterson in Thompson, ed., *Portraits*, p. 123

55. Bock, *National Security Assistant*, p. 34; Henderson, *Managing the Presidency*, p. 26

56. Bock, *National Security Assistant*, p. 34.

57. Prados, *Keepers of the Keys*, pp. 66–67.

58. Ibid.

59. Jones Oral History, DDEL.

60. "Good Staff Work" brochure, Organization (2), WHO, Staff Secretary, DDEL.

61. Summary of an interview with Harold Ickes, 28 April 1948, E.O.P. Misc. Memos, 1939–1952, E2–5, Series 39.32, RG 51, NA.

62. Conference with the President, 31 January 1946, Diary—January 1946, Smith Papers, Harry S Truman Library.

63. Richard E. Neustadt, *Presidential Power: The Politics of Leadership* (New York, 1960), p. 174.

64. "The Presidential Job in Organizing and Managing the Executive Branch," 1953, E2–50/52.2, Series 52.6, RG 51, NA.

65. Flemming Oral History, DDEL; Minnich Memo for the Record, 4 August 1954, ACW Diary Aug 54(4), Whitman File, DDEL.

66. "Looking Ahead, Supplement No. 2, 1955," 13 December 1955, Burns Papers, DDEL.

67. Jones Oral History, DDEL.

68. Henderson, *Managing the Presidency*, pp. 52–54.

69. Flemming Oral History, DDEL.

70. Sloan, "Management and Decision-Making Style," pp. 300–301.

71. Ambrose, *Eisenhower: The President*, p. 509.

72. Hess, *Organizing the Presidency*, pp. 73–74

73. "A Staff Plan for the President," Organization(9), WHO, Staff Secretary, DDEL.

74. "A Staff Plan for the President," 23 April 1956, Organization (9), WHO, Staff Secretary, DDEL.

75. Ibid.

76. Memo of Conference with the President, 23 April 1956, April 56–Goodpaster, DDE Diary Series, DDEL.

77. "A Staff Plan for the President," 23 April 1956, Organization (9), WHO, Staff Secretary, DDEL.

78. Ibid.

79. Memo of Conference with the President, 23 April 1956, April 56–Goodpaster, DDE Diary Series, DDEL.

80. "Looking Ahead," 13 December 1955, Correspondence with Hauge, Burns Papers, DDEL.

81. Joseph Dodge to the President, 13 October 1959, Dodge 1959, Whitman Administrative, DDEL.

82. Dodge to Sir Leslie Rowan, 25 January 1955, Agency Subseries R(2), CFEP, DDEL.

83. "Looking Ahead," 13 December 1955, Correspondence with Hauge, Burns Papers, DDEL; Finding Aid, DDEL; Cullen to Patterson, 21 July 1959, OCDM(3), CFEP, DDEL.

84. Cutler to President, Operations of NSC, January 53–April 55, NSC(2), Whitman Administrative, DDEL.

85. Dodge to President, 13 October 1959, Dodge 1959, Whitman Administrative, DDEL.

86. Henderson, *Managing the Presidency*, pp. 14–15.

87. Sloan, "Management and Decision-Making Style" p. 301; Director's Opening Statement, 13 June 1955, 52.2, B1–6/1, RG 51, NA.

88. Memo for Adams from BOB, 28 September 1955, 52.2, B1–3/1, RG 51, NA; Policy Committee on Hoover Reports, 27 October 1955, Hoover Commission, WHO, Cabinet Secretariat, DDEL.

89. Sander, *A Staff for the President*, pp. 54–55.

90. PACGO Memo, "Presidential Level Organization," 25 October 1960, 52.6, E2–50/57.2, RG 51, NA.

91. Rocco C. Siciliano Oral History, DDEL; Functions of Assistant for Personnel Management, WHO, Staff Secretary, DDEL.

92. OMO Discussion Notes, 20 February 1959, 52.2, B1–13/2, RG 51, NA.
93. Jones Oral History, DDEL.
94. Ibid.
95. Hess, *Organizing the Presidency*, pp. 72–73.

2

The Reorganization of the Council of Economic Advisers

In January 1953 the Council of Economic Advisers was in an endangered state. Congress had appropriated just enough money for council operations through the end of March. Eisenhower had to decide before then whether he wanted the agency to continue to exist and, if he did, what form it should take, what its functions should be, and who should be appointed to it.

The council had been created shortly after the end of World War II at a time when there was fear that the widespread unemployment that characterized the depression years would soon return. The council's main purpose was to recommend policies and actions that would relieve the expected unemployment. But the joblessness did not develop so the CEA had to invent a new role for itself. It began to interpret the act generally to mean that the CEA should give economic advice designed to preserve existing economic conditions so that it would not be necessary for it to recommend measures for dealing with unemployment. As a result the function originally assigned the CEA was never carried out and the ideas behind the Employment Act have never been tested.[1]

To anticipate and avert economic difficulties required the taking of a series of steps in which the whole executive branch would be involved and which would be coordinated by the Executive Office of the President. What should the role of the CEA be in this process? Was the council a presidential staff agency like the Bureau of the Budget or was it a group of technical advisers whose responsibility ended with a statement of views about the nation's economic health? There had been widespread disagreement by council members and others about the correct answer to this question since the establishment of the CEA in 1946.[2] One of the basic decisions Eisenhower had to make about the CEA was the definition of its staff role.

The council as established by Congress was to consist of three coequal members. One was to be designated chairman and another vice chairman but neither was given any additional authority with the title. The equal status led to organizational difficulties and interminable squabbles among the members. These inherent problems were exacerbated when Truman appointed an academic economist and two partisan activists to the CEA. The resulting battles and publicity led to early calls for abolishing the council. When the Hoover Commission studied the executive branch in 1948 it recommended that the CEA be replaced by a single economic adviser in the White House.[3]

During the Truman period the CEA operated under two different program assumptions. Initially Chairman Edwin Nourse sought to shape the council into a professional advisory group solely responsible for presenting objective economic advice to the president with no responsibility for taking a position before the public or Congress. As the election of 1948 approached, the partisan members of the council demanded that the CEA become a more active spokesman before Congress and the public for the economic measures recommended by the president.[4]

The council's principal activities were to prepare annual and midyear economic reports to the president. It also assisted the White House staff to prepare the president's annual Economic Message to Congress as required by the Employment Act. In addition, the CEA presented informal reports at more frequent intervals to the president and conducted special studies when requested. The council served as a focus point for federal economists through an interdepartmental committee on the economic outlook and operated a seminar-type program with business and labor leaders to obtain their viewpoints on the problem of maintaining full employment.[5]

The status of the CEA became precarious when Norse resigned as chairman to be replaced by the most voluble and vociferous of the partisan activists, Leon Keyserling. His actions soon made the council the target of conservative elements in Congress, both Democrats and Republicans. Many who had no quarrel with the CEA on ideological grounds had doubts that a three-person group of equals was the best way to provide economic advice to a president.[6] A large number in Congress began to feel that council members were playing a role in political matters that was more active and more direct than they thought appropriate.[7]

Truman's budget request for the CEA for the 1952 fiscal year was for $349,000. The House Appropriations Committee recommended that this amount be reduced to $309,900. When the question reached the floor of the House in February 1952 Representative Edward H. Rees of Kansas, supported by Congressmen Jon Phillips and John Taber, got the appropriation reduced another $100,000. A cut of this size would lead to an immediate sharp staff reduction and seriously cripple the council. The CEA appealed to the Senate committee for restoration, but it was clear that the House would never approve the larger amount. To save the council, the Senate committee recommended an appropriation of $225,000 with the proviso that it be spent during the first three quarters of the fiscal year. The Senate and the House accepted this compromise.[8]

The CEA had some powerful friends among the senators including Taft, Ellender, Maybank, O'Mahoney, and Saltonstall. When O'Mahoney hit upon the happy compromise that would allow the Council to continue to operate until a new president was installed, the others were able to push it through. The rationale for the action was to give the new administration an opportunity to reexamine the role of the CEA. It was clear, however, that Taft and the others wanted to keep the council once Keyserling was gone.[9]

Some members of president-elect Eisenhower's entourage sought to convince him that he did not need a CEA. Reputedly this was the view of Sinclair Weeks, the soon to be named secretary of commerce and at one time the new budget director. Hauge told Eisenhower that such an idea was "for the birds" and that a president needed his own coordinating group. Hauge believed his part in convincing Eisenhower that the Council of Economic Advisers should be retained was one of his most important contributions.[10]

Before the inauguration the President's Advisory Committee on Government Organization began looking at the organizational problems that the new president would face. The economic council was a high priority because its funds would be exhausted in a few months and decisions had to be made. PACGO recommended that Eisenhower make the CEA "in practice the staff of the President responsible for analysis, interpretation, and reporting to him on economic matters." They did not agree with the Hoover Commission recommendation for the president to rely on a single economic adviser. As an interim move, PACGO suggested that Eisenhower appoint a chairman for the CEA and ask his "considered opinion in the matter."[11] When PACGO discussed the matter with the president he reluctantly agreed with their suggestion but admitted that he was leaning toward a single economic adviser. To achieve balance in the advice he received, Eisenhower thought he could call on economists from around the country for opinions on an ad hoc basis.[12]

The pre-inauguration advice given by Eisenhower's budget director-designate was similar to that offered by PACGO. Joseph Dodge said:

There is general agreement that the present form of this organization [CEA] is completely unsatisfactory, particularly in the way it has functioned publicly in giving conclusions and recommendations as to legislation and testifying to this effect. It should not give recommendations separate from those made by the President, but has been in the habit of doing so. This is the same as though the Budget Bureau were to make recommendations contrary to those of the President whom it serves. There is general agreement, even among some of the highest representatives of the present [Truman] administration, that there should be a fundamental change here. These views vary from eliminating it entirely to including it in the Budget Bureau, and to an agency with a single head. The organization undoubtedly has value, properly administered and under certain restrictions as to its activities. . . . [P]robably the first step should be to appoint an outstanding person to the Council as Chairman and not appoint the two other members until the future role of the agency is determined. . . . This would put the CEA immediately under control while plans were being made for its future prior to March 31, 1953.[13]

ARTHUR BURNS

Eisenhower accepted the recommendation of PACGO and Dodge that he name "an outstanding person" to study the CEA and asked Gabriel Hauge who it should be. Hauge suggested that Arthur Burns of Columbia University would be ideal for the position.[14] As director of research at the National Bureau of Economic Research, Burns was heavily involved in the study of business cycles. When asked to come to Washington Burns "did not jump for the job, but took [his] time to accept." He was drawn to the post by the opportunity to rebuild the CEA while serving a "president who thought he needed me."[15]

At that time Burns was a prominent economist who was well known for his work with Wesley Mitchell and for his disenchantment with Keynesian economics. As a champion of empirical, or inductive economics, he drew his conclusions from observable facts rather than deductively from theoretical relationships and models. His knowledge of history served as the foundation for his anti-Keynesian beliefs. Outside of some brief consulting visits during the New Deal, this was to be his first Washington assignment.[16]

Burns, who was born in Austria, received his Ph.D. in economics from Columbia. He taught at Rutgers until 1945 when he returned to his alma mater as a professor and became research director of the National Bureau. In 1953 he was to begin an on and off government career of more than thirty years, during which he advised four presidents, served as chairman of the Federal Reserve Board and as ambassador to West Germany.[17]

Before Burns had his conference with Eisenhower, Hauge brought him in to meet Sherman Adams. The chief of staff was shocked.

I said to myself, "This is exactly the kind of candidate whose image is anathema to a good many Republicans." Burns had overabundant hair, thick glasses, and a typical professorial Ph.D. But I found Burns had some characteristics that were exceptional. He answered questions in succinct and knowledgeable language that immediately impressed his interviewer. In short he knew what he was talking about. After he left, I turned to Hauge and we had a discussion, and I asked, "Who's going to support him?" Phenomenally, Burns was interviewed by George Humphrey and Joseph Dodge and others concerned with hard fiscal matters with whom Burns had no difficulty at all. . . . Whatever doubt there may have been concerning Arthur Burns' qualifications were soon dissipated by his adept manner in dealing with various committees of Congress and, just as important to us with conservative Republicans.[18]

While Burns was preparing to come to Washington, there were members of Congress who were trying to administer the coup de grâce to the CEA. Eisenhower's coattails were broad enough in the election of 1952 to permit the Republicans to control both houses of Congress—for the last time in forty years. An implacable foe of the council, John Taber of New York was the new chairman of the House Appropriations Committee. He was outraged when he learned that Eisenhower was considering continuing the "Economic Adviser set-up." A member of the budget bureau reported that Taber believed that

neither the President or Sherman Adams know what they are doing. He said the Council was loaded with "a gang of nitwits and numbskulls . . ." He said finally the "decent people" on both sides of the aisle got up their courage and decided to cut the whole business out on March 31. Mr. Taber said that if the President wants economic advisers what he ought to do is go out and hire a good economist and put him on the White House payroll and let him build up whatever staff he wants to build right there. The President, said Taber, should let the Council die because it is worthless and would always be worthless.[19]

Taber was convinced that Keyserling had done "his best to wreck the economy" and with a staff that was "totally incompetent and totally without any capacity to grasp economics."[20]

Once Burns was chosen to decide what to do with the council, it was necessary to get some money from Congress to keep the agency in existence until he had completed his analysis. The budget bureau tried to get a supplemental appropriation to secure time for Burns to develop firm plans.[21] Taber scheduled hearings on the request before one of his subcommittees for 5 February but no Eisenhower appointees appeared. Its administrative officer, a relatively junior civil servant, who made a routine justification for the supplemental appropriation, represented the CEA. Chairman Taber said he was only interested in discussing a liquidation of the council staff and warned the hapless bureaucrat

that he would be personally liable for any funds spent after 31 March. No
Democrats came to his defense.[22]

Taber got the House to approve only $25,000 for the CEA while admitting
candidly that his purpose was "to get rid of that gang that is in there now." The
budget bureau then went to Senators Robert Taft and Styles Bridges for help in
saving the CEA. The Senate voted to raise the amount to $60,000, but in the
conference committee the House held firm. Taber was able to force a "compromise" that provided no money for the council. Instead the Supplemental Appropriation Act which was approved on 28 March 1953 provided $50,000 for
an economic adviser to the president and a small staff for the remainder of the
fiscal year.[23] The administration believed that "we did the best we could under
rather difficult and complicated circumstances."[24] Burns was appointed to the
new post and continued, as best he could, to perform the functions previously
performed by the council.

THE LIQUIDATION OF THE COUNCIL

While the Senate and House were composing their differences, Burns had
been nominated by Eisenhower to be chairman of the council. He appeared
before a Senate committee on 11 March and was quickly confirmed. Burns
spent the rest of the month liquidating the agency. He was placed on the payroll of the White House as economic adviser, taking a half dozen of the CEA
staff with him. But more than twenty staffers of the council were dismissed. By
agreeing to this action, the administration was at least able to preserve the concept of the CEA if not its continuity.[25]

A former senior member of the CEA staff recalled that his colleagues were in
a state of shock. "It was like seeing a bunch of people who didn't know what had
hit them, wandering around the hall, not knowing whether they were to stay or
not. And most of them in the end did not stay, and were extremely embit-
tered." He thought the initial attitude of the Eisenhower administration "was
that the people who were working in the government under the Democratic
administration were sort of incompetent loafers."[26] Burns was able to retain
only three of the professionals from this staff: Francis James, a longtime civil
servant, was a statistician; Collis Stocking, an economist who became the
CEA's executive officer; and David Lusher, a brilliant econometrician and national income analyst.[27] Burns had told a Senate committee that "a fairly large
proportion" of the staff were good scholars who should be retained but he obviously was not a free agent in the matter.[28]

THE REORGANIZATION PLAN

After salvaging what he could from the existing council, Burns set to work designing the new one. When the CEA's money expired on 1 April, Burns ceased to be its chairman and became instead the economic adviser to the president. The council's functions were transferred to his office along with its records and remaining employees.[29] Of the questions Burns had to consider, the most important was whether he should remain a one-person operation or attempt to revive a three-person council.

Dewey Anderson, one of those who had helped design the original council, still felt strongly that a "balanced" but divergent team of three members that included one Keynesian was vital.

The reason we set up the Council of Economic Advisers separately from the President's direct associates, and independently of the various cabinet and other government agencies was that there was great need of not only a correlating function being performed that brought out the common views and reconciled the differences of the government departments, but actually formulated economic policy which took all factors into account. No single adviser can do that, and no officer subservient to any of the departments or responsible for the daily advising of the President and housed as one of the White House staff can do that either.

He agreed that members of the council must be loyal to the president, but "economics is not exact science" so the chief executive needs to know various views.[30]

Burns came to the same conclusion but for different reasons. During a committee hearing Senator Barry Goldwater asked Burns what he thought about a three-person council versus a single adviser. Burns replied:

When I turned to this question, turned it over in my mind for the first time a few weeks ago, it seemed very clear to me that a three-man Council would be preferable. My principal reason for that was that in writing law and studying up on these situations it is desirable not to project individuals against the frailty of their own nature. I can think of an economic adviser winning the ear of a President and becoming a little careless, extemporizing, voicing opinions, and not subjecting his thinking to the discipline that the important questions to be dealt with deserve and require.[31]

Burns and Hauge then prepared a draft reorganization plan which, if approved, would reestablish the CEA. The essential change that the plan would make was to fix the responsibility for the administration and policy of the council with the chairman. The chairman would be tied more closely with the president, and the position of vice chairman would be eliminated. By centralizing authority it was expected that the endemic organizational problems of the original CEA would be vitiated.[32]

The Burns/Hauge plan was sent to the budget bureau for review and suggestions. William Finan, the bureau's organizational expert, favored the changes but opposed seeking congressional approval by means of a formally submitted reorganization plan. He thought the same objectives could be achieved by first getting Congress to fund the council, and then having the president announce that he intended to recognize the chairman as the principal spokesman of the council and give all his instructions through him. The instructions could give the chairman sole responsibility and authority for the internal operation of the council and specify that the annual report of the CEA to the president should deal with the operations of the council rather than substantive economic or policy matters.[33]

Finan convinced budget director Dodge to oppose the submission of the reorganization plan to Congress. Dodge told Hauge he would "make certain this situation is thoroughly understood by the President before the plan is sent up" to Congress. He summarized his objections as follows:

1. All of the objectives of the plan except raising the chairman's salary could be achieved by other means.

2. The attorney general has yet to decide whether salary changes can be achieved by reorganization plan.

3. Burns was in a hurry to get a budget and recruit new council members, yet a reorganization plan requires sixty days to clear Congress.

4. The presidential message that Burns drafted "is not consistent with those used by the President in connection with other plans insofar as it specifically mentions difficulties with the past setup which are not necessarily corrected by the plan."

5. The whole effort is not warranted by the rather slight organizational change proposed.[34]

Hauge and Burns won this particular bureaucratic battle and Reorganization Plan No. 9 of 1953 was sent to Congress on 1 June. The Reorganization Act specified that unless one of the houses of Congress rejected the plan within sixty days it would go into effect with the force of law. Burns appeared in support of the plan before the Special Subcommittee on Reorganization of the House Committee on Government Operations on 14 July. He explained that he had devised the plan after a careful study of the history of the CEA and an analysis of the kinds of problems it will have to deal with. Its main effect would be to give more authority to the council chairman who would have the sole responsibility of reporting to the president on behalf of the CEA. John McCormick, the future Speaker, suggested by his questioning that a powerful chairman would mean that the council would be run like a military organization. Ignoring the implied reference to the general in the White House, Burns assured the congressman that if a serious disagreement developed between himself and the other Council members he would take them along with him when he reported to the president. He said he could run the revamped CEA with six to eight of the top economists of the country, a dozen statisticians, five or six junior economists and supporting clerical staff for a total complement of twenty-five to thirty.[35]

Burns tried to reassure the Congress that, if they approved the reestablishment of the CEA, there would be no repeat of the squabbling that characterized the earlier council. He said,

My own personal feeling or my inclination would be to stay out of the limelight, make my recommendations to the President, indicate to him what the basis for the recommendation is and do that in the light of the national interest as I, after consulting with very many people, many of them abler than I, can discover, and having done that, to remain eternally quiet.[36]

What was designated Reorganization Plan No. 9 of 1953 was a simple one-paragraph document. It transferred from the council to the chairman the functions vested in the CEA by section 4(b) of the Employment Act of 1946. These functions involved the employment and the fixing of compensation of officers and employees of the council. It also transferred to the chairman the function of reporting to the president defined in section 4(c). This section dealt with assisting and advising the president in the preparation of the economic report, the gathering of information concerning economic development and trends, and the appraisal of the contribution of various federal programs and activities to the achievement of the policy of the Employment Act. It abolished the position of vice chairman.[37]

The thrust of the reorganization was to centralize in the chairman administrative control of the council and total responsibility for reporting to the president. The effect was to make the chairman preeminent. He had the authority to deal with the other council members as senior members of the staff rather than as colleagues. In a real sense Eisenhower ended up with the single economic adviser that he preferred. The president met with the other members of the council at the time that they were appointed to welcome them aboard but all substantive matters were handled by the chairman. He was the only one who ever went to the White House on council business.

Congress approved the plan without major opposition, and it entered the records of Congress as 67 Stat. 644.[38] The elimination of the former staff and

Eisenhower's support for the reorganization was apparently enough to over-come the concerns of Taber and his cohorts. By the end of July 1953 Congress had approved the plan and the Senate had confirmed Burns as the new chairman. Although Burns said he found he had "perhaps unfortunately, no taste" for lobbying and had refrained from engaging in it, his relations with Congress were proved effective.[39] By the end of the year the CEA was a going concern.[40]

ABEGS

The reorganization plan was but one part of the structural changes that Burns made trying to improve the effectiveness of the CEA. He also convinced Eisenhower to establish the Advisory Board on Economic Growth and Stability (ABEGS), made up of under secretaries and assistant secretaries from the departments and a member of the Board of Governors of the Federal Reserve System. Its purpose was to assure participation by all-important elements of the executive branch in the formulation of economic advice. It was one way to deal with the perennial problem of obtaining cross-departmental considera-tion of policy questions and maintaining liaison between the CEA and other parts of the government having important economic responsibilities.[41]

ABEGS was a coordination device designed to enhance the CEA leadership role in federal economic policy. One of Eisenhower's budget directors found:

It's quite easy for different Departments and pockets of the government to go ahead with their own plans, and develop new ideas and work them into a system without co-ordinating with the other Departments. I think the President was particularly con-cerned about this. . . . Practically every department had its own economists. I think one of the reasons that he picked Arthur Burns to head the Council of Economic Advisers was that he had such a high standing among economists generally that he was recog-nized as an authority, which made it a lot easier to get them to work together.[42]

Eisenhower announced his plan to establish ABEGS in the letter that he used to transmit Reorganization Plan No. 9 to Congress. He said the purpose of ABEGS was to keep the president "closely informed about the state of the national economy and the various measures necessary to aid in maintaining a stable prosperity."[43] During the hearings on the reorganization plan Burns ex-plained the reason for ABEGS.

That board is essentially an advisory committee to the Council. It is designed to meet a very concrete problem in government, namely, to regularize the channels through which economic thinking, that is thinking on economic policy, can be pooled and tested. Now, the old Council did not have the advantage of any such governmental machinery. This had the result of restricting the influence of the old Council on economic policy. The new advisory board is designed to prevent the Council from becoming a report-writing or purely research agency.[44]

The board was established under the chairmanship of Burns and included Hauge as a member. Burns used ABEGS to get ideas, but probably its greatest contribution was in giving the agency people some sense of the overall economic effects of their actions. During the early months of the board's existence it was the principal means Burns had for developing departmental associations.[45] However, Hauge's replacement at the White House, who became a member of ABEGS during its later years, did not think the board served a very useful role.[46]

For the remainder of the Eisenhower years, ABEGS met every Tuesday at four o'clock in the office of the CEA chairman. Since most of the members were presidential appointees, they shared Eisenhower's broad ideology and worked harmoniously together. The board's supporting auxiliary staff did much of the work. This group was made up of some very able economists, including the head of the Bureau of Labor Statistics, the budget bureau's economic adviser, and the monetary adviser and director of research of the Federal Reserve Board.[47] The auxiliary staff in turn provided a contact between the CEA and the network of federal economists.

The board met a very concrete need previously unmet in the executive branch. It provided a forum for the comparison and coordination of the thinking of the various departments and agencies on economic policy. It also provided the one place in the government where all questions concerning the maintenance of production, employment, and economic growth could be jointly considered.[48]

ABEGS was designed to permit the participation of all concerned elements of the executive branch in the formulation of economic advice. It was a forum for discussing policy questions in depth and for exploring the need for deeper studies. The board kept no minutes and had no coordinating function since it served essentially as an informational and communicative device. Other administrations have used the Domestic Economic Policy Board for similar purposes.

NOTES

1. Ed Strait to Files, 30 October 1952, 52.6, E2–50/52.1, RG 51, NA.
2. Bureau of the Budget to PACGO, draft memo, 6 May 1953, 52.6, E1–30, OMO, Govt. Org. Br., RG 51, NA.

3. Herbert Hoover, *General Management of the Executive Branch*, part 2, *The Executive Office of the President* (Washington, D.C., 1949), pp. 16–17.

4. "The Presidential Job in Organizing and Managing the Executive Branch," 1953, 52.6, E2.50/52.2, RG 51, NA.

5. Ibid.

6. Laurin L. Henry, *Presidential Transitions* (Washington, D.C., 1960), p. 548.

7. Raymond J. Saulnier Oral History, DDEL.

8. Elmer Staats to Director, 3 February 1953, E3–1/1, 52.1, RG 51, NA.

9. Ibid.; Ed Strait to Files, 30 October 1952, E2–50/52.1, 52.6, RG 51, NA.

10. Gabriel Hauge Oral History, Columbia University, pp. 52–53.

11. PACGO Memo for the President, 11 February 1953, NSC Organization & Functions(5), WHO Clean Up, DDEL.

12. Joseph Dodge and Nelson Rockefeller to the President, 14 February 1953, E2–50/42.2, 52.6, RG 51, NA.

13. Dodge Memo, "Most Immediate Organization Problems, Executive Office," BOB 1952, OF 72–B, NA.

14. Saulnier Oral History, DDEL.

15. Edward S. Flash, Jr., *Economic Advice and Presidential Leadership: The Council of Economic Advisers* (New York, 1965), p. 103.

16. Ibid.

17. *Britannica Book of the Year, 1988* (Chicago, 1988), p. 90.

18. Kenneth W. Thompson, *Portraits of American Presidents*, vol. 3, *The Eisenhower Presidency* (Lanham, Md., 1984), pp. 200–201.

19. W. D. Carey to Director, 6 February 1953, E3–11, 52.1, RG 51, NA.

20. John Taber to Sontag, 24 March 1953, OF 72–E, CEA 53 (1), DDEL.

21. Elmer Staats to Director, 3 February 1953, E3–1/1, 52.1, RG 51, NA.

22. Henry, *Presidential Transitions*, pp. 548–549.

23. CEA Annual Report for 1953, 30 December 1953, Report to the President, CEA Records, DDEL.

24. Ibid.; Joseph Dodge to James K. Murray, 26 March 1953, CEA 53(1), OF 72–E, NA.

25. Henry, *Presidential Transitions*, pp. 548–549.

26. Walter Salant Oral History, October 1970, Harry S Truman Library.

27. Neil Jacoby Oral History , pp. 42–43, DDEL.

28. Henry, *Presidential Transitions*, p. 551.

29. 1953 Annual Report of the CEA to the President, 30 December 1953, CEA 1954, OF 72–E, NA.

30. Dewey Anderson to Rockefeller, 4 February 1953, CEA 53 (1), OF 72–E, NA.

31. Hearings, Senate Committee on Banking and Currency, 11 May 1953, 52.6, E1–30, RG 51, NA.

32. Lester G. Seligman, "Presidential Leadership: The Inner Circle and Institutionalization," *The Journal of Politics* 18, no. 3 (August 1956): 425.

33. William Finan to Director, 22 May 1953, 52.6, E1–30, RG 51, NA.

34. Dodge to Hauge, 22 May 1953, 52.6, E1–30, RG 51, NA.

35. Hearings, House Committee on Government Operations, Special Subcommittee on Reorganization, 14 July 1953, 52.6, E1–30, RG 51, NA.

36. Hearings, Senate Committee on Banking and Currency, 11 May 1953, 52.6, E1–30, RG 51, NA.

37. Dodge memo for the President, 29 May 1953, 52.6, E1–30, RG 51, NA.

38. Flash, *Economic Advice*, p. 105.

39. Arthur Burns to Ralph Flanders, 23 July 1953, Congressional Correspondence, Burns Papers, DDEL.

40. 1953 Annual Report of CEA to President, 30 December 1953, CEA 1954, OF 72–E, DDEL.

41. Raymond J. Saulnier, "On Advising the President," *Presidential Studies Quarterly* 15, no. 3 (summer 1985): 585.

42. Percival Brundage Oral History, DDEL, p. 5.

43. Burns version, Reorganization Plan, 52.6, E1–30, RG 51, NA.

44. Hearings, House Committee on Government Operations, Special Subcommittee on Reorganization, 14 July 1953, 52.6, E1–30, RG 51, NA.

45. Flash, *Economic Advice, 170.*

46. Don Paarlberg to author, 7 March 1995.

47. Neil Jacoby Oral History, DDEL, pp. 85–86.

48. 1956 CEA Annual Report, Report to the President, CEA Records, DDEL.

3

Eisenhower and the
Economic Council

The concept of an institutional presidency implies that a new president should accept and use the executive office that exists when he arrives. In fact each president is remarkably free to give or withhold his time and attention and to seek or avoid advice from any source.[1] The contrast in the attitude of Truman and Eisenhower toward the Council of Economic Advisers provides a striking illustration of this point.

Edwin Nourse, the first chairman of the CEA, was bitter and frustrated by his inability to establish a satisfactory personal relationship with Truman or to engage the president in a dialogue on economic matters. Years later he and Arthur Burns compared notes of how they had fared in dealing with their respective presidents. Nourse wistfully recalled the quite different experience that Burns enjoyed with Eisenhower. He considered those years as the high mark of the council's performance because of the relationship Burns established with Eisenhower.[2]

A good part of the difference must be attributed to Eisenhower. The president was not an economist but he was quite bright and he learned to evaluate the indices of economic situations. He could grasp the forces at play and was reasonably intelligent about them.[3] One of his assistant secretaries of the treasury "recalled that the President had a good understanding and definite views on the specific contents of the tax program and a full grasp of its significance."[4] There were many other evidences of the president's command of economic matters.

Raymond J. Saulnier, who served as chairman of the CEA after Burns left in 1955, recalled that Eisenhower was, first of all,

extremely interested in economic matters. Second, he was well informed about many aspects of the economy. Third, he was deeply concerned that we promote economic growth in ways that would give maximum encouragement to the enterprise system, and to the role of the individual and private groups in the economy. Fourth, he was concerned that we get under control the inflationary psychology that existed when he became President. . . . He was deeply concerned about stabilizing the price level, avoiding inflation. And he was deeply interested in business conditions.[5]

Eisenhower's fascination with economic matters was intense. Saulnier found that when he would go into the president's office "for a half-hour talk with him; typically, the President would become so involved in the discussion that it would have to broken up by the appointments secretary as the next visitor came along."[6]

By the time Saulnier began to deal with Eisenhower on a regular basis, the president had been a student of Drs. Burns and Hauge for three years. One of Eisenhower's few fixed appointments was with the two economists each Monday morning at 11:00. In these meetings the president displayed a keen interest in being kept current on economic developments and having things that he learned through his other conferences explained to him and evaluated.[7] These conferences had "two major purposes: to brief the president on current economic developments and needs and to increase the president's grasp of economic affairs generally."[8]

After Burns and Hauge left the administration the nature of these meetings changed. The subject was still economics, but they were no longer weekly and the regular participants were "the troika": the Chairman of the CEA, the secretary of the treasury and the chairman of the Federal Reserve Board. Sometimes Paarlberg would join the group and sometimes the director of the budget would be invited.[9]

Nourse and Burns compared notes on how each got on with his respective president. Burns told Nourse:

Eisenhower has a good mind and is an excellent listener. As questions come up that he is interested in, or that I raised because I think he ought to be interested in, people have told me, don't bring him any memorandum any longer than one page and I bettered that advice by not bringing him any written memorandum at all. I had my memorandum, I had it worked out very carefully, of the agenda that I want to discuss with him and the way I want to approach it. So, he expects me to do that. We know what the question is that I have raised or he has raised, and he says, "Well how about it Arthur?" I go ahead and after a time he'll interrupt me and say, "Now hold on, I wonder if I under-stand just where you are there or what the implications are."[10]

In these weekly conferences Burns provided constant and expert counsel. Edward Flash believes that it was through these sessions that the CEA chair-man made his greatest contribution to the president's program. They gave Burns "the opportunity to widen the President's own dichotomous view of lib-eral welfare and conservative economics to include the divergent but not neces-sarily conflicting concerns of the Treasury and the Council. These briefings, conducted with tact and restraint, paid off."[11]

Eisenhower was so impressed with Burns's briefing skills that he not only made him a regular at his Cabinet meetings but also frequently made him a star performer. Economic issues were always important at these meetings, and Burns was an analyst of economic phenomena without peer. According to one economist, no one could match Burns in the "skillful use of statistical data."[12] The Cabinet was a genuine agency of consultation during the Eisenhower years so the prominent part that the CEA played in its deliberations increased the council's stature in the executive branch. The department heads saw "that from time to time the President would ask Arthur Burns what his view was about this or that, and that he listened attentively to Burns's advice. Now these episodes were not lost on the Secretaries of the different departments."[13]

The influence of the CEA was also enhanced by Eisenhower's attitude to-ward it. He wanted to reestablish the prestige of the council by giving it inde-pendence in its work. The president thought that the CEA had become "a political football" during the Truman years when he thought it had been used to find economic justification for executive actions taken for political reasons. He promised never to do this. Eisenhower told council members that he would view them

as experts, as professionals. I don't want you ever to give me an assessment of the econ-omy that you think will please me. I want you to tell me the truth about the state of the economy at all times, as you see it, and what policies you think are needed to help the country move towards its economic goals, whether you think that they're politically palatable or not. You're not involved in politics. You're a professional in this job.[14]

The president was an active participant in the development of his admin-istration's economic policy. He even involved himself in the work of the CEA. The Employment Act required the president to send an annual economic re-port to Congress. The council drafted the report, but Eisenhower was deter-mined to make it his report as well. In December 1958 the president called the chairman of the CEA to his office and told him that he had read the first two chapters of the proposed economic report. He liked them, but felt there was one very definite omission. He felt that in these two chapters there should be some account of the history of the weakness of the automobile market. He thinks it very important to say what caused this weakness—and he listed the causes as (1) lack of statesmanship in the search for market and (2) over extension in the use of credit terms. This latter had the effect of encouraging buying and unusual wage demands. He did not want this to be "opinions" rather a recounting of history.[15]

This was not merely a reflection of Eisenhower's penchant for editing but the expression of a person confident of his understanding of economic forces. Burn's most famous student had come a long way.

STAFFING THE COUNCIL

As soon as Burns had decided the council should be retained and had secured Eisenhower's support for the idea, he set to work recruiting new members and staff. He considered several candidates but clearly decided that Neil Jacoby was the man he wanted to serve on the council and to help him build a staff. As early as mid-April 1953 he called Jacoby about coming to work with him in Washington. At that time the council had no money so Burns could not be specific whether he could offer Jacoby a full-time appointment, a temporary summer assignment, or just occasional consulting. Jacoby was then a professor and dean of the School of Business Administration at the University of California at Los Angeles with many consultation commitments. He told Burns that he could only join the government if he was offered a major assignment at a policy-making level.[16]

Neil H. Jacoby, who was born in Canada, received his Ph.D. from the University of Chicago in 1938 and taught there for ten years. He became a naturalized citizen in 1937. During World War II, he was also a member of the research staff of the National Bureau of Economic Research at Columbia that Burns later headed. In 1948 he was appointed dean at UCLA. A background investigation by the Republican National Committee revealed that he registered as a Republican in 1952 and was "somewhat active" in the "Citizens for Eisenhower" movement but had not taken a "very vigorous part in the campaign." Informants regarded "him as a middle-of-the-road conservative leaning, insofar as he leans at all, slightly toward the right."[17]

Before Eisenhower became president Jacoby had developed definite views about the council's role. Soon after the election, Raymond Saulnier, who was to succeed Burns as chairman of the CEA, asked Jacoby for his views on the organization, functioning, and staffing of the CEA. He replied that his thinking about the Council starts from the premise that it is a staff advisory agency to the President. Implications of this concept of the Council are extremely important and it is my view that most of the compromises and difficulties under which the Council has fallen have arisen from failure to grasp these implications. One of them is that the Council gives advice to the President and not to the Congress or to the public or any section thereof. Any staff advisor to a chief executive in a business or military or political organization acts as the counselor of his principal and does not broadcast his advice by public reports or appearances before Congress or any other agency. I doubt whether it is wise for the Council to publish its own reports. Persistent adherence to its proper role as a staff adviser would require that it make its report to the President, and that the President alone should determine whether or not it ought to be published, either by itself or with such additional comment and suggestion as he determines would be necessary or appropriate. In case of publication, it is the *President's* report that is published and not the Council's.

He believed that members of the council should have a "passion for anonymity" and great technical skill as economists. His prescription for an effective council would also require a president who would accept their advice most of the time.[18]

Burns must have found Jacoby's version of the CEA to his liking, for he suggested that he be offered an appointment to the council in the spring at the time when he recommended that a three-person CEA be retained.[19] In August 1953 Jacoby traveled to Denver for his interview with the president who told him that the "boys had checked you thoroughly and I am satisfied that you are qualified." Jacoby told Sherman Adams at the time that he could only promise to come to Washington for a year. The chief of staff merely replied, "It's a changing world and a year is a long time."[20] Jacoby actually stayed two years, but it was his appointment that began the practice of relatively short tenures on the Eisenhower CEA. In contrast, two-thirds of the Truman council had served until the end of his administration. Jacoby was formally appointed a member of the CEA on 15 September.[21]

Although the position of vice chairman no longer existed on the council, at Burns's request, Jacoby served as a kind of chief of staff. This meant that while the chairman became "Mr. Outside," dealing with the White House and Federal Reserve, he relied on Jacoby as "Mr. Inside" to organize the committee structure that was so important to the council's function and to take the principal responsibility for rebuilding the council staff.[22]

Selecting the new staff of the CEA was of critical importance, and because of the legislative maneuvers of Taber and company, Jacoby "had to start building personnel de novo. . . ." As to selection criteria:

We were not looking for a group of yes-men. We wanted men of creative and original minds, not people that would simply rubber stamp ideas that we had. We were looking for creative ability, for fresh thinking. On the other hand, we didn't want to have to spend our time debating fundamental articles of ideology . . . we want a common ground . . . for this reason we did not consider it efficient to go out and deliberately look for people who might be labeled as radicals. This would introduce inharmonious elements.[23]

The CEA had always been a relatively small body of highly trained and skilled professional economists. By end of 1953 the staff, including full and part time, detailed personnel and consultants who reported frequently, numbered thirty-three. Of this number, seventeen were expert economists.[24]

The Truman CEA staff was composed almost entirely of career government economists. Only three survived Congressman Taber's budget maneuver. Jacoby turned to the universities to recruit the dozen or so new senior economists. But by the time Jacoby began trying to sign up a staff, it was late in the academic year and many professors felt committed to their institutions for the coming year. The best he could do was get those who could obtain a leave of absence and commit some others for the next year. The resulting rotation system was later touted as the appropriate way to staff the council, but it was primarily motivated by necessity.[25]

They came to Washington for one or two years in what was deliberately a temporary assignment. Their primary functions were as teachers, consultants, and researchers rather than as operating economists. Their career focus continued to be the universities and colleges from which they came rather than the bureaucracy. The combination of great turnover and lack of government experience and contacts had a catastrophic effect on the relations between the CEA and the agencies.[26]

Raymond J. Saulnier, Burns's successor, recognized the problem of relying on short-term academics to staff the council. In retrospect he thought: "A certain amount of staff turnover is desirable to keep fresh viewpoints alive in council work, but my preference is for a staff largely, but not entirely, of permanent civil service appointees. This gives the staff the best chance of achieving the seniority and standing in government which it should have to function most effectively."[27]

By Washington standards the CEA was always a small agency and thus was characterized by informality and considerable staff interaction. The senior economists who made up the professional staff each covered a specific field such as labor, agriculture, housing, prices, money and finance, international trade, etc. Once a week the council members, with the chairman presiding, met with the staff but informal meetings between the members and the staff were irregular and frequent.[28]

Chairman Burns believed that the staff "functioned primarily to advise me; it was not supposed to go around selling programs." But in fact he really did not rely on the staff for economic evaluation and judgment. Because of his own strong intellectual traditions, he was skeptical of staff members whose training represented other schools of thought. He only worked intimately with the three members of the staff whom he had known before his Washington years. As long as Burns was chairman, the work of the CEA centered on him with little separate identity for the staff or even the other members of the council.[29]

THE OTHER COUNCIL MEMBERS

Finding and recommending the appointment of council members was typically Hauge's responsibility in cooperation with the chairman. In making his selections Hauge was always under pressure to have them represent various economic areas such as industry or agriculture. Generally he resisted such pressure but on most of the councils there was someone from agriculture. Hauge did try to avoid too much concentration in one city or region or in one particular academic tradition. His primary concern was to obtain broad-gauge people who were general economists and who were well informed on the business, financial, and international picture. Staff appointments rather than council members would cover specialties.[30]

During the fall of 1953 Hauge, Burns and Jacoby turned their attention to the selection of the third member of the council. They chose a man who had served as an economic adviser to Presidents Calvin Coolidge, Herbert Hoover, and Franklin Roosevelt. Walter Stewart, who was sixty-eight at the time of his appointment, was then a successful investment banker who had begun his career as a professor at the University of Missouri and had taught at the University of Michigan and Amherst College. Although he did not have a Ph.D., he had been described as "a gifted economic theorist." Hoover's treasury secretary said Stewart was the "greatest living authority on gold and foreign exchange." He was first associated with the federal government during World War I when he served with the War Industries Board and then during the twenties he became the Director of the Federal Reserve Board's Division of Research and Statistics. Later he served as president of the Rockefeller Foundation. He retired from business in 1938 when he accepted an appointment as a professor at Princeton's Institute for Advanced Study. In 1950 he became an emeritus professor.[31]

In 1953 Stewart was still at Princeton where he was engaged in "rather a recondite study of monetary and banking theory." He naturally became the elder statesman of the council. Jacoby said Stewart was "truly a man of immense breadth of knowledge, who had refined it into a good deal of wisdom." But he was not in vigorous health. He participated fully in council meetings and policy decisions but he was not able to work the long hours that Burns and Jacoby were obliged to put in.[32] Both Jacoby and Stewart were given recess appointments during the fall of 1953 and were confirmed by the Senate early in 1954. Both served on the council until the spring of 1955 when Raymond J. Saulnier and Joseph S. Davis replaced them.[33]

Saulnier, like Burns, was a product of Columbia University. He had become an instructor there in 1934, and after he received his Ph.D. in economics in 1938 he was appointed an assistant professor at Barnard College. That same year he joined the research staff of the National Bureau of Economic Research. During the war years he coauthored many publications with Neil Jacoby. In 1946, the year after Burns was made director of the bureau, Saulnier was appointed director of the bureau's Financial Research Program that studied banking and finance. In the early 1950s Saulnier did some Washington consulting with the Federal Reserve System and the Farm Credit Administration. When Burns moved to Washington in the spring of 1953, he brought Saulnier along as a member of his staff. In April 1955 he was made a member of the council, and when Burns left in December 1956, Saulnier replaced him as chairman of the CEA, a position that he held for the remainder of the Eisenhower administration.[34]

Saulnier replaced Jacoby who had resigned on 9 February 1955. Stewart resigned from the council on 29 April 1955 but continued as a consultant to the CEA for a period of time. Dr. Joseph S. Davis, the retired director of the Food Institute of Stanford University, succeeded Stewart. When Davis left in 1958 he was replaced by Karl Brandt, another Stanford agricultural economist from the Food Institute.[35]

Burns's resignation in 1956 and Saulnier's elevation to the chairmanship provided an opening on the council for Paul W. McCracken. At the time of his appointment McCracken was serving as a member of the council's senior staff on leave from the University of Michigan where he was professor of business conditions.[36] When McCracken went back to Michigan in 1959 he was replaced by Henry C. Wallich, a Yale economist who, with Saulnier and Brandt, stayed until the end of the Eisenhower administration.[37]

CONGRESS AND THE COUNCIL

The Employment Act of 1946 specified that the president send to Congress at the beginning of each regular session a report on the country's economic levels and trends together with his program for dealing with these conditions. As the name of the law implies employment was to be the main thrust of the report. The law also established the Joint Committee on the Economic Report, made up of seven members from the Senate and seven from the House of Representatives. The committee's primary function was "to make a continuing study of matters relating to the Economic Report."[38]

The question whether members of the CEA should testify before this committee and other committees of the Congress was a cause célèbre in the latter years of the Truman council and led to a well-publicized debate between Nourse and Keyserling. Nourse declined to testify while Keyserling was anxious to support the administration before Congress.[39] Elmer Staats, former member of both the Truman and Eisenhower administrations, did not think Keyserling was the best person to head the CEA, but he did agree with his position on appearing before Congress. He did not believe that the Nourse view that the council's "advice ought to be confidential . . . was compatible with the law."[40]

The squabble between Nourse and Keyserling was well publicized, and it was one of the factors that led to the congressional disenchantment with the council. In December 1952, as the Eisenhower administration prepared to take office, a senior member of the CEA staff attempted to put the issue in perspective and offer advice.

I have felt that the disagreement between Mr. Nourse and Mr. Keyserling over the issue of Council appearance before congressional committees was greatly exaggerated, both by the two persons involved and by the public generally. It seems to me that agency responsibility requires that the Council members appear before the Joint Economic Committee to discuss the economic report and at any other times the Joint Committee wishes the Council to appear. In fact, this has been done since the beginning of the Council. The difficulty arose as to whether the Council should place itself in a position of being called to testify before other committees. Here I think no hard and fast precedent should be established.[41]

The reorganization of the CEA simplified the issue by assigning to the chairman the responsibility of representing the council before outside groups. There would be no more public disagreements between council members. Burns tried to avoid the testifying controversy by arranging with the chairman of the Joint Committee to testify before the committee only in executive session without a transcript. When invited to appear before a Senate subcommittee on housing, Burns declined because he felt "a certain hesitation, serving as I do as the President's adviser, to make any public pronouncements just before the President submits his recommendations on economic matters to the Congress."[42] The new council tried to "remain aloof from the legislative branch, and be reticent about making statements to the general public."[43] This low profile approach was effective as long as the Republicans had control of the Joint Committee.

This cozy arrangement ended in 1956 when Democratic Senator Paul Douglas began demanding that Burns testify in open session before the committee. The two began a heated correspondence that continued through the spring. Burns began by reviewing the Nourse/Keyserling controversy and then stated his position.

I have pondered this problem for a long time, both before assuming my present post and since then. It is entirely clear to me that members of the Council must always try to be helpful to the Joint Committee. I therefore feel that they should respond affirmatively to an invitation to testify before the Joint Committee. It is equally clear to me that—except in the case of technical discussions such as those of the Subcommittee on Economic Statistics—the testimony should be given at an executive session and without a transcript.

Burns told Douglas that, while the legislative history of the Employment Act inferred that CEA members should not testify before congressional committees, he personally did not accept that interpretation. He held that the CEA and the Joint Committee should work together but if a member testified on the record, he

would almost necessarily have to appear as an advocate of the President's program, not only in general but down to every detail. Once a member of the Council becomes a public spokesman for the Administration, and that is what testimony in print implies as a practical matter, his objectivity in handling economic facts and policies—which is essential to the proper performance of his duties under the law—may be impaired. When that happens, and I am not imagining remote possibilities when I say this, the Employment Act itself is put in jeopardy.[44]

Douglas continued to press for open testimony and Burns continued to resist, as their letters became increasingly hostile.[45] Burns resigned from the council on 1 December 1956 and was replaced by Saulnier who soon worked out a compromise with Wright Patman, the chairman of the Joint Committee. Patman suggested that Saulnier testify in executive session

at which a transcript would be taken of those parts of the meeting which the Council felt would not jeopardize its position of anonymity. At any point in the hearing when the Council felt it was getting into an area where it wished to "roll up its sleeves" it would be given permission to go off the record—with no stenographic notes made. Upon completion of this delicate point the discussion could go back on the record.

The part of the hearing that was transcribed could then be typed, and the Council could edit it to provide additional elaborations or to delete portions that on further consideration were felt to jeopardize its position.[46]

Saulnier replied that, although he preferred to testify in executive session without a transcript, he accepted Patman's proposal as "a fair and workable one."[47]

Saulnier considered the relationship between the council and the Joint Committee as an agreeable and useful partnership. In practice he testified in open hearings. The compromise was essentially a face-saving device for the CEA. While Saulnier always had the privilege of requesting an executive session for all or part of a given testimony, he never found it necessary to exercise it.[48]

DEPRESSION BULWARK

The Employment Act and the Council of Economic Advisers were designed to help avoid an expected postwar depression. The CEA was to estimate annually for the president and the Congress the number of jobs that the private sector was expected to provide and compare that figure to the size of the workforce. The implication was that the government would provide employment for the surplus workers. Since the depression did not reappear after the war, the Truman council found itself focusing on inflation rather than unemployment.

The Great Depression had begun the last time a Republican was in the White House. The Democrats had been so successful in demonizing Herbert Hoover that many Republicans feared that if it happened again it would mean the end of the party. Eisenhower shared these fears and he was determined that it would not happen on his watch. The new president made it clear that he wanted to have in his executive office a

staff for the purpose of keeping a close watch on our domestic economy, with the particular objective of anticipating signs of decreasing economic activity tending in the direction of either a recession or a depression; and with the further objective of proposing remedial measures before the economy gets into serious difficulties.[49]

Burns had little doubt that the CEA was the staff that the president expected to use to keep the country out of a depression. He repeatedly talked to Burns "about the need for keeping in a high state of readiness all applicable plans for combating or rather preventing, depression or serious deflation." As a result of the Monday morning sessions Eisenhower was aware that many of the Government's weapons against recession are ready for prompt and current action, such as credit measures, debt management, alternation in certain permissive terms in mortgages Federally insured, and some variation in the rate of authorized budget expenditures. Others, such as reduction in taxes and other modifications in tax laws together with changes in the social security and unemployment insurance programs, require Congressional action. There are others that require a varying length of preparatory work before they can be effective either in employing large numbers of people or in otherwise making money available for stabilizing and stimulating the economy. In this later group must be included all types of public works.[50]

The council had the task of watching the economy and recommending to the president when to apply any of these "weapons."

Although the above was a memo from the president to the chairman of the council, clearly this was really Burns's analysis of the countercyclical measures the federal government might take when recession threatened. This was the area of Burns's academic expertise and one of the reasons he was named chairman. Burns made a major effort to achieve a modification and liberalization of the traditional Republican conservatism about the role of the government in managing the economy.[51] The president's memo cited above is evidence that he succeeded. The president had told his brother that the "maintenance of prosperity is one field of governmental concern that interests me mightily. . . . I am sure that the government has to be the principal coordinator and, in many cases, the actual operator of the many things that the approach of depression would demand."[52]

In the battle for the president's mind, George Humphrey was Burns's biggest rival. Humphrey was the president's good friend. A lawyer by training, he had become a wealthy industrialist and in 1952 the chairman of the finance committee of the Republican party. In this role he raised a great deal of money for the Eisenhower campaign. He then became secretary of the treasury and Eisenhower's favorite in the Cabinet. Both men were ebullient, vital, and energetic with engaging personalities. Humphrey did not like professors. He considered them impractical dreamers and theorists. And they did not like him. Jacoby considered Humphrey an arrogant, uneducable, economic illiterate who "hadn't learned anything from the Keynesian Revolution."[53]

Even those professors who tended to agree with Humphrey's views did not like the way he arrived at them. Saulnier did not consider Humphrey

a reflective kind of person. He had his positions pretty well formulated and could and would give you his judgment on a question pretty fast. This doesn't mean his positions on economic question are not thought out, much less that they are wrong. He is a man who, while he does a lot of thinking about questions of public policy, can give you his position on them very quickly. This tends to be a little disconcerting to the academic and reflective mind. He quickly judges a new problem by reference to established positions, churning out of his mental computer an answer to the question at hand.[54]

There is little doubt that Humphrey, the hard-shell businessman, and Burns, the egg-head professor, were Eisenhower's primary economic advisers. Their views frequently differed in more than detail and emphasis. Burns recalled, "We fought hard at times and each lost some battles to the other." One suspects that in these battles Humphrey won more than he lost. Usually both men were prudent enough to avoid forcing the president to choose between them.[55]

PUBLIC WORKS PLANNING

While Jacoby was getting the new council staff organized during the fall of 1953, Burns was gathering information from the departments about the status of their plans for undertaking public works. He knew that during the depression and World War II serious deficits had developed in the country's infrastructure. He did not expect to use public works as an anti-depression measure, but because of the lead time that was necessary to plan these activities, he wanted to be ready should they be needed.[56]

The president's memo laid out the council's role in public works planning and emphasized his commitment to it.

Your function in the preparation of such plans will be largely coordinating and supervisory in character. The Departments will in general prepare specific plans. In order that there may be no misunderstanding of the importance I attach to this work, we will, as we also agreed this morning, take it up at the next meeting of the Cabinet. I shall do everything possible to make certain that this work is pushed vigorously so that we may be assured of a reasonable state of readiness in this regard certainly no later than July first.[57]

Armed with this presidential mandate Burns organized a public works task force charged with developing criteria for the volume of projects under various conditions and the advance planning of desirable projects in terms of their organization and financing. The group's job was to prepare for the rapid and effective expansion of public works in case of a recession.[58]

The public works unit together with the Bureau of the Budget completed an inventory of federal public works plans, showing the status of both planning and financing, also the estimated cost of the projects, their type, location, urgency, the time required for getting them under way and for completion, and the employment that would be afforded by their execution. To broaden the scope of public works planning and make it more effective the function was transferred to the White House staff on 12 August 1955.[59] In typical Eisenhower fashion a new special assistant to the president was created. Retired Major General John Bragdon was appointed as the administration's public works planner and remained in that post until 1961.[60]

THE ECONOMIC REPORT

The Employment Act of 1946 required the president to transmit to Congress at the beginning of each regular session an Economic Report setting forth the levels of employment, production, and purchasing power currently prevailing in the economy; current and foreseeable economic trends; and the levels of employment required to carry out the declared policy of the Employment Act.[61] For the first two years President Truman signed the reports that had been drafted by the CEA and rewritten by the White House staff. Then, beginning with a midyear report in July 1948, the practice was begun of sending to Congress every six months a detailed report written by the council. To meet the requirements of the Employment Act the president supplemented this with a short and general annual report to Congress.[62] This change coincided with the bitter election campaign of 1948. Many felt that this practice had contributed to the negative congressional reaction to the CEA.

The rationale for the change was that an economic report to Congress from the president would inevitably be labeled "political" whereas a CEA report could be objective and scientific. Nourse had resisted the change because he feared it would politicize the council and his misgivings turned out to be well founded. Neil Jacoby wrote that:

the notion that a cold, scientific objectivity is possible in evaluating alternative courses of economic policy is itself a will-o-the-wisp. Economic analysis rests on certain "values" which are themselves open to debate; it does not lead to unique and unambiguous results. What is important is that the president and his advisers hold a certain set of values in common and that they reason logically from them, utilizing the best data at hand.

He felt that a short and general report from the president allowed "an administration to avoid the difficult but highly desirable discipline of evolving a coherent economic doctrine and policy."[63]

The Burns council reverted to the earlier practice of having the president annually send Congress a detailed analytic Economic Report. The CEA's own annual report to the president was limited to council administrative matters.

Eisenhower resisted signing a report that had obviously been written by professional economists because he did not want to say anything in the first person unless he was personally familiar with it. He felt that if he "signs a report containing a lot of things he does not understand, he can expect a press conference question about some involved part of it—and he then is at a loss to answer and put in a bad light." But Burns insisted that the president had to sign the report, and Eisenhower did—but under protest. After Burns left, the president won part of the battle when Saulnier agreed that Eisenhower need only sign the introduction to the report itself.[64]

During Burns's tenure the writing of the report was an internal council project dominated by the chairman. The staff contribution was limited to providing information and reviewing drafts. The process began in October with discussions between the council and the staff. Burns then wrote from scratch the initial draft of the major chapters with some specialized chapters drafted by others under Jacoby's direction. Later Burns rewrote everything except the appendices—and these he carefully reviewed and edited. Interdepartmental clearance of the Economic Report was superficial, being limited to a general discussion in ABEGS and a review of drafts. The focus of Hauge's White House review was the letter of transmittal that was a three- or four-page summary of the report.[65]

The president's signature on the Economic Report converted the document from a working paper into the official statement of economic doctrine and policy of the administration.[66] Since the report in turn was essentially the work of Arthur Burns it was a measure of his influence in the Eisenhower administration.

THE SAULNIER YEARS

The departure of Burns in 1956 inevitably reduced the influence of the Council because much of it depended on the chairman's relationship with the president. Saulnier, who had served as a member of the staff and council before becoming chairman, inherited the enhanced stature that Burns had built up for the position. He attended meetings of the Cabinet and the National Security Council and periodically chaired Cabinet committees. Economic matters were always an important topic in the administration, and he ended up reporting to the Cabinet more than any other person. He was also a regular participant in the weekly meeting with legislative leaders.[67]

The new chairman was very protective of his role as economic adviser to the president.[68] He saw Eisenhower several times a week and considered the president an ideal man for a professional economist to work with because of his interest in the subject and his skill in using staff. His contacts were frequent and intimate, both in person and by telephone, since the president often used Saulnier as a member of White House staff as well as his chief economic adviser. For example, Eisenhower had his staff brief him before his weekly press conferences to work out his positions: the chairman always participated in these sessions.[69]

Eisenhower's systematic approach to his use of staff meant that the council would have an opportunity to comment on all economic matters. Saulnier recalled that:

no bill presented for presidential signature that had economic significance failed to pass under Council review. Nor any presidential speech, statement, or paper dealing with economic questions. Likewise, no economic or financial proposal designed to be part of the "President's program," failed to come under Council review. Nor any of the wide range of actions to be taken by the President having economic implications, such as determinations on import damage to U.S. industry. Furthermore, the President expected no department or agency to take an action with significant economic policy impact without first reviewing it with the Council.[70]

Saulnier's contemporaries thought his interests were limited and specialized compared to Burns, who was thought to be much broader-gauged person. Like his predecessor, Saulnier was considered a "one-man operator" who did not make effective use of the council staff. He had little communication with the staff and never took a member of the staff to meetings, even of ABEGS. The other two council members under Saulnier functioned more as senior members of the staff rather than as the chairman's colleagues.[71]

Though the staff and the other members had no personal contact with the president they considered themselves a presidential staff unit rather than an operating agency. Primary emphasis was placed on writing the council's quarterly and annual reports. The annual report alone took the major part of staff time for about three months. In preparation for its writing the staff used task forces to make across the board studies.[72]

Saulnier's personal background was in the housing credit field so he tended to over-emphasize its importance. While chairman he served on the board of the Federal National Mortgage Association and was intimately involved in all significant actions taken by the Housing and Home Finance Agency. In this area Saulnier had the staff take on an operational role and do much work that was not productive as far as policy was concerned. The staff also resented the "minutiae" they had to engage in to support Saulnier in his role as chairman of the Cabinet Committee on Small Business.[73]

In summary the Eisenhower years saw the transformation of the Council of Economic Advisers. When the administration began, the CEA was on the road to extinction. Burns saved it by winning the respect of Eisenhower and the Congress, but its resurgence was essentially due to the president's attitude toward it. When Eisenhower signaled that he was interested in the advice that the chairman could provide, everything else fell into place.

NOTES

1. Stephen Hess, *Organizing the Presidency* (Washington, D.C., 1988), pp. 86–87.
2. Edwin Nourse Oral History, 1972, Harry S Truman Library, p. 54.
3. Sherman Adams Oral History, DDEL, pp. 190–191.
4. Edward S. Flash, Jr., *Economic Advice and Presidential Leadership: The Council of Economic Advisers* (New York, 1965), p. 123.
5. Raymond J. Saulnier, Oral History, DDEL, p. 20.
6. Ibid., p. 16.
7. Gabriel Hauge, Speech to National Planning Association, 13 December 1955, Burns Papers, DDEL.
8. Flash, *Economic Advice*, pp. 168–169.
9. Don Paarlberg to author, 7 March 1995.
10. Nourse Oral History, Harry S Truman Library.
11. Flash, *Economic Advice*, pp. 122–123.
12. Ibid., p. 160.
13. Neil Jacoby Oral History, DDEL.
14. Conference with the President, 21 August 1953, Neil Jacoby Papers, DDEL.
15. Memo for the Files, 24 December 1958, Staff Notes Dec 58 (1), DDE Diary Series, DDEL.
16. Phone conversation, 18 April 1953, Personnel 53–55, Burns Papers, DDEL.
17. Flash, *Economic Adivce*, p. 109; W. L. Crum to Burns, 1 July 1953, Personnel 53–55, Arthur Burns Papers, DDEL; Jacoby c.v., Admin-Council Staff, CEA 1956–1961, DDEL.
18. Jacoby to Saulnier, 29 December 1952, CEA Appointment, Jacoby Papers, DDEL.
19. Telephone Conversation, Burns and Jacoby, 28 April 1953, Jacoby Papers, DDEL.
20. Memo of Conference with the President, 21 August 1953, CEA Appointment, Jacoby Papers, DDEL.
21. 1953 Annual Report of the CEA to the President, CEA 1954, OF 72–E, NA.
22. Jacoby Oral History, DDEL, pp. 41, 93.
23. Ibid.
24. 1953 CEA Annual Report to the President.
25. Flash, *Economic Advice*, p. 109.

26. Ibid.; Bureau of the Budget meeting, 4 April 1958, 52.6, E1–31/54.1, RG 51, NA.

27. Saulnier Oral History, DDEL, pp. 7–8.

28. Ibid.

29. Flash, *Economic Advice*, p. 126.

30. Hauge Oral History, pp. 92–93.

31. Flash, *Economic Advice*, p. 109; Stewart c.v., Administration-Council Staff, CEA 1956–61.

32. Jacoby Oral History.

33. Millardi to McCaffree, 4 May 1955, White House Correspondence, 1955, Burns Papers, DDEL.

34. Saulnier c.v., Administration-Council Staff, CEA 1956–1961, DDEL; Jacoby c.v., Ibid.

35. 1958 CEA Annual Report, 29 December 1958, Report to the President, CEA Records, DDEL.

36. 1956 CEA Annual Report, ibid.

37. 1959 CEA Annual Report, 31 December 1959, Ibid.

38. U.S. Code, 1946 edition, pp. 1509–1510, CEA Appointment, Jacoby Papers, DDEL.

39. Jacoby, "The Operation of the Council of Economic Advisers," Role of the Council, Jacoby Papers, DDEL.

40. Elmer Staats interview with author, 10 September 1979, GAO Bldg, Washington, D.C.

41. Fisher, 72–E, 1955, OF72E, DDEL.

42. Burns to John Sparkman, 18 November 1955, Congressional Correspondence 1953–55, Burns Papers, DDEL.

43. Jacoby Oral History, DDEL, p. 77.

44. Burns to Paul H. Douglas, 3 February 1956, Congressional Correspondence 1956, Burns Papers, DDEL

45. Ibid., 12 March and 15 May 1956.

46. Wright Patman to Saulnier, 11 December 1956, Joint Committee Hearing, CEA Records, DDEL.

47. Saulnier to Patman, 19 December 1956, ibid.

48. Raymond J. Saulnier, "On Advising the President," *Presidential Studies Quarterly* 15, no. 3 (summer 1985): pp. 585–586.

49. Cover for draft memo to PACGO from BOB, 6 May 1953, Series 52.6, E1–30, OMO, RG 51, NA.

50. Dwight D. Eisenhower to Burns, 2 February 1954, DDE Diary-February 54(2), DDE Diary Series, DDEL.

51. Flash, *Economic Advice*, p. 158.

52. DDE to Milton Eisenhower, 6 January 1954, DDE Diary-January 54(2), DDE Diary Series, DDEL.

53. Jacoby Oral History, p. 79, DDEL.

54. Saulnier Oral History, pp. 58–59, DDEL.

55. Flash, *Economic Advice*, p. 164.

56. Burns to Maxwell Rabb, 14 November 1953, White House Correspondence, Burns Papers, DDEL.

57. DDE to Burns, 2 February 1954, DDE Diary-February 54(2), DDE Diary Series, DDEL.

58. Public Works Task Force Agenda, 7 April 1954, Public Works, Jacoby Papers, DDEL.

59. 1955 CEA Annual Report, 30 December 1955, Report to the President, CEA Records, DDEL.

60. John W. Sloan, "The Management and Decision-Making Style of President Eisenhower," *Presidential Studies Quarterly* 20, no. 2 (spring 1990): 300.

61. Saulnier to Senator Ralph Yarborough, 19 September 1958, Congressional Correspondence, CEA Records, DDEL.

62. Neil Jacoby, "The Operation of the Council of Economic Advisers," Role of the Council, Jacoby Papers, DDEL, p. 11.

63. Ibid., p. 12.

64. Diary entry, 22 January 1958, ACW Diary, January 58(2), Whitman File, DDEL.

65. Flash, pp. 167–168.

66. Jacoby, "The Operation of the Council of Economic Advisers," Role of the Council, Jacoby Papers, DDEL, pp. 11–12.

67. Saulnier Oral History, DDEL, p. 15.

68. Paarlberg to author, 7 March 1995.

69. Ibid.

70. Saulnier, "On Advising the President," pp. 583–584.

71. Bureau of the Budget meeting on CEA, 4 April 1958, 52.6, E1–31/54.1, RG 51, NA.

72. Ibid.

73. Ibid.; Saulnier, "On Advising the President," p. 587.

4

The Reorganization of the National Security Council

By 1952 the Cold War had reached a new level of intensity. With the explosion of the Soviet atomic bomb in 1949, Americans, for the first time, began to feel physically threatened. In 1950, NSC–69, a major foreign policy planning document, had posited the possible outbreak of war with the Soviet Union for 1954. The North Korean invasion of South Korea confirmed for many the validity of this prediction. In these perilous times Eisenhower's military background was one of the sources of his popularity. The candidate's promise to visit Korea personally was enough to assure his election. The climate that existed made the formulation of foreign policy a sensitive political issue, and the National Security Council was supposed to be the president's primary mechanism for the development of this policy.

BOBBY CUTLER

General Robert Cutler had been added to the Eisenhower campaign train as a companion because the candidate wanted someone to talk to and no one else would have time to do so.[1] Bobby Cutler was an amusing fellow who liked to joke and quip. He had been his class's poet while an undergraduate at Harvard and then a published novelist by the age of twenty-three. These youthful diversions were put aside when he became a lawyer and a Boston banker. Active in Republican politics, he was one of the group that had pressed General Eisenhower to seek the Republican nomination.[2]

During World War II Cutler had served as an army staff officer working in the Pentagon on high-level policy and political problems. There he got to know Henry Stimson, George Marshall, and Gordon Gray and became known as an effective organization man. Through these contacts he also got to know Dwight Eisenhower. In 1951 Gordon Gray became the director of the Psychological Strategy Board (PSB) which Truman had established to work with the National Security Council on Cold War strategy. Gray was able to enlist Cutler to serve as his deputy for a three-month stint. One of Cutler's duties at the PSB was to attend meetings of the National Security Council's senior staff. Cutler's work with the PSB introduced him to the structure, procedures, and problems of the NSC.[3] By the spring of 1952 he was convinced that "the NSC should be shaken up, vitalized, given a driving force."[4]

Cutler was too much of an activist to be content serving as a companion for the candidate on the campaign train. Soon he was quite busy writing speeches and serving as general handyman. He and Hauge would work over drafts prepared by a group of speechwriters in New York and teletyped to the train.

Based on his experience with the PSB and discussions with Eisenhower, Cutler drafted a speech that the candidate delivered in Baltimore.[5] In it Eisenhower was critical of the NSC. He suggested that its membership should not be limited to Cabinet officers but should include civilians of the highest capacity, integrity, and dedication to public service who would have no other official duties.[6] (Using civilian consultants on the NSC was not an idea that Cutler was ever comfortable with.)

On 8 October 1952 in San Francisco, candidate Eisenhower delivered another speech written by Cutler that focused on the National Security Council and the need to adapt the nation's foreign policy to a Cold War strategy that was "unified and coherent." He said, "We must bring the dozens of agencies and bureaus into concerted action under an over-all scheme of strategy" directed by "a revitalized and reconstructed National Security Council."[7] With these two speeches Eisenhower not only made the operation of the president's staff a campaign issue but also promised, if elected, to make some improvements in the operation of the White House.

TRUMAN'S NSC

An objective appraisal of the effectiveness of the NSC in 1952 had to take into account the fact that, compared to the foreign policy mechanism that existed on the eve of World War II, it was a tremendous step forward. Truman had said that it had been invaluable to him and that he could not see how his predecessors had got along without it. Yet, in 1952, the Bureau of the Budget cautiously admitted, "On balance . . . it is possible to draw the conclusion the NSC has not yet achieved working procedures which permit it to meet fully all of the criteria set for its performance."[8]

The budget bureau found the NSC a beneficial interagency group because it permitted the Department of Defense, short of going to the president, "to force State to deal with problems and has likewise permitted State to force Defense to give it a whack at problems which would otherwise be bound up in Defense alone." But the bureau believed that the NSC was frequently assigned the wrong problems and was handicapped by an organization that permitted logrolling. As a result the council gave the president not independent staff advice "but the lowest-common-denominator of advice from the participating agencies."[9]

As the Eisenhower administration was preparing to assume office, the budget bureau drafted a document designed to provide the president-elect with background on the problems then existing in the Executive Office of the President. In regard to the NSC the bureau found that

many of its policy pronouncements seem vague and general when attempts are made to link them with the realities of departmental operations. The NSC plays a very limited role in following up on policy execution. It likewise plays a very limited role in questioning the adequacy of the departmental positions presented. Thus, policy issues are stated and resolved by default in terms of any effective challenge to the position of the major department concerned. Particularly when there is a latent feeling of opposition among other departments concerned, but no effective center of debate, this situation results in a "sterile" product from the NSC activity with each agency following its own course as a practical matter.[10]

DODGE ASSESSES THE NSC

Shortly after the election Eisenhower announced that he planned to designate Joseph Dodge as his director of the budget. He then sent Dodge off to Washington to gather data about the Truman budget that was to be submitted in January. After he set up shop in the budget bureau Dodge began to gather information for Eisenhower on other problems he would be facing.

One of these problems was the National Security Council. Dodge reported that the NSC was a policy committee that operated at the presidential level but was not in the chain of command. At that time the statutory membership of the NSC was the president and vice president, the secretaries of state and defense, the chairman of the National Security Resources Board, and the director for mutual security. By presidential invitation the secretary of the treasury and the director of defense mobilization also attended all meetings. The chairman of the Joint Chiefs of Staff (JCS) and the director of Central Intelligence attended the meetings in a supporting advisory capacity. The small NSC staff then numbered twenty-three including James Lay, the council's executive secretary.[11] The NSC budget for 1952 was $145,000.[12]

In an effort to make the NSC more effective Truman had, in July 1950, approved a reorganization of the council's supporting mechanism that created a "Senior Staff." This group was composed of high-level representatives of each of the council's statutory members (except the president), the chairman of the Joint Chiefs of Staff, and the director of Central Intelligence. The purpose of the Senior Staff was to develop policy papers for consideration by the NSC. It was hoped that the NSC members would designate as their representatives persons who had their full confidence and would provide them with enough time to engage in the thinking, exchange of views, and deliberation needed for devising national policy. These expectations were not realized. One of the members of the Senior Staff recalled that every paper they produced "was so compromised and watered down to avoid disagreement that when it was finished it had about as much wallop as cambric tea."[13] Dodge summarized the principal problems facing the NSC as:

a. composition and organization,

b. domination of policy decisions by the agency in the area where the problem falls.

c. effective implementation of policies,

d. limitation on policy and staff work predicated on the levels and applied time of the agency individuals assigned to work on the problems before the Council,

e. time delays and lack of action on program projects,

f. a general absence of relating policy decisions to the feasibility of implementation or the costs.

The main difficulty that he identified was the tendency to allow the agency in whose area the policy fell to dominate the decision made because the staffs of the other agencies failed to give the problem adequate consideration. An even more serious deficiency was implementation of policies after they were enunciated. That is, after the president accepted a policy proposed by the NSC, there was no machinery to insure that it was carried out.[14]

Both of these problems could be traced, Dodge believed, to the nature of the departments' representation on the NSC's Senior Staff.

The difficulty here was that it turned out to be a part-time effort on the part of those assigned, while full-time effort and application are indicated. This could be satisfied by the appointment of "Special Assistants" to the head of each agency for assignment to the NSC Office of the President on a full time basis and with full recourse to all the resources of the agency. Preferably he should not be a career man and he should not solely represent the Department from which he is appointed but primarily represent National Security and freely collaborate with similar representatives of other agencies.[15]

Dodge held that the departments would pay more attention to NSC policy directives if they were represented on the NSC Senior Staff by people with higher departmental status. Dodge also suggested that the membership on the council should be altered by dropping the director of mutual security and by merging the National Security Resources Board and the Office of Defense Mobilization and combining their seats on the NSC. He further proposed that the president-elect consider adding to the council one or more representatives of the domestic policy problems relating to national security.[16]

Another critique of Truman's NSC was provided by W. Y. Elliott. Professor Elliott, a noted political scientist on leave from Harvard, was then representing the Office of Defense Mobilization on the Senior Staff of the NSC. (Elliott had been involved in the organization of the Executive Office of the President since he worked as a staffer for the Brownlow Committee in 1936.)[17] He characterized the council as "more a secretariat and a routine method of clearing matters of interagency concern" than the high-level policy mechanism it was supposed to be. He found that the members of the council avoided their responsibility and passed "down the line to subordinates the kind of policy decisions that deserve and must get top-side consideration and settlement." Elliott recommended that the new administration create an Executive Director for the NSC and provide him with adequate staff. He also suggested that Vice President-elect Nixon preside over the NSC and oversee congressional liaison.[18]

Elliott was particularly critical of the NSC Senior Staff of which he was a member. He complained that while it was supposed to consist of departmental representatives at the level of undersecretaries, in practice its members were considerably junior to assistant secretary rank. This group's primary function was to review the papers presented by the departments and prepare the issues for presentation to the council. Another important part of their job was to brief their bosses before they attended NSC meetings. But, said Elliott, "the general evidence is that in practice the principal members of the Council spend a half-hour or less in many cases on this type of briefing and that the sessions of the Council are often somewhat perfunctory and the discussions are by no means searching or thorough, even on very important issues of policy." Elliott thought the only remedy for this situation was to have the president "insist upon the kind of presentation which shows that the principals on his National Security Council are taking seriously the functions of the Council and the advice which is to be presented to him."[19]

CUTLER'S STUDY

After his election Eisenhower's interest in the NSC and its problems remained high on his agenda. He confided to a friend:

I look upon the Council as the most important single agency in the Executive Department and . . . do not believe it has had the staff and prestige to do its job in the past. With this in mind, I gave a good deal of thought to finding a man to head the senior staff who would have the stature, experience and ability to energize the operation and command the respect and cooperation of the Cabinet and military services. I think we have such a man in Robert Cutler.[20]

In late December 1952 Eisenhower offered, and Robert Cutler accepted, the job of restructuring the NSC. He did so humbly because he knew that Eisenhower considered "the Executive of the National Security Council as one of the most critically important posts in the effective functioning of the National Government." In his acceptance letter Cutler laid out his frame of reference for reorganizing the council by summarizing ideas he derived from the Baltimore and San Francisco speeches and the subsequent conversations he had had with Eisenhower about the NSC and Cold War strategy.[21]

A few weeks later Cutler went to Washington to look at his future office and talk shop with his former colleagues on the staff of the Psychological Strategy Board. He also met with James Lay, the executive secretary of the NSC, and his assistant, Everett Gleason. Both men agreed to stay at their posts if requested to do so. Cutler then described for Eisenhower what he intended to do during his first months on the job. These plans included:

1. an inquiry into NSC authorizing documents, operational procedures, and administrative matters;

2. examining past, present, and pending security policies;

3. working with a committee chaired by William H. Jackson looking into the programs of the federal government "for giving information to the world and conducting cold war";

4. interviewing present and former members of the NSC and Senior Staff and individuals experienced in governmental operations for ideas to improve the NSC;

5. finally, to submit to the president recommendations for modification and improvement of the NSC operation.[22]

Cutler sought and weighed the views of a variety of observers of the council. In response to his request for ideas on improving the NSC, James Lay prepared for Cutler a paper identifying what he considered the council's four major organizational and operational problems. Lay, who had been with the NSC since its origin and had replaced Sidney Souers as its executive secretary in 1950, was a career bureaucrat who had been struggling for years to make the NSC more effective. He was the author of the 1950 reorganization of the council and the creator of its Senior Staff.

Lay considered the current membership of the NSC too broad. He thought it should be limited to the president, the vice president, the secretaries of state and defense and someone representing the National Security Resources Board-Office of Defense Mobilization area. These five, supported by the CIA and the JCS, should meet to develop the nation's foreign-military policies.[23] Lay admitted that the character, responsibilities, and position of the Senior Staff was still a problem in spite of his best efforts to remedy them. He also noted that the provision of integrated intelligence evaluations on which the council based its development of policy and program needed to be improved. Finally he pointed to the absence of means by which the president could be assured that the policies approved by him were actually being executed.[24]

The President's Advisory Committee on Government Organization, came up with its own diagnosis for the NSC's failure to fulfill its promise. One problem it found was that the council gave insufficient attention to the domestic implications of the policies it recommended. Another was a general failure to relate policy recommendations to either the feasibility of their implementation or their costs. PACGO also faulted the NSC for straying into areas that were not closely related to national security. Its growing inefficiency was traced to its constantly growing membership. Delay and the lack of precision in the council's recommendations were attributed to its efforts to come up with unanimous recommendations.[25]

In a meeting early in February 1953 PACGO gave the president its organizational recommendations for the NSC. The committee suggested that the secretary of the treasury join the NSC as a statutory member and that the NSRB be dropped. PACGO also proposed that a new position of "Executive Officer for the National Security Council" be established and that he be provided with an adequate staff. Eisenhower thought this officer should be called director "so he can call on big shots in his own right." General "Beetle" Smith, Eisenhower's wartime chief of staff, thought "Director" an inappropriate title for the coordinator of what was essentially an interdepartmental committee.[26] Whatever this official's title PACGO thought he should be

an individual with high qualifications and recognized stature, whose functions would be to prevent delays, follow-up decisions, and keep the Council ahead of crises; second, in addition to its present functions, use the NSC staff, augmented in size as necessary, to develop for the President specific analyses which may be presented directly to him by the Executive Officer. It should be made clear that this recommendation makes the Executive Officer responsible to the President. He is not merely the head of the Secretariat of the Council.[27]

THE STUDY GROUPS

A technique that Cutler used to gather the views of knowledgeable people about how the NSC could be improved was to assemble "study groups" into round table discussions about the organization, operations, and problems of the NSC. Each of these groups then developed recommendations for improving the council and its product.

One group included academics that had become old government hands such as Vannevar Bush, W. Y. Elliott, and Marx Leva. They met on 13 February from early afternoon until late in the evening. Their recommendations included changing the NSC staff from a secretariat into a dynamic staff headed by a director who had direct access to the president and enjoyed his confidence. Such a so-called "thinking" (in contrast to "clerical") staff should include specialists in atomic energy, logistics, mobilization, economics, military affairs, and psychological warfare. In respect to the membership of the NSC, this study group thought "the ODM-NSRB function was important and merited representation more than the Treasury function." Bush suggested that some meetings of the NSC be held without the CIA and the JCS present to emphasize that their status in the NSC was advisory only.[28]

The next study group that Cutler assembled supported his opposition to civilian participation in NSC meetings because "ivory tower advice may be screwball" and "advice disassociated from responsibility is not, over a long period, apt to be helpful." Members of this group included Sidney W. Souers, the man who had first organized the NSC for Truman; Paul Nitze, the principal author of NSC–69 and secretary of state Dean Acheson's policy chief; and Allen W. Dulles, the brother of the secretary of state and the soon to be named head of the CIA.

According to Souers, a loyal friend of Harry Truman, Cutler had invited him to the brain storming session just "to make it look as if the Eisenhower administration had made good its promise to revolutionize the set up of the council but in effect not to change the way it was being run." He also reported that *everyone* in the group agreed that it had been a mistake to raise the NSC issue in the campaign speeches. But Souer's comments were made many years after the event and may have been colored by politics. All the other evidence indicates that Cutler was quite sincere in his efforts and achieved a genuine reform of the NSC. It is not likely that as the author of the campaign speeches he would have joined in denigrating them. Souers had one thing right: he was only invited to the one meeting and never saw a draft of the final report. He recalled, "That paper Bobby must have done on his own."[29]

Professor Barton Leach, who also attended this session, thought the recent performance of the NSC had been "seriously inadequate." He believed that since the NSC was the agency for ultimate policy review, it had to have a staff adequate in quality and quantity to be able to exercise an independent review of the papers approved by the Senior Staff.[30] The entire study group agreed that the NSC "think staff" should be increased by six to eight qualified top people. The enlarged staff should then be used to "(1) ferret out facts, state issues fairly, isolate crucial issues, i.e. to examine and comment and prepare; (2) examine the totality of our policies and see where gaps occur."[31]

Eisenhower was an active participant as Cutler gathered views about reorganizing the NSC. In his campaign speech in Baltimore in September, Eisenhower had said that the membership of the NSC "should not be limited to Cabinet officers and heads of administrative agencies." In early February the president reminded Cutler of how important it was to get an outside point of view from respected men such as Roy Roberts, the publisher of a Kansas City newspaper, Governor Alan Shivers of Texas, Governor Earl Warren of California, etc. The president continued to press this idea and Cutler resisted it for the next several years. Eisenhower was also still insisting that Cutler's new title be "Director" so he could "command respectful attention of big shots when he telephoned or visited." When Cutler continued to demur, the president agreed that his title might be "Director and Special Assistant to the President for NSC Affairs."[32]

George Marshall had been secretary of state in 1947 when the NSC was established. Then, while secretary of defense during the Korean War, he again sat as a statutory member of the council. These unique experiences together with Marshall's status as Eisenhower's mentor made it inevitable that Cutler would seek his advice about improving the NSC. The interview, which took place in mid-February 1953, revealed a Marshall who was extremely critical of the existing council and "worried about how to improve its functioning."[33]

Marshall characterized Truman's NSC as "too much concerned merely with papers; too much a meeting of busy men who had no time to pay to the business before them, and, not being prepared, therefore took refuge either in non-participation or in protecting their own departments." He said that Truman had not been a leader in council discussions who tried to bring out discussion. The president simply "came in, sat down, went out." Marshall found that the policy papers the council considered were too much compromised before they reached the NSC. They simply presented "a *fait accompli* to be accepted or rejected or modified a little." While a member of the council Marshall had thought its performance could have been enhanced if three distinguished civilians were added to the NSC membership. He had since decided that this was not a good idea because the civilians "would not be knit together to the Council. They would be without responsibilities."[34] Cutler could be counted on to use this argument in his continuing effort to dissuade Eisenhower from diluting the council membership with nongovernment appointees.

Both of Cutler's "study" groups had advocated strengthening the NSC "thinking" staff but Marshall rejected this approach. He did not believe that any "permanent staff of NSC can possibly take the place of a staff representative of the agencies." But he stressed that the departmental representatives who made up the Senior Staff "must be active in their agencies and in the stream of things in order to be useful."[35]

NITZE'S VIEWS

Paul Nitze, director of the Policy Planning Staff for Acheson's State Department, provided Cutler with a thoughtful analysis of the NSC problem. He advocated a council that would not only work out for the president areas of agreement among the departments but also discover "the issues between possible alternative courses of action, sharpening their definition, and bringing to light the whole range of impacts, costs, and possible losses, as well as gains" which the president had to consider in making decisions. If it adopted this function, Nitze argued, the NSC would become "a vital arm in relation to decisive matters rather than a forum for deliberation on the relatively obvious and unexceptionable aspects of policy."[36]

The State Department typically saw the NSC as an invader in its area of foreign policy. To minimize interference and maximize its influence, state usually favored limiting the membership of the council to its statutory minimum. Nitze supported this position and cautioned against adding a civilian component because "the crux in policy making is the establishment of a practical relationship between ends and means—a task requiring exacting and intimate knowledge of the means such as is likely to grow only out of familiarity with and closeness to the realities of operations." He also opposed the participation of members of Congress in NSC deliberations.[37]

Nitze recommended that the policy papers the NSC considered should initially be prepared by the department primarily concerned with their substance. He thought most of this work would fall to the Departments of State and Defense and Nitze hoped that it would be common practice to assign the tasks to them jointly because "sharing in the authorship of policies tends to heighten devotion to its success."

A central review of the papers thus prepared should be performed by a staff identified with the Council. This staff might well be similar to the present Senior Staff in so far as line of responsibility is concerned. In this event, however, it would be considerably reduced in size to enable it to serve as a working group rather than as a forum. It should consist of not more than five permanent members, one each from the State Department, the Defense Department, the Joint Chiefs of Staff, and the Central Intelligence Agency, with a chairman functioning as a servant of the National Security Council proper. Representatives for other departments and agencies could be drawn in for Senior Staff work or on an *ad hoc* basis as required. Under this arrangement, the chairman should have the assistance of two or three assistants of such standing as to be able to spell him in presiding over the Senior Staff and share with him the attributes essential to the performance of his tasks in general.[38]

The purpose of the central review, according to Nitze, should be to apply broad standards such as insuring that the issues have been spelled out and that the papers reflect a realistic appreciation of the relationship between means and purposes. But, cautioned Nitze, the NSC staff should have, with respect to the departments, "only such authority as derives from the utility of their work rather than that authority derived from being placed at a higher level in a chain of command." In regard to Cutler's own role Nitze urged him to "exercise leadership in the substance and dispatch of business instead of functioning as a merely passive presiding officer."[39]

Cutler also had access to the views of those then working in the NSC apparatus. One of these was William P. Bundy (MacGeorge's brother and Acheson's son-in-law) who was then working for the CIA and representing that agency among the NSC Staff Assistants. His description of the current nature of the NSC papers was a strong argument for arguing the issues in the presence of the president.

NSC papers have had a tendency to present a deceptively monolithic appearance. This tendency (a) fudges or ducks issues; (b) derogates the President's constitutional responsibilities for decision. If there is an initial real difference, e.g. between State and Defense, an agreed paper means that State (Defense) has decided that military (diplomatic) reasons outweigh its own contrary diplomatic (military) arguments. Yet it is the *President* who should weigh the relative importance of the two. Even more important, the President must consider a third element—what the American people will accept and support—that is not directly involved in the recommendations of either State or Defense. If State and Defense present a falsely united front, the President may well hesitate to overrule them; but if the differences are presented frankly to him, he may well decide that domestic considerations tip the scale in favor of the party who would have yielded otherwise.[40]

CUTLER'S REPORT

By early March Cutler had gathered his data, completed his analysis of the problem, and prepared his recommendations to improve the operations of the National Security Council. The structural changes he proposed were rather modest. One of these was the establishment of a new position, an executive officer of the NSC bearing the title of "Special Assistant to the President for National Security Affairs." Even though Eisenhower said he wanted "Director" to be part of the title, Cutler did not include it and the president did not insist. This aide, who would serve at the president's pleasure, would help him run the NSC meetings and preside over the Policy Planning Board. He would supervise, but not be a member of, the NSC staff.[41] It was clear that Cutler would be appointed to the new position.

The title Cutler devised was later assumed by McGeorge Bundy and Henry Kissinger but the positions they occupied were far different from the one Cutler had designed. The Cutler version would focus his energy on making the NSC a viable organization. He and his successors in the Eisenhower White House were not national security advisers. "Their function was to coordinate and facilitate the planning and policies that constituted the work of the NSC." There was no thought that the NSC would handle operational matters.[42]

The new position, special assistant for national security affairs, did not replace the existing executive secretary of the NSC and his deputy. The budget bureau organizational experts told Cutler:

The role of the Special Assistant to the President will depend largely on the relationship and degree of personal participation of the President in the Council. In any case, the role of the Special Assistant should be one primarily aimed at true Presidential staff assistance—that is, being wholly the President's man as in contradistinction to being the Council's assistant. This is largely a matter of orientation but also involves attention toward not becoming too routinely involved in NSC machinery. Special attention should be given to the relationship between the Special Assistant and the Executive Secretary of the NSC so that full appreciation is given to their relative duties. The Executive Secretary's role should therefore relate primarily to serving the Council and seeing to it that its staff is effectively operating.[43]

Both Eisenhower and Cutler tended to follow this advice.

The major decision that Cutler had to make was whether to try to revitalize the Senior Staff, whose personnel came from the departments, or create a presidentially oriented "thinking" (professional) NSC staff to prepare the materials for the council to consider. Both of his study groups had told Cutler to build up the NSC staff. The budget bureau also thought the best way to improve the NSC was to encourage its staff

to take a more positive and aggressive role in relation to the appropriateness of agenda items and to the content of papers submitted by the departments. The NSC staff should develop into a substantive and institutionalized Presidential staff facility in the field of national security policy. This does not mean that they should detract from the policy positions of the members of the Council. Rather, they should be more the agents of the President in securing more from the deliberations of the Council and in stimulating through its staff work, more effective Presidential policy formulation than is currently the case.[44]

But Cutler disagreed. In his recommendation to Eisenhower he deliberately rejected the idea of considerably enlarging the NSC and giving it the function of working up policy papers. Cutler thought it preferable

that representatives of the interested operating agencies (which would eventually be responsible for carrying out a policy) actually and fully participate in the preparation and formulation of that policy. Such a "participant" procedure was—and still is—thought superior to a procedure under which experts, however qualified, who are divorced from agency responsibility and operations, act in the preparation and formulation of a policy.[45]

He suggested that the discredited Senior Staff be replaced by a new organization called the Planning Board. (The name was specifically chosen by Eisenhower.)[46] To remedy the problems that had developed with the Senior Staff, Cutler proposed two basic changes. One was that the new special assistant (Cutler), as the representative of the president, would be the chairman of the Planning Board rather than someone from the State Department (as was the case with the Senior Staff). As chairman he would "lead the discussion at Board Meetings in such manner as to bring out the most active participation by all present and the most expeditious dispatch of business." The special assistant would also try to improve the NSC's record for the implementation of policies by bringing "to the President's attention . . . lack of progress on the part of a department or agency in carrying out a particular policy."[47]

The second change involved the selection, rank, and duties of the members of the Planning Board. Members of the board were to be nominated by members of the NSC, approved by the Special Assistant, and appointed by the president. They would have a rank in their departments similar to that of an assistant secretary. Each would have as his "principal responsibility, which overrides all other duties and with which no other can interfere, his work with the Board; yet at the same time continue to be sufficiently in the stream of activity of his department or agency so as to be capable of representing its views." The members of the board were to have direct access to, and the personal confidence of, the NSC member, that they represented. To deal with the problem (that Marshall and others had pointed out) of unprepared NSC members the board members were to "have an unbreakable engagement to brief the head of the department or agency before every Council meeting."[48]

The only other major change that Cutler recommended was to add a few high-caliber "think" personnel to the career NSC staff. These people would permit the staff to perform the following new functions: "(a) independent analysis and review of Planning Board reports before submission to the Council; (b) continuous examination of the totality of NSC policies to discover gaps, insufficiencies, etc.; (c) continuing integrated evaluation of free world versus Soviet-satellite capabilities." This group, under the direction of Lay's deputy, was called the Special Staff. Any gaps it identified in NSC policies were to be sent to the Planning Board for consideration. This staff would also be responsible for briefing the vice president before each council meeting and providing him with staff assistance on NSC matters.[49]

Basically, Cutler's plan would have the structure of the NSC remain substantially the same. The Planning Board (Senior Staff) would continue to be the principal body for the formulation and transmission to the NSC of policy recommendations (papers). There would be no change in the statutory position of the NSC, and its executive secretary and his deputy (James Lay and Everett Gleason) would continue as career employees of the council. Cutler said that no members of Congress should attend NSC meetings nor should civilians become participant members. He suggested that Eisenhower get his civilian advice by appointing individuals to serve as ad hoc consultants on specific subjects.[50]

It seems clear that Cutler thought that the primary element in the "revitalization" of the NSC would be his personal skills as executive officer at the NSC meetings, presiding officer of the Planning Board, and briefer of the president before NSC meetings. He was also depending heavily on Eisenhower's interest and background in foreign affairs and the president's skill and energy as presiding officer of the NSC.

Cutler prepared a one-page summary of his recommendations for the NSC and met with Eisenhower for an hour and twenty minutes on Sunday morning 8 March 1953.[51] The president accepted the recommendations without change and told Cutler that he would be appointed to the new special assistant position.[52] Cutler's recommendations were formally submitted to the president on 16 March. Eisenhower approved these recommendations the next day.[53]

CIVILIAN CONSULTANTS

While Cutler was preparing his NSC reorganization recommendations Eisenhower continued to pursue his idea of incorporating wise men from outside the government into NSC deliberations. He had committed himself to this during the 1952 campaign and believed that these men could add perspectives untainted by bureaucratic biases to the advice he received from the council. He was also anxious to get the NSC to consider the costs of the policies they recommended to him. At its meeting on 25 February 1953 the NSC established an ad hoc committee of civilian consultants to study the basic national security policies and programs and advise the NSC in relation to their costs.[54]

It was agreed that the committee would consist of about six consultants chosen, in order, from Dillon Anderson, James B. Black, John Cowles, Eugene Holman, Deane W. Malott, Charles A. Thomas, Arthur W. Page, and Howard Bruce. There was also to be in the group a labor representative to be proposed by Secretary of Labor Martin Durkin and approved by the secretaries of state, treasury and defense. (Eisenhower suggested the labor representative be from the Congress of Industrial Organization [C.I.O.] and mentioned Walter Reuther as a possible candidate.) Those selected would be invited to come to the White House on 11 March for a period of three weeks.[55] Cutler was given the job of contacting the first six who would accept the appointment. It was not a task he welcomed, because Cutler personally remained opposed to the inclusion of nongovernmental personnel in the deliberations of the council.

After spending twenty-four "unhappy hours" working on the president's suggestion that Reuther be the labor representative, Cutler concluded that there were "good reasons" for not inviting him. Instead he proposed David Robertson (who was neither CIO nor American Federation of Labor [AFL]) and got him approved by Durkin and the other departments. He also secured the acceptance of Anderson, Cowles, Malott, Black, Holman, and Thomas.[56] This group of "Seven Wise Men" included the president of Cornell, a prominent scientist who had played a major role in the Manhattan Project, and the CEO of Pacific Gas and Electric. After they received security clearances they were given intensive briefings by the CIA, military officers, and State Department analysts. During its first two years the administration used outside consultants to the NSC half a dozen times.[57]

MEMBERSHIP

The original membership of the NSC, as established by the National Security Act of 1947, was the president, the chairman of the National Securities Resources Board, and the secretaries of state, defense, army, navy, and air force. In 1949 Congress dropped the service secretaries from the council's membership and added the vice president.[58] From the very beginning of the NSC Truman had asked the secretary of the treasury (who also happened to be a personal friend) to attend all meetings of the NSC.

The budget bureau had never been happy with the idea that Congress should tell a president who his advisers should be. This was one of the reasons the bureau had always held that the membership of the NSC should not be established by statute. When Cutler began his study of the NSC, the budget bureau won him over to their position. That is, statutorily, the council should consist of the president and the vice president and anyone else the president wished to appoint. But Cutler and the bureau soon decided that they probably could not sell Congress on the concept of giving the president complete power over the council's membership, and if they tried to accomplish it through a reorganization plan, it "would be misunderstood, especially by the press." It was agreed to live under the then de facto arrangement for a time.[59]

Eisenhower, like Truman, was more interested in having his treasury secretary added to the NSC as a statutory member than in the philosophical question of whether Congress should specify the minimum membership of the council. However, since the president could invite anyone he chose to NSC meetings, it was not deemed worth the bother or expense to submit a reorganization plan to make the treasury secretary a member by law.[60] The only change in NSC membership made by law at this time was to replace the chairman of the National Security Resources Board with the director of the Office of Defense Mobilization when those two agencies were combined in 1953.

THE BUDGET BUREAU JOINS THE NSC

Eisenhower came into office determined to give greater emphasis to budgetary considerations in the fashioning of national security policy. The primary responsibility of the ad hoc committee of civilian consultants to the NSC that was formed in the spring of 1953 was to "advise the Council on basic national security policies and programs in relation to their costs."[61] This effort became but one aspect of Eisenhower's determination to use the NSC machinery as part of the budget process.

During the Truman administration the NSC repeatedly struggled (but never very successfully) with the problem of establishing the national security funding level. It first became involved in 1948 when, as a ploy to raise a presidentially imposed ceiling on the defense budget, Secretary James Forrestal asked that the matter be placed on the NSC agenda. Truman saw this move as a challenge to his control over the council and a budget issue rather than a foreign policy question. While Truman allowed the item to be added to the agenda for discussion, he simultaneously reiterated his imposition of a budget ceiling on Forrestal's department. In this way he effectively took the NSC out of the budget-making loop.[62]

After Forrestal resigned there were no further challenges to presidential control of the NSC. Truman then felt more comfortable with the council and decided to use the NSC in his desperate efforts to restrain the federal budget. In July 1949 he asked its members to help him make the national security budget decisions for fiscal year 1951 by recommending the relative priority and emphasis for programs ranging from the military budget to foreign aid. For this exercise Truman invited the chairman of the economic advisers and the Economic Cooperation administrator to sit with the NSC. The effort failed when the NSC was unable to agree on priorities and instead recommended that the budget ceiling be raised by over $2 billion. Truman never formally approved or disapproved this recommendation and never again involved the NSC in the budgetary process.[63]

Truman established his defense budget by inviting the Defense Department to state its needs and then personally working out the final amount with the budget bureau. Eisenhower, however, insisted that the budget bureau take part in the planning discussion of the costs of policies at the NSC meeting rather than merely being involved after the fact. In June 1953, at the president's request, the director of the Bureau of the Budget became a standing request participant in *all* NSC meetings and he was represented at all Planning Board meetings by a bureau official.[64]

Prior to the Eisenhower administration it had always been the policy of the budget bureau to avoid participation in interagency committees such as the NSC because it feared that its independent powers of review and its responsibilities for staff advice to the president would be compromised by such committee involvement. After 1953 the bureau began to be regularly represented in meetings, not only with the NSC but also with the Cabinet and the Council for Foreign Economic Policy, because it found itself working for a president who preferred to have policy issues reviewed "interdepartmentally in his presence and determined with finality in the interdepartmental forum rather than having them presented unilaterally through Presidential staff channels for decision."[65] If the bureau had not participated in these meetings it would have lost much of its influence on shaping the budget.

To give more meaning to its participation in the NSC process, the bureau proposed to periodically supply the council with data on the fiscal outlook of the country so that the members could gauge whether fiscal and security affairs were in balance. The bureau sought to keep the NSC out of the regular budget process, however, by limiting the cost estimates to only a rough order of magnitude. The bureau also suggested that any NSC paper that involved high costs include in a financial appendix an estimate of the effect of that policy on the cost of the government.[66] The Planning Board was required to provide a budget appendix to all policy proposals it forwarded to the council in an effort to determine their financial implications. In practice, the effort to get the NSC to maintain an awareness of the relationship between its recommendations and fiscal policies proved difficult to accomplish.

The NSC reorganization plan that Cutler implemented in 1953 remained in effect until the Kennedy administration dismantled it in 1961. In chapter 5 we will explore how it functioned in practice.

NOTES

1. Robert Cutler, *No Time for Rest* (Boston, 1956), p. 272.

2. John Prados, *Keepers of the Keys: A History of the National Security Council from Truman to Bush* (New York, 1991), pp. 61–62.

3. Cutler, *No Timer for Rest*, p. 271.

4. Cutler to Gordon Gray, 10 March 1952, PSB Personnel(4), Gordon Gray Papers, DDEL.

5. Cutler, *No Time for Rest*, pp. 282–83.

6. Cutler to Dwight D. Eisenhower, 27 December 1952, Cutler 52–55(5), Whitman Administrative Files, DDEL.

7. Proposed Reorganization of OCB, 22 December 1955, OCB Organization, WHO, Special Assistant for National Security, DDEL; Cutler to DDE, 27 December 1952, Cutler 52–55(5), Whitman Administrative File, DDEL.

8. BOB Appendix B, NSC, 1952, 52.6, E2–50/52.1, RG 51, NA.

9. Ed Strait to Files, 30 October 1952, 52.6, E2–50/52.1, RG 51, NA.

10. "The Presidential Job in Organizing and Managing the Executive Branch," 52.6, E2–50/52.2, RG 51, NA.

11. Joseph Dodge to DDE, 22 December 1952, BOB 1952, OF 72–B, NA.

12. Memorandum II, 4 November 1952, Executive Office Reorganization(1), Whitman Name File, DDEL.

13. Alfred Dick Sander, *A Staff for the President: The Executive Office, 1921–1952* (Westport, Conn., 1989), pp. 319–324.

14. Dodge to DDE, "National Security Council," 22 December 1952, BOB 1952, OF–72–B, NA.

15. Ibid.

16. Ibid.

17. W. Y. Elliott to Charles Stauffacher, 19 November 1952, NSC Organization and Functions(4), WHO Clean Up, DDEL.

18. Elliott to Arthur S. Flemming, 23 December 1952, NSC Organization and Functions(2), WHO Clean Up, DDEL.

19. Ibid.

20. DDE to Admiral Charles M. Cooke, 18 February 1953, NSC(2), Whitman Administrative Files, DDEL.

21. Cutler to DDE, 27 December 1952, Cutler 52–55(5), Whitman Administrative Files, DDEL.

22. Cutler to DDE, 10 January 1953, ibid.

23. James S. Lay, Jr., "Suggestions for Further Strengthening of the National Security Council," 19 January 1953, NSC Organization and Functions(6), WHO Clean Up, DDEL.

24. Ibid.

25. PACGO to DDE, "White House and Executive Office," 11 February 1953, NSC Organization and Functions(5), WHO Clean Up, DDEL.

26. Ibid.

27. Ibid.

28. NSC Study, Notes of Study Group Conference, 13 February 1953, NSC Organization and Functions(5), WHO Clean Up, DDEL.

29. Prados, *Keepers of the Keys,* pp. 61–62, 70.

30. NSC Study, 3 February 1953, NSC Organization and Function(6), WHO Clean Up, DDEL.

31. NSC Study, 17 February 1953, ibid.

32. NSC Study, "The President," 9 February 1953, NSC Organization and Functions(5), WHO Clean Up, DDEL.

33. NSC Study, 19 February 1953, NSC Organization and Functions(3), WHO Clean Up, DDEL.

34. Ibid.

35. Ibid.

36. Paul Nitze to Cutler, 17 February 1953, NSC Organization and Functions (3), WHO Project Clean Up, DDEL.

37. Ibid.

38. Ibid.

39. Ibid.

40. William Bundy to Assistant Deputy Director/Intelligence, 2 March 1953, NSC Organization & Functions(3), WHO, Clean Up, DDEL.

41. Cutler to DDE, 7 March 1953, NSC Organization and Functions(3), WHO Clean Up, DDEL.

42. Anna K. Nelson, "The Top of the Policy Hill: President Eisenhower and the National Security Council," *Diplomatic History* 7 (fall 1983): 318–319.

43. Bureau of the Budget, Office of Management and Organization to Cutler, draft memo, 16 March 1953, 52.6, M1–21, RG 51, NA.

44. "The Presidential Job in Organizing and Managing the Executive Branch," 52.6, E2–50/52.2, RG 51, NA.

45. Cutler, Report to the President, 1 April 1955, NSC(2), Whitman Administrative Files, DDEL.

46. Ibid.

47. Ibid.

48. Ibid.

49. Ibid.

50. Ibid.

51. Cutler to DDE, 7 March 1953, NSC Organization and Functions(3), WHO Clean Up, DDEL.

52. Cutler, *No Time for Rest*, p. 299.

53. DDE to Cutler, 17 March 1953, Presidential Papers, 1953, WHO, Special Assistant for National Security Affairs, DDEL; James S. Lay to J. K. Mansfield, "An Organizational History of the National Security Council," 30 June 1960, NSC.

54. Cutler, 26 February 1953, Cutler 52–55(5), Whitman Administrative Files, DDEL.

55. Ibid.

56. Whitman Note, February 1953, Cutler 52–55(5), Whitman Administrative Files, DDEL.

57. Philip G. Henderson, *Managing the Presidency: The Eisenhower Legacy—From Kennedy to Reagan* (Boulder, Colo., 1988), p. 73.

58. Public Law 216, 81st Congress, 1st sess., chapter 412.

59. Cutler Memo, 14 May 1953, 52.6, M1–21, RG 51, NA.

60. Ibid.

61. Cutler memo, 26 February 1953, Cutler 52–55(5), Whitman Administrative Files, DDEL.

62. Sander, *A Staff for the President*, pp. 252–253.

63. Ibid, p. 254.

64. Henderson, *Managing the Presidency*, pp. 73–74.

65. Reid to Director, 10 March 1958, 52.1, M1–1/2 RG 51, NA.

66. Memo for the President, William Finan draft, 25 June 1953, 52.6, M1–21, RG 51, NA.

5

The NSC in Operation

While the NSC was being reorganized according to Cutler's proposals it continued to function as Eisenhower's long-range national security policy mechanism. In November 1953 Cutler took stock of the council's work up till that point. He proudly reported that

we held more Council Meetings than in any *full* year of the Council's previous existence and about *twice* as many meetings as in the last year under Truman. In the first nine months of this Administration, the action numbers (i.e. separate items considered at Meetings) constituted 25% of *all* from the beginning of the Council in 1947 through October 1, 1953.[1]

There were several reasons for the heavy workload. One was the decision in the "Solarium" project to review all of the existing policies that the new administration had inherited. Cutler and "Beetle" Smith were the prime movers of Project Solarium. It produced three different scenarios for dealing with the Soviets, ranging from cooperation to rolling them back. The scenarios, which were produced by three different teams, were then debated by the NSC that ended up modifying one of them and then adopting it. Finally a committee headed by Bromley Smith drafted a paper based on this decision that, after being debated and approved by the NSC, became the basis of a new policy toward the USSR.[2]

The work pressure on the Planning Board was particularly severe. Cutler complained that the board regularly met three times a week in sessions lasting from three to five hours. In addition to "Solarium," the tense international situation in 1953 contributed to the heavy workload that year. But the most important reason the NSC was very busy throughout the Eisenhower administration was "the emphasis placed by the President on the Council's deliberative and advisory process."[3]

EISENHOWER AND THE NSC

Eisenhower came into office believing that the National Security Council was "the most important single agency in the Executive Department."[4] The NSC was well suited to the way Eisenhower liked to make decisions because he preferred to have matters decided once and for all when all the agencies involved were present and had a chance to express their views. For example, if a policy being considered by the council required a particular level of army manpower he wanted the budgetary aspects of the matter considered as part of the overall policy question. The budget bureau, which in the past tried to avoid being involved in NSC and cabinet meetings, now found that if it was "to 'get its licks in' it must do so in these forums at the time policy is made."[5]

In the popular mind the NSC is the command post where the president makes crucial decisions during foreign policy crises. But this was not true for Eisenhower (or for most of his successors). Eisenhower normally considered his critical command judgments as operational problems and usually dealt with them informally in the Oval Office. Many of Eisenhower's advisers, particularly those not invited to the more select Oval Office meetings, complained about the president's practice of ruling out certain subjects from NSC consideration. They told him that the public, press, and Congress assumed that foreign policy crises received full NSC consideration. The president resisted this pressure to use the council to deal with command decisions and continued to focus the NSC on long-range planning and interdepartmental decisions. (John Foster Dulles supported Eisenhower's practice of excluding crises or day-to-day subjects from the council because they might tie the hands of the secretary of state.)[6]

A more mundane reason why Eisenhower did not use the National Security Council as the forum in which he dealt with foreign policy crises was that the meetings got to be so large (usually more than twenty people present) that the president was reluctant to discuss extremely sensitive material in that arena. He was also irritated by the tendency of the Dulles brothers to play to the gallery. The larger the group the greater the temptation for Allen and Foster Dulles to attempt to impress the audience. The president felt "real impatience" with the CIA chief's overly philosophic, laborious, and tedious briefings while he found those of the secretary of state "too long and in too much detail in historical account." Eisenhower did nothing to rein them in because "one must recognize the personality of the individual involved."[7]

Bobby Cutler did not agree with Eisenhower's policy of refusing to use the NSC as the arena for foreign policy crisis decisions. While Cutler admitted that the bulk of the council's time should be devoted to the fashioning of long-range national security policy recommendations, he argued that

the Council is also a convenient forum in which to get a coordinated answer to a crash or short-range problem. Every so often history takes charge. Then there is no time for papers to be properly staffed through the Planning Board and decisions must flow from oral discussion. That the Council members have been trained in the customary council procedure serves to condition them for crash problems which must be decided without the usual background material.

Cutler also suggested that the NSC mechanism would offer "a perfect refuge to a President from one-sided pressure to decide some issue. An *ex parte* presentation may or may not present all the facts."[8] Eisenhower apparently decided that he did not need this sort of protection from his advisers and continued to deal with foreign policy crises outside of the NSC mechanism.

Gordon Gray became the special assistant for national security affairs in the middle of the second term. In an effort to improve the operations of the NSC, he interviewed many of the members and sought their suggestions. The main thing all except Foster Dulles complained of was Eisenhower's policy of excluding the NSC as a forum for foreign policy crisis decisions. Dulles supported the practice because he did not think the council was an appropriate place for such a discussion. Since Dulles was almost always present when these decisions were made in the Oval Office, his position was understandable. Gray retorted that since the press, the public and the Congress assumed that crisis decisions had received full NSC consideration, the president should change his way of seeking advice on these matters.[9]

When Dulles entered the hospital with the cancer that was to take his life, Gray urged Eisenhower "to change his habits and begin making his policy decisions in NSC meetings, rather than in private meetings with two or three others, or over late-afternoon cocktails with Dulles alone." The president said the NSC was too big and cumbersome to explore the decision-making options. He told Gray he wanted to discuss the issues with Acting Secretary of State Christian Herter, Secretary of Defense Neil McElroy, Chairman of the JCS Nathan Twining, science adviser James Killian, his son John, and always with staff secretary Andrew Goodpaster.[10]

Otherwise the National Security Council was a congenial device for Dwight Eisenhower for several reasons. One of the most important of these was the great emphasis that the former general put on the planning process. To him, the significant product was not the plan but the process. It was this process that would keep his advisers and staff involved, fully informed and ready to assist the president when the occasion required their counsel. By holding regular NSC meetings, Eisenhower believed that its members "became familiar, not only with each other, but with the basic factors of problems that might on some future date, face the President." Then, when the inevitable crisis arose, "his advisers, accustomed to expressing their views to the president, would be prepared to offer critical judgement instead of simply becoming 'yes-men.'"[11]

Eisenhower also saw the NSC as an essential mechanism to improve the coordination of the state and defense departments. As a result of his World War II experience he knew well both the difficulty and the importance of coordinating the attitudes and efforts of diverse groups. He did not believe that state and defense had known enough about what each other was up to prior to the Korean War. Most of the work Eisenhower did as president involved these two departments, and he used the NSC to improve their ability to work together.[12]

This president believed the NSC was the appropriate mechanism to provide the chief executive with long-term advice in foreign policy. In this role, he told the members, he hoped they would be able to take off their departmental hats and function

as a corporate body composed of individuals advising the President in their own right, rather than as representatives of their respective departments and agencies. Their function should be to seek, with their background of experience, the most statesmanlike solution to the problems of national security, rather than to reach solutions which represent merely a compromise of departmental positions.[13]

John Foster Dulles, for one, took this request literally and in NSC discussions, on occasion, disagreed with the position his representative on the Planning Board had taken.[14]

Eisenhower was comfortable with the NSC procedures that Cutler developed. Since the national security assistant technically ran the meetings, Eisenhower was much more relaxed during NSC sessions than he was at Cabinet meetings where he had to function as chairman.[15] But, while Cutler or one of his successors functioned as the ringmaster at council meetings, Eisenhower was always in charge. One observer recalled that "Eisenhower ran the show, and he was very meticulous about staff work. Foster [Dulles] wouldn't dare try to avoid the issue and go off on tangents because the boss would bring him right back again."[16] Dulles never got used to the fact that there was a NSC involved in his foreign policy area. On occasion he would try to get Gordon Gray to remove an item from the NSC agenda. When this would happen, Gray would raise the matter with Eisenhower. The president would invariably reply, "Ask Dulles whose council he thinks this is. Of course put it on the agenda."[17]

THE ROLE OF THE NATIONAL SECURITY ASSISTANT

The position of special assistant to the president for national security affairs came into existence when Eisenhower approved the recommendations that Bobby Cutler made in March 1953 to reorganize the National Security Council. That document described the job as follows:

The Special Assistant to the President for National Security Affairs should be the principal executive officer of the Council; should preside as Chairman at and actively participate in meetings of the Council's Planning Board; should be appointed on the White House Staff by the President; and should be compensated at $20,000 a year. . . . During the afternoon before each Council Meeting, the President should be briefed by the Special Assistant, assisted by the Executive Secretary. . . . The Special Assistant should bring to the President's attention, with recommendations for appropriate action, lack of progress on the part of a department or agency in carrying out a particular policy.[18]

These words not only defined the position but also in a sense established a contract between the incumbent special assistant and the president insuring a close personal relationship between the two.

It should be borne in mind, however, that this job description was only in effect during Eisenhower's time. During subsequent administrations the occupant of this position became, in practice, the president's national security adviser rather than merely an assistant. One of them, Henry Kissinger, believes that

in the final analysis the influence of a Presidential Assistant derives almost exclusively from the confidence of the President, not from administrative arrangements. . . . For reasons that must be left to students of psychology, every President since Kennedy seems to have trusted his White House aides more than his Cabinet. It may be because they are even more dependent on him; it may be that unencumbered by the pressures of managing a large bureaucracy the Presidential Assistants can cater more fully to Presidential whims; it may be as simple as the psychological reassurance conferred by proximity just down the hall.[19]

But this was not the case with Eisenhower.

Eisenhower was always careful to keep his policy-making machinery separate from operations. His special assistants for national security were essentially limited to the coordination and facilitation of the planning and policies that constituted the work of the NSC.[20] Perhaps this president simply felt that he was so well qualified in the field that he did not need a national security adviser. He certainly did not attempt to fill the position with individuals who were foreign policy experts.

Eventually Eisenhower considered his special assistant for national security the most important job, after the secretaries of state and defense, in his administration.[21] During his eight years he was served by four quite different men in this position. They were Robert Cutler, Dillon Anderson, Gordon Gray, and William H. Jackson, who served in the post temporarily for a few months in 1955. Each brought to the position his own talents and background and developed his own unique relationship to the president.

ROBERT CUTLER

Initially Bobby Cutler, who had defined the position, served as the national security assistant from March 1953 until April 1955. He returned to the position in January 1957 and stayed this time until July 1958.[22] Both times Cutler, who was something of a hypochondriac, left the position pleading exhaustion. Even those who liked Cutler found him to be a difficult person to work with. Bromley Smith, whom Cutler had hired, "thought him a flawed man, the runt of his family, and he could be extremely rude." (He once hung up on the president's wife!)[23]

Cutler came into the position without much substantive knowledge of world affairs or of national security problems and made no pretensions that he had much background in these fields.[24] However, Eisenhower thought that the members of his NSC and the Planning Board should visit military and naval installations to get a better feel for the reality of what they were establishing policy for.[25] As a result, in 1954 Cutler, at the president's direction visited Argentina, the Azores, Rabat, Naples, Heidelberg, Wiesbaden, Paris, and London conferring with American officials.[26] Apparently his trip was a great success for one of Eisenhower's fellow generals wrote

I feel someone should tell you about the activities in Morocco of your emissary of goodwill, Brigadier General Robert Cutler. I have no doubt he has done a superior job as your Special Assistant, but after having seen him operate here for two days, I think he is presently miscast and should be "Ambassador at Large." He has completely captivated the entire French colony here and left with the entire Air Force in Morocco in his pocket.

A pleased Eisenhower sent a copy of this letter to Foster Dulles with the comment, "Possibly we have Bobby in the wrong place!" Dulles replied that he would be glad to take Cutler "any day, anywhere."[27]

Most of the State Department hated Cutler, but he managed to preserve a good working relationship with Dulles.[28] But Cutler did not mollycoddle the secretary of state. At a NSC meeting in May 1958 Dulles complained that he had not had enough time to study a document that was scheduled for discussion. Cutler sent Dulles a scathing memo the next day in which he pointed out how long it had taken the Planning Board to develop the document and that Dulles had had it to read for fifteen days before the meeting. Cutler sent a copy of this memo to the staff secretary "to note and swallow."[29] (Actually state should have been grateful to Cutler because he helped to preserve the department's position by firmly resisting all efforts to create in the White House a permanent staff concerned with the substance of national security policy.[30])

Cutler was successful in his job because he gave it everything he had. Hauge, who considered Cutler one of the great citizens of the country, said that he "worked harder than any man I have ever known."[31] Another associate saw him as "an expert procedures man" who really knew how to get results. He was able to develop a staff that was very good at collating information and points of view so that the president could make his decisions and then Cutler would see to their implementation.[32] He was very loyal to Eisenhower. Cutler was quite intelligent, had strong views and great drive, and excelled as a facilitator.[33]

Cutler really believed in the role of coordinator. He would give Eisenhower his policy views if pressed, but essentially he was the president's assistant in charge of the NSC rather than national security policy. He was very aware that "the desire for advancing a cause could be a very dangerous attribute" for one in his position.[34] Cutler himself thought his role was "to administer, to serve, to get things done, and to be trusted."[35]

Eisenhower and Cutler did not always see eye to eye as to how the NSC should function. The president continually pressed (and Cutler resisted) to give civilian consultants a major role in council proceedings. During his second term Eisenhower became increasingly bored with the NSC's focus on the production of Cutler's precious policy papers and pushed his special assistant to make the procedures more flexible to encourage free debate among the council members.[36] He told Cutler he wanted the NSC to spend more time discussing issues rather than documents. He hoped the council would discuss provocative issues that required high-level thought.[37]

Cutler was hurt and obviously bothered by this criticism but in typical fashion took the blame by admitting "it has been my lack of skill not to evoke as sharply as you wish the issue, rather than the text which expresses the issue. I shall certainly try to do better." But Cutler was convinced that the very heart of the NSC system he had constructed was the basing of council discussions on written papers that would serve as the basis for planning and budgetary expenditures throughout the government. He lectured the president on the necessity for these papers and claimed that the most fruitful discussion in the NSC "results when it is addressed to a carefully-prepared paper, circulated and studied in advance." Cutler told Eisenhower that the debate he sought took place in the meetings of the Planning Board where "all the resources, all the strong views, all the passionate advocacies, of the Executive Branch agencies meet and clash in this broad spectrum. As President you see only the end-result, often with many divergent and unresolved views." About the only concession Cutler offered Eisenhower was the suggestion that the policy papers could serve as a springboard for discussing at the council meetings "the basic issues they covered rather than concentrating attention on the papers themselves."[38]

Seemingly Cutler won this battle. Eisenhower still complained privately to his secretary that because of the papers and briefings he knew every word of the NSC presentations before they were made. But as a conscientious leader he continued to sit through these long sessions in order to maintain interest among the others present.[39]

Cutler served as chairman of the Planning Board, which met three afternoons a week for many hours. Bromley Smith, a former State Department intelligence officer whom Cutler had hired, "postured" Cutler for these meetings as well as the weekly NSC meeting. The Planning Board was a high-level group that Cutler ran like a schoolteacher. He was frequently rough on the members and could be truly murderous. For example, he might compliment a beautiful paper written by the State Department and then say how well it stated the French point of view.[40]

Midway through his first stint as Eisenhower's assistant for national security, Cutler wrote a personal letter to the president that reveals a lot about the job and the relationship between the two.

Because there have been stories in the press about my wishing to quit, I thought I should write this letter. . . . I have a few observations about my job. It is a real back breaker, as I have to do it, because my equipment is limited. There have been many times when I thought this 10–11 hour schedule couldn't be kept up any longer. But you have set such a high standard and you repose so much undeserved confidence in a fellow, there is no other way but to keep on. My intellectual equipment is really not adequate to this task. My will to work for infinite hours and a flashy (but ordered) loquacity partially conceal my many deficiencies. There must be someone who could perform better than I. If we could find and train him, he could run for you this Juggernaut we've developed much better than my poor powers can. I'm not trying to be a cry-baby or down-in-the-mouth. I just say what I honestly believe.[41]

About a year later Cutler felt physically exhausted, found a replacement, and sent the president his resignation. The reasons for his resignation, which he believed the president was familiar with, were "wholly related to my personal and private concerns."[42] After what turned out to be his first stint as special assistant, Cutler said that he hoped Eisenhower would think of him "as (perhaps) one who got the engine turning over from its dead center."[43]

When Cutler left in the spring of 1955, Dillon Anderson replaced him. He was a lawyer Eisenhower had originally sought as one of the "Seven Wise Men," civilian consultants to the NSC. The president asked him to take Cutler's place in the spring of 1955, and he stayed until the latter part of 1956. Apparently it was not a pleasant experience for him. Anderson recalled that if the president was not happy with a paper the Planning Board had developed, he would hear from him. The president "asked the questions and he uttered the convictions in the privacy of his office, when there were just the two of us there, with considerable vehemence." Anderson did not like being away from his law business and his family, and he remembered his stint as special assistant as "a hell of a job, awfully hard work, long hours."[44] Bromley Smith does not think that Anderson ever understood the job while Eisenhower thought his approach to his duties had been "too legalistic."[45]

Cutler returned for his second tour as national security assistant in January 1957 but stayed only half as long as the first time. He finally left the government in July 1958 but apparently missed the excitement. A year later he stopped by the Oval Office because he wanted "to get back to the Washington scene on some appointment that will not end" with the Eisenhower administration.[46] In retrospect Eisenhower was not too sorry to see Cutler resign. He still felt admiration and affection for him but noted that "tension in Council meetings and related activities had largely disappeared since Bobby Cutler's departure."[47]

By the time Cutler left the second time many of the NSC members were disenchanted with his leadership. Attorney General Herbert Brownell complained that because Cutler spent so much time reading documents aloud during the NSC meetings they had become pedantic in nature. "He felt that the President had been awfully bored and some times irritated, and that this was true of other members of the Council." Because most of the time was spent discussing papers, Brownell believed that the members did not have any real opportunity to exchange views on policy questions.[48] Secretary of the Treasury Robert Anderson agreed that too much of the president's time was being taken up in unimportant language changes during the NSC meetings.[49]

GORDON GRAY

Gray's father, Bowman, a onetime chairman of R. J. Reynolds, had made a fortune in the tobacco business. Gordon Gray, who had been the publisher of two newspapers by the age of twenty-eight, was wealthy, well educated, and urbane. He had initially joined the federal government during World War II as an official in the Pentagon. There he got to know Cutler. After the war he served in the Truman administration as secretary of the army and then, in 1951, he became the first director of the Psychological Strategy Board (PSB). One of his first actions was to recruit Cutler as a temporary employee of the board. After getting the PSB organized he left in January 1952 to return to his hometown of Winston-Salem to become the president of the University of North Carolina. Reportedly a man who combined modesty with wit, intelligence, and a gracious manner, Gordon Gray was in some contrast to the fussy Cutler.[50]

During Eisenhower's first administration, Gray was named Assistant Secretary of Defense for International Affairs. In this position he was a member of the NSC Planning Board and again worked with Cutler. When Arthur Flemming became secretary of the Department of Health, Education and Welfare in the spring of 1958, Gray succeeded him as the Director of the Office of Defense Mobilization (ODM). This unit in the Executive Office of the President, which was a remnant of Truman's Korean War mobilization effort, had once wielded great power over the economy. It was now primarily engaged in strategic material stockpiling, but (reflecting its earlier power) its director was still a statutory member of the NSC.

ODM turned out to be a brief assignment for Gray. When he arrived he found that office was in the process of being merged with the federal civil defense administration. Gray told Sherman Adams, Eisenhower's chief of staff, that he did not want to remain as director of the new organization because there were parts of the civil defense effort that he "would not have his heart in" and would thus be somewhat "disabled." By this time Gray knew that Cutler had decided to again resign as special assistant and that he had recommended Gray as his successor. Although he told Adams he knew that the appointment of the special assistant for national security was necessarily a "very special choice" for the president, bowing out at ODM may have been Gray's way of encouraging Eisenhower to name him to the post. He assured Adams he would do anything the president wanted.[51]

A few weeks later Cutler and Gray met with Eisenhower. Cutler reminded the president that he was leaving his position in July and told him that Gray, by reason of character, experience, familiarity with the work, and ability to deal with the "big shots," was the best-equipped person he knew to replace him. Gray protested that he was anxious to leave the government and so was not interested in the job. Eisenhower interrupted to say that he did not want to lose Gray from the government and that this was the ideal arrangement: "that Gray would have his fingers on almost everything; and that Gray's experience in Defense, in working with State, in ODM, and in working with Budget made him the man for the job."[52] Gray accepted the assignment.

The appointment of Gray marked the only time Eisenhower had a special assistant for national security who was actually an expert in national security matters. After Gray had been in the job for a year and a half, the president told Gray that under his leadership the NSC "was operating better now than at any time in his experience."[53] Although Gray was much more knowledgeable of international affairs than Cutler, it was probably his other qualities that made the council run smoother.

The death of Dulles and Eisenhower's confidence in Gray resulted in a significant increase in the special assistant's power. In the spring of 1959 one of the many crises over Berlin came to a head. Meeting privately with the president, Gray asked Eisenhower to give him the authority to force the departments to conform to NSC procedures in handling the problem. Eisenhower agreed. As John Prados has observed, Eisenhower thus

permitted the emergence of the modern national security adviser, an official with virtual command powers over the range of policy planning and crisis management. Hitherto, Ike had carefully restricted [the NSC] to policy planning, using Goodpaster for current operations. Gray's limited function was to make crisis management flow as smoothly as did policy planning, and he largely confined himself to this. His successors have not always been so judicious. . . . Previously Ike had scrupulously separated his personal staff from the policy machinery; now he was allowing, indeed requiring, cooperation under difficult circumstances. Ironically, Eisenhower, the staff expert, established a precedent here for the unparalleled accumulation of power by the NSC staff.[54]

THE PLANNING BOARD

Bobby Cutler believed that one of the principal dangers policy-makers could face at the top level of government would be to have their decisions based on one-sided information and not be subjected to critical analysis. His design of Eisenhower's NSC mechanism was an effort to ensure that the product of the council would escape this danger. It was his hope that carefully staffed papers which provided background, together with policy options, searchingly prepared by their own representatives on the Planning Board, would enable the NSC members to avoid the risk attending decisions based on inadequate preparation. Cutler believed that without the opportunity to have studied and grasped the kind of material prepared by the Planning Board few men would have enough overall perspective to deal with long-range security issues.[55]

But Cutler realized there was a downside to basing the work of the NSC entirely on the presentation of carefully staffed papers. Such a procedure led to a tendency for formal, stylized work, which eliminated the possibility for the informal "kicking about" of a problem at a council meeting. However he believed this was a luxury that had to be sacrificed in the interest of obtaining a more sure and decisive result. Cutler insisted that NSC discussions be based "on an exactly prepared and commonly understood statement of facts and of recommendations."[56]

The NSC, Cutler believed, could only be successful if the Planning Board was effective. He believed the board's effectiveness turned

on four principal criteria: (a) the intellectual capability and integrity of the Planning Board Members. (b) the responsibility of each Member's position in his department or agency (at the Assistant-Secretary level) and his continuous, direct access to his department or agency chief. (c) each member's faithful attendance at all Planning Board meetings. (d) the vigor and penetration with which Planning Board Meetings are conducted by its Chairman.

Cutler was determined to bring it to the president's attention if he was unable to have the Planning Board maintain these standards.[57]

Not everyone thought that this was the best way to analyze foreign affairs problems and develop policy. Paul Nitze, who during the Truman administration had served as chief of Acheson's policy group and later was an adviser to many other presidents up to and including Reagan, did not think it possible

to do first class, rigorous, analytical work that close to the White House. There has to be some distance between analytical work and the final decision making authority, otherwise they become too involved with one another. While you are trying to do the analysis you corrupt it in order to win your side of the argument. So those meetings of the NSC staff with interdepartmental representatives were the most bitter, miserable, nonsensical meetings that I can remember.[58]

The meetings might have been bitter but to Cutler they were anything but nonsensical. So, three times a week during the first term, and twice a week during the second, the Planning Board met in a large room in the Old Executive Office Building for three or four hours of "red hot debate and cross examination of experts."[59] About a dozen individuals, who were the third- or fourth-ranking persons in their departments, would take the position papers developed by their organizations and try to fashion them into a document that purported to be the policy of the United States on a subject or area in foreign policy. To do this they had to eliminate "all of that which was nonsense—in other words, all of that which was just departmental prerogative or anything else—and really get something which would represent . . . a policy that all could agree to. Of course this means argumentation of the toughest kind."[60]

The task was particularly difficult for board members who represented complex departments. Karl Harr recalled:

I went over there [to the NSC] with a mandate to defend the views of the Defense Department, and each of the three military services would have been in lobbying with me as to their own particular service point of view, and the same thing was true with the State [Department] representative. We'd get in there and have different perspectives, perhaps, or even personality differences, departmental differences, and try to evolve from these different points of view something that we agreed represented the best overall policy for the United States.[61]

Harr had replaced Gordon Gray as the assistant secretary of defense for international security affairs. As such his main responsibility was to provide the secretary of defense with staff support for his NSC membership.[62] In the Defense Department an anomaly existed in that the Joint Chiefs of Staff, an element within the department, had been specified, in the legislation establishing the NSC, as the council's military adviser. For this reason it was necessary for the JCS to be separately represented on the Planning Board.

The situation was further complicated by the fact that the JCS was a "corporate" entity that could not take a position until the members had voted as a unit. While none of the other Planning Board members could bind their chiefs to a position before a council meeting, they were supposed to have such a close relationship with them that the views they expressed in board meetings substantially reflected their chiefs' positions at that time. As a result of the corporate nature of the JCS their Planning Board representative (who participated in all the board's deliberations) presented what he believed to be the views of the chiefs but he did not have the authority to commit the JCS before the chiefs themselves addressed the issue and voted on it. As a result, all the other departments had to be brought into agreement on each paper before the JCS would consider it for formal comment. Cutler wryly admitted that this procedure was not always "pleasing" to the other departments and agencies.[63]

Inevitably the quality of the representation among the members of the Planning Board varied. The State Department usually got high marks for its staff work. Its Planning Board member was normally accompanied to board meetings by the head of the regional bureau and the desk officer involved in the issue being considered. The defense representative did well considering the complexity of the department he represented. In contrast, W. Y. Elliott, who represented the Office of Defense Mobilization, frequently presented his personal views and was often overruled by his boss when the matter came to the NSC. The Treasury Department was not well represented because its board members had heavy operating responsibilities in their department which caused them to frequently send alternates to meetings and made it difficult for them to get staff work done. The CIA did a good job in providing the Planning Board with intelligence background for planning, which was supposed to be the agency's only role at the meetings. However, the other members resented it when the CIA sought to enter their substantive discussions. The Foreign Operations Administration representative was usually well briefed and gave clear evidence that the paper had been fully coordinated within his agency and was seldom repudiated by his principal in NSC meetings.[64]

The budget bureau was represented on the Planning Board by Ralph W. E. Reid. (One of his colleagues recalled that he was a "tough cookie" who ably spoke for that "arrogant bunch" over at the bureau.)[65] Reid, who was appointed as an assistant to the director of the bureau, served on the Planning Board throughout the Eisenhower years. He had previously been the chief of the economic division in the Army of Occupation in Japan. Reid had received a Ph.D. from Harvard in 1948.[66]

It was the Planning Board's job to identify problems and situations that affected the security of the United States, analyze those problems, and then draft policy statements to deal with them. These statements were then sent to the NSC for consideration. A group drawn from the various departments and known as the NSC Board Assistants aided the board in the drafting of papers. This group, which was chaired by Marion Boggs, attended all of the board meetings. Boggs was director of the board's secretariat and the head of the Policy Coordination group of the NSC staff.[67]

Cutler and his successors presided at the Planning Board meetings. They normally began the meetings by setting the frame of reference and analyzing the problem. After a preliminary discussion by the board, the issue was assigned by it to a department to develop a draft paper. When the redrafted paper came back to the board it was again discussed and then given to the Board Assistants for revision in the light of the discussion. The revision was then approved, amended, or rejected by the board.[68]

The traffic of ideas that the board considered arose from one of three sources. Items for study normally originated in the departments or agencies or, on occasion, they came from a board member. Infrequently the NSC itself identified a problem it wished to consider and asked the Planning Board to study the issue and report back.[69] In addition to preparing papers for consideration by the NSC, the Planning Board also convened for background briefings by other members of the administration. For example, Arthur Burns came by to give the board the high points of the CEA's annual economic report to the president.[70] Another example of board activities was the establishment of ad hoc committees to consider the need for policy papers on various subjects. In 1958 such a committee was set up with members from state, defense, ODM, and the JCS to prepare a staff study on U.S. relations with Canada. The study was then discussed by the Planning Board, which, in turn, prepared points to be discussed in the NSC.[71] In sum, problems of foreign policy, the care of alliances, the encouragement of the nonaligned, and the restriction of Communist power dominated the work of the Planning Board.[72]

Many had criticized the Truman NSC because they considered it simply a mechanism for papering over policy differences within the administration. But Eisenhower wanted each member of his NSC to be "just as free to express his opinion as a man can be" so that "nobody is barred from bringing up any fear or any matter, any preoccupation on his mind, any anxiety or conviction." The Planning Board was Eisenhower's mechanism for ensuring that each member had the opportunity of placing before the president "precisely the language it wishes against whatever background of common agreement has been reached."[73]

However, not all of the members of the NSC wanted their differences debated before the president. Secretary of the Treasury Robert Anderson complained that the president's time was being wasted by "Bobby Cutler's insistence of bringing the splits developed in the Planning Board to the Council which otherwise could be clearly resolved by the heads of the agencies concerned."[74] But Cutler did insist. As he reported to the president:

On many national security issues there are naturally divergent views between agencies. At the Planning Board, honest effort is made to settle such differences, but never with a view to watering-down a basic split or to "sweeping it under the rug." In fact, it has become a recognized function of the Planning Board, when a difference is stoutly held, to sharpen and make as precise as possible the expression of this conflict to the end that the Council can make an effective decision between the opposing views.[75]

As a result of this attitude more than half of the papers the Planning Board sent on to the NSC contained split views, largely on important issues, in which one or more of the departments represented on the council indicated a strong divergence of opinion. Reid recalled one paper dealing with a fundamental issue that contained nineteen splits when the Planning Board sent it to the NSC and then required five council meetings to resolve.[76]

THE NSC STAFF

The NSC staff that Eisenhower inherited from the Truman administration was headed by Executive Secretary Lay and was composed of civil service employees hired by him and employees detailed full time from the member agencies for work at the NSC. Prior to 1953 the number of NSC employees never exceeded twenty-three.[77] During the Truman years the discussions and recommendations of the National Security Council were based on policy options that originated in the departments. One of the major questions facing Cutler when he undertook to refashion the NSC for Eisenhower was whether to continue to rely on the departments to initiate items for the council to consider or to try to build the NSC staff into an entity capable of providing the council with these policy options. In the end Cutler rejected this latter idea and maintained the existing practice of relying on departmental initiative. That is, the representatives of the agencies who would eventually be responsible for carrying out the policy would develop the policy proposals.

For Cutler the key NSC staff function was to provide "permanence and experience; it carries on continuously through changing Administrations, providing a background of invaluable and otherwise unobtainable knowledge."[78] Lay's assistant summed up this function as "to remember, not to recommend." However the work of the NSC was not entirely of a passive secretarial and recording nature since there were a few members of the staff who did have a professional background in national security matters. This so-called "thinking" staff was used to identify gaps in national security policy that the Planning Board had not addressed and to suggest items for it to consider. This group was responsible for reviewing the product of the Planning Board for coherence, completeness, and applicability in the light of past experience.[79]

Another function of the "thinking" staff was to provide technical support for Cutler personally in his effort to know as much as possible about the matters he had to present to the NSC and to get the Planning Board to produce the best possible papers. A special staff within the policy coordination group prepared the briefing notes that Cutler and his successors used in introducing policy papers in the NSC. They also did an independent analysis of the Planning Board's papers at each stage of their development.[80]

Both Eisenhower and Cutler wanted the NSC to assume the role of presidential advisers rather than merely representing the views of their departments. To give the NSC an independent capability Cutler made being on the NSC staff a career. The staff was made up of former military people and onetime employees of the treasury and defense departments who had economic or regional specialties. These people considered themselves servants of the NSC (of which the president happened to be chairman). They worked exclusively for the NSC and did not get involved in other presidential business. To maintain separation from the rest of the White House staff all contact with other elements of the presidential staff flowed through the Special Assistant for National Security Affairs.[81]

As he neared the end of his first tour as special assistant, Cutler was feeling very over-worked. On his recommendation, his successor added a few more people to the professional "thinking" staff.[82] With other accretions over the years, by 1960 the staff had assumed a formal organizational structure that included: (a) the Office of the Executive Secretary, (b) the Policy Coordinating Staff (which included the Planning Board Secretariat), (c) the Internal Security Coordinating Staff, and (d) the Research and Intelligence Staff.[83]

There was constant pressure from those dissatisfied with the work of the Planning Board to have it replaced by a large NSC staff at the White House as the mechanism for developing the papers that the NSC considered. But Cutler and his successors resisted these ideas. Gray for example argued:

A large super-staff, once established, is likely to settle into a relatively fixed pattern of advocating particular policy approaches or pet projects, thereby becoming just another participating agency. Moreover, I do not believe that the American people would approve or be best served by experimentation with ivory tower policy proposals when they involve the security or even the survival of our nation.[84]

A decade later Henry Kissinger created such a "super-staff" that resulted in many of the bad results Gray predicted.

Among those urging the expansion of the NSC staff was a commission headed by ex-president Hoover which, in 1954 and 1955, was charged with studying the federal government and recommending organizational changes to improve its efficiency. One of the commission's working groups, Task Force 1A on Procurement (headed by a onetime CIA official named Franklin Lindsay who had served on the Jackson committee before joining the Ford Foundation), examined the NSC. The task force found fault with the quality of the council's recommendations and with its ability to place them in a context with other elements of the country's foreign policy. Lindsay thought the NSC should try to balance its total requirements against national resources. To remedy these problems the task force recommended: "(a) that the existing NSC Staff be expanded into a larger new 'national staff' [size not specified] reporting directly to the Special Assistant, and (b) that a critical study be made of the continuous use by the Council of external research organizations for analytical research."[85]

Cutler rejected the idea of a larger national staff. He argued that the staff could not accomplish what Lindsay sought unless it was of a size and character that duplicated the staffs of the Operations Coordinating Board (OCB), Office of Defense Mobilization and the other staffs currently responsible for coordination. If Lindsay's recommendation was adopted he feared it would significantly change his own job. Cutler told Eisenhower that it was "inadvisable formally to give greater responsibility to and increase the functional prestige of the Special Assistant for National Security Affairs."[86]

THE NSC AND THE BUDGET

While Eisenhower supported Cutler's view about the proper role of the NSC staff, he had long sought a way to implement the task force's suggestion that the NSC should consider resource requirements when it made its recommendations. To this end he tried to inject budget considerations into the council's deliberations by naming the Director of the Budget as a standing-request member of the NSC and by installing a budget bureau representative on the Planning Board. After these assignments were in place, the president directed that the Planning Board include a budget appendix with each proposal it sent to the NSC. He hoped that the result would be that the financial implications of policy proposals would be considered before they were adopted.[87]

Forcing the Planning Board to consider costs when devising national security policy caused some concern and resentment among its members. After a year's experience with this procedure one departing member, Paul Morrison, told Cutler,

I have become increasingly concerned with the trend toward detailed program and fiscal management in Planning Board activities. . . . Unless you are careful operating agencies will be running to the NSC for approval of each little program change. Then the system will collapse. Neither budgets nor programs can be executed by totaling a series of unrelated actions during a year. At some point the details must be fit into certain maximums established by the President and by the Congress. . . .

I am sympathetic with the attempt to make NSC actions more specific but it is not desirable to use NSC machinery, particularly the Planning Board, too precisely for this purpose. If, however, NSC actions are interpreted as policy directives of the President to the Executive agencies of government to execute them to the best of their abilities within the limitations otherwise imposed, real progress is possible. If you attempt to make the policy statements more than that, it will be necessary to change the composition of the Planning Board so that the fiscal and program people in the respective agencies can have greater participation in the making of policy. This would be very cumbersome and, in my opinion, unsound.[88]

Soon the NSC was so heavily involved in the budgetary process that one of its policy documents, NSC 162/2, was used to set forth the administration's fiscal objectives. These included reducing expenditures not associated with national security and maximizing the economic potential of private enterprise by minimizing government controls. NSC 162/2 also projected the budgetary situation for fiscal years 1954 through 1957.[89] This was pretty far afield from national security affairs and showed that Morrison's fears were well founded.

The budget bureau soon found problems with this mixture of national security and budgetary affairs. In Planning Board discussions the bureau stood alone in trying to get qualifying phrases added to proposals that would emphasize the idea that new expenditures would be balanced by revising other priorities. The purpose of the proposed language was to "prevent what might otherwise very well be taken down the line as an encouragement to disregard established budget programs and to feel that an indefinite number and an indefinite amount of add-ons are invited."[90]

Roland Hughes, the budget director, took his concerns to the president. The result was that on 4 August 1954 the NSC adopted a statement that the council "cannot take over the budgetary operation nor can the budgetary process take over NSC responsibilities. They are closely interrelated, but each has its separate function in aiding the President in carrying out his responsibilities relating to national welfare and safety." Eisenhower noted that "a general understanding had been reached by the Budget staff and others concerned."[91]

Keeping the NSC out of the establishment of the budget required constant vigilance. At the urging of the budget bureau Eisenhower approved a memo to Cutler which stated:

Despite the care which you used in sending out notices for the meetings to prevent any implication that the meetings would be a means of fixing the budget figures for the coming year, our people find that the agencies are inclined to such a view. Any attempt to make such a corruption of the purpose of the meetings would be, of course, not only in violation of the procedures and methods provided for overall budget decisions by the President, but would be in direct contradiction to the established policies of the NSC.[92]

By insisting that all NSC documents contain a financial appendix Eisenhower was able to make the NSC the administration's battleground for its budgetary versus security concerns.[93] But the procedure still had flaws. The appendices frequently did not cover principal elements of cost for major programs and suffered from a lack of critical review. Since each program was considered separately it was difficult to balance one program against competing and supporting programs. According to the Hoover Commission task force, "Neither the Council nor any other organ of government is adequately formulating broad programs involving expenditure of funds, with a balancing of each program against the other, and the balancing of total requirements against national resources."[94]

MEETINGS OF THE NSC

During the Eisenhower administration the NSC met in the Cabinet Room at 9 A.M. each Thursday for two or more hours. A typical meeting would begin with an intelligence briefing by the CIA director, Allan Dulles, followed by a short military report by the chairman of the JCS. After hearing progress reports on the follow-up to prior council actions, the special assistant for national security affairs [Cutler, et al.] would move to consideration of the papers on the agenda. He would summarize the papers (paying particular attention to splits) and then invite discussion of the important issues. Usually at this point Eisenhower would take control of the meeting by making comments and raising questions. After what was frequently a lively discussion and spirited exchange, the president would usually reach a tentative decision. Within forty-eight hours the NSC staff would reduce this to a written "Record of Action" which Eisenhower would review, frequently amend, and sign. The official policy thus established was then distributed to the other members of the NSC.[95]

The regimented weekly schedule for the NSC, as well as for cabinet meetings and sessions with congressional leaders, was a reflection of Eisenhower's organizational philosophy. "It was the commander's duty to regularly review the troops, to encourage teamwork, to check that routine obligations were being fulfilled, to be accessible to a number of advisers, and to be knowledgeably prepared for any new or emergency decisions that might be required."[96] Dillon Anderson thought that Eisenhower used the NSC

as an arena within which he would have the benefit of the comments by those Cabinet ministers who headed the Departments with national security responsibilities of one sort or another—an arena in which, by give and take in his presence and in the presence of each other, there would be a full airing of their views before the determination of our country's posture or policy in any given subject area, geographical or otherwise. It was a place, in other words, for the formulation of long term policy guidelines and identification of long term policy objectives.[97]

In 1953 when Cutler made his initial recommendations to the president concerning the NSC he suggested that not more than eight persons participate in council discussions. These should be the statutory members and officials that the president invited to participate. The secretary of the treasury was invited to all meetings but others just to meetings whose agendas contained items of interest to their departments or agencies. These officials included the attorney general, the chairman of the Atomic Energy Commission, and the Federal Civil Defense administrator. As a minimum, others attending all council meetings would be the advisers: the director of Central Intelligence, the chairman of the Joint Chiefs of Staff, and the president's special assistant for the Cold War (C. D. Jackson or Nelson Rockefeller)—and of course NSC staff officials, Cutler, Lay, and Gleason.[98]

At most of the NSC meetings (until his death) Foster Dulles, after the president, was the most important actor. He seemed to regard the meetings as official sessions rather than confidential or private ones. Dulles did not always end up supporting the position that the State Department had taken at the Planning Board meetings and frequently played a key role in working out compromise wording for NSC recommendations. Next to Dulles, Secretary of Treasury George Humphrey was the most influential participant. Disarmament adviser Harold Stassen was quite voluble ("a terrific presenter") at meetings, but there is a real question as to whether anyone listened to him. Vice President Nixon was not very significant at these sessions because Eisenhower used him primarily as a domestic political expert rather than as a foreign policy specialist. Secretary of Defense Charles Wilson's "greatest contribution used to be asking questions. He would often ask a question that would sort of blow a proposition out of the water." The NSC meetings became the battleground for the administration's budgetary problems versus its security concerns.[99]

During the first two years of the administration the task of reviewing, revising, and updating all the policies approved by the Truman administration so overburdened the NSC agenda that they frequently dealt with six or seven items at a meeting, and the time extended considerably beyond the two and one-half hours allotted. In 1955 Cutler recommended that, except where "crash events" intervened, agendas be limited to two or three principal items. He "believed that better work is done, and the President's working schedule is better accommodated, if Meetings do not exceed approximately 2½ hours." This type of scheduling would also "permit more time for 'free talk' which the President has from time to time desired."[100]

Holding down attendance at NSC meetings was a perpetual problem. An invitation to attend a NSC meeting added to the prestige of the official so honored. High-level officials of the justice department pressed Cutler to recommend regular council membership for Attorney General Herbert Brownell because of his internal security responsibilities. There was also sporadic public and congressional agitation to make the heads of civil defense and atomic energy regular members. Cutler sought to keep attendance at a minimum so that "intimate, frank and fruitful discussion can take place." He resisted pressure by pointing out the "basic fact" that the NSC "is a body advisory to the President and that, accordingly, attendance at its meetings must conform to his needs and desires. No other criteria for Council membership merits consideration."[101]

Despite Eisenhower's desire to limit attendance at NSC meetings to those persons "with a need to know" and Cutler's best efforts, because of bureaucratic pressures the number present at the meetings continued to grow throughout the tenure of the administration. We have already seen how the director of the Bureau of the Budget joined the secretary of the treasury as a regular participating member. Observers who had a standing invitation to attend for items of interest to them included the assistant to the president, the deputy assistant to the president, the director of the United States Information Agency, the under secretary of state (as coordinator of the mutual assistance program), the special assistants to the president for foreign economic policy and science and technology, and the White House staff secretary. Usually there were many more in attendance but the above were there even when matters of a "highly sensitive nature" were being considered.[102] Dillon Anderson recalled that when Eisenhower looked around the table at NSC meetings "and saw more people than he expected there, pretty soon after the meeting I'd have to explain to him why."[103] It is no wonder that Eisenhower was reluctant to use the NSC as the forum for dealing with foreign policy crises.

EVALUATION

Many members of the NSC were not happy with the mechanism that Cutler had created. Attorney General Brownell complained that the council meetings were too much characterized by Cutler reading documents in a pedantic fashion that bored and sometimes irritated the president and other members. He would have welcomed less discussion of papers and more opportunity for the members to exchange views on policy questions. Maurice Stans, Eisenhower's last budget director, thought that busy people were spending entirely too much time in the weekly NSC meetings and suggested biweekly sessions instead. Vice President Nixon did not think Cutler's procedures were well designed to use the brains and creative abilities of the busy people who were members of the council. He thought the members should be stimulated by the process so "that they may use their creative thinking on policy issues and less of their time spent on language disputes."[104] Even Dillon Anderson conceded, "If there was a weakness that developed in the process, we probably got ourselves into more papers than we were comfortable with."[105]

Basically the above participants were unhappy with Cutler's procedures that focused council meetings on the papers generated by the Planning Board. According to Cutler these procedures were designed to yield through the NSC the following values for the president:

a) a clearinghouse for national security issues;

b) integration of foreign, domestic, economic and military policy;

c) resolution of divergences among departments;

d) long- and short-range policy recommendation capability;

e) a refuge from *ex-parte* actions for the president;

f) NSC records which provide a clear directive to departments, and

g) a flexible mechanism that the president can adjust to the tempo, volume, emphasis and quality he prefers while the NSC Staff provides continuity from administration to administration.[106]

Cutler was aware that his emphasis on policy papers had a tendency to produce formal, stylized work that frequently bored NSC members, but this was necessary, he argued, to produce a more sure, decisive result and a commonly understood statements of facts and recommendations. As a result, by 1955, "the fundamental validity of policy integration is so generally recognized by Council participants and has become so well established that what was often strange and suspect before 1947 is now 'second nature' to those who work on national security problems."[107]

By the Eisenhower years the national security operations of the federal government had grown to massive proportions. The NSC that Cutler constructed was an exercise in trying to find a practical way to do a job for which the federal government was not basically designed. From the prospective of one who tried to make this system work,

The value of having major policy questions thrashed out and put in writing, however general the terms, was that it laid to rest throughout this monstrous government of ours debate on these issues. It allowed people to go forward, instead of having every Deputy Assistant Secretary of State arguing with every ambassador overseas as to whether we should or should not recognized Red China or something like that. Such things would have been fought out in the proper forum and decided and we could get on with the job.[108]

Elmer Staats, who spent more than forty years in the federal government, in retrospect concluded that Eisenhower's efforts to systematize the NSC machinery "worked on the whole pretty well."[109]

NOTES

1. Robert Cutler to Charles E. Wilson, 11 November 1953, NSC Organization and Functions, WHO Project Clean Up, DDEL.

2. Bromley Smith Interview, 6 September 1979, Old Executive Office Building, Washington, D.C.

3. Cutler to Charles E. Wilson, 11 November 1953, NSC Organization and Functions, WHO Project Clean Up, DDEL.

4. Dwight D. Eisenhower to Admiral Charles Cooke, 18 February 1953, NSC(2), Whitman Administrative Files, DDEL.

5. BOB Study Group Major Findings, B1–13/2, Series 52.2, RG 51, NA.

6. John Prados, *Keepers of the Keys: A History of the National Security Council from Truman to Bush* (New York, 1991), p. 78.

7. Stephen E. Ambrose, *Eisenhower: The President* (New York, 1984), p. 469.

8. Cutler, Report to the President, 1 April 1955, NSC(2), Whitman Administrative Files, DDEL.

9. Prados, *Keepers of the Keys*, p. 78.

10. Ambrose, *The President*, p. 509.

11. Ibid., p. 248.

12. Karl G. Harr Oral History, OH-34, DDEL.

13. DDE to NSC, 15 October 1953, President's Papers 1953(2), WHO, Special Assistant for National Security, DDEL.

14. Anna K. Nelson, "Before the National Security Adviser: Did the NSC Matter?" SHAFR Conference, Washington, D.C., 10 June 1988.

15. Robert Cutler, *No Time for Rest* (Boston, 1956), p. 304.

16. Philip G. Henderson, *Managing the Presidency: The Eisenhower Legacy—From Kennedy to Reagan* (Boulder, Colo., 1988), p. 84.

17. Joint Staff Interview, OH-508, DDEL.

18. DDE to Cutler, 17 March 1953, Presidential Papers(3), WHO, Special Assistant for National Security, DDEL.

19. Henry Kissinger, *The White House Years* (Boston: Little, Brown and Company, 1979), p. 47.

20. Nelson, "The Top of Policy Hill: President Eisenhower and the National Security Council," *Diplomatic History* 7 (fall 1983); 318.

21. Memo for the record, 1 December 1959, Miscellaneous 58–59, Gordon Gray Papers, DDEL.

22. Joseph G. Bock, *The White House Staff and the National Security Assistant: Friendship and Friction at the Water's Edge* (Westport, Conn., 1987), p. 32.

23. Bromley Smith Interview, 6 September 1979, Washington, D.C.

24. Harr Oral History, DDEL.

25. Cutler, *No Time for Rest*, pp. 347–348.

26. Cutler memo to President, 20 July 1954, Cutler 52–55(3), Whitman Administrative Files, DDEL.

27. F. E. Glantzberg to DDE, 12 July 1954, Cutler 52–55(3), Whitman Administrative Files, DDEL.

28. Smith Interview; Nelson, "Top of Policy Hill," p. 313.

29. Cutler to John Foster Dulles, 2 May 1958, Cutler vol. 1(1), WHO, Staff Secretary, DDEL.

30. Nelson, "Top of Policy Hill," p. 313.

31. "Looking Ahead," 13 December 1955, Correspondence with Gabriel Hauge, Burns Papers, DDEL.

32. Harr Oral History, DDEL.

33. Smith Interview.

34. Nelson, "Top of Policy Hill," p. 313.

35. Cutler, *No Time for Rest*, p. 315.

36. Ibid., pp. 347–48.

37. Cutler to DDE, 7 April 1958, ACW Diary April 58(2), Whitman Diary, DDEL.

38. Ibid.

39. Ann Whitman to Milton Eisenhower, 28 August 1956, Whitman Name Series, DDEL.

40. Smith Interview.

41. Cutler to DDE, 20 March 1954, Cutler 52–55(4), Whitman Administrative Files, DDEL.

42. Cutler to DDE, 8 March 1955, ibid.

43. Cutler to DDE, 7 April 1955, Cutler 52–55(2), Whitman Administrative Files, DDEL.

44. Dillon Anderson Oral History, 31 December 1969, OH-165, DDEL.

45. Smith Interview; Memo for the Record, 1 December 1959, Miscellaneous 58–59, Gordon Gray Papers, DDEL.

46. Whitman Diary, 23 July 1959, ACW Diary July 1959(1), Whitman Diary, DDEL.

47. Memo for the Record, 1 December 1959, Miscellaneous 58–59, Gordon Gray Papers, DDEL.

48. Memo of discussion, Herbert Brownell and Gordon Gray, 4 August 1958, NSC General(1), WHO Clean Up, DDEL.

49. Memo of conversation, Robert Anderson and Gray, 21 July 1958, NSC General(1), WHO Clean Up, DDEL.

50. Prados, *Keepers of the Keys*, p. 77.

51. Gray Memo for the Record, 25 April 1958, Miscellaneous 58–59, Gordon Gray Papers, DDEL.

52. Gray, Memo for the Record, 9 May 1958, Miscellaneous 58–59, Gordon Gray Papers, DDEL.

53. Gray, Memo for the Record, 1 December 1959, Miscellaneous 58–59, Gordon Gray Papers, DDEL.

54. Prados, *Keepers of the Keys*, pp. 89–90.

55. Cutler to the President, "Operations of NSC," 1 April 1955, January 53–April 55, NSC(2), Whitman Administrative Files, DDEL.

56. Ibid.

57. Ibid.

58. Kenneth W. Thompson, ed., *The Virginia Papers on the Presidency: The White Burke Miller Center Forums 1979* (Washington, 1980), pp. 38–39.

59. Cutler, *No Time for Rest*, p. 312.

60. Harr Oral History, OH-34, DDEL, pp. 11–13.

61. Ibid.

62. "Relationship of the Secretary of Defense to the NSC," 31 October 1960, series 52.6, M1–21, RG 51, NA.

63. Cutler to Charles E. Wilson, 11 November 1953, WHO, Project Clean Up, NSC Organization and Function, DDEL; Cutler to the President, Operations of NSC, January 1953–April 1955, NSC(2), Whitman Administrative Files, DDEL.

64. Finan's OCB Study, 21 September 1954, 52.1, M1–1/2, RG 51, NA.

65. Smith Interview, 6 September 1979.

66. BOB Office Memo 391, 3 August 1953, Series 52.2, B2–5, RG 51, NA.

67. Prados, *Keepers of the Keys*, p. 72.

68. NSC Structure and Functions, 25 February 1960, NSC Misc(2), CFEP(Randall), DDEL.

69. Ibid.

70. Cutler to Arthur Burns, 5 February 1954, White House Correspondence, Burns Papers, DDEL.

71. C. Edward Galbreath to Clarence Randall, 16 June 1958, NSC Misc(5), CFEP, DDEL.

72. "Some Thoughts on the NSC Planning Board," undated, NSC General(2), WHO, Project Clean Up, DDEL.

73. Ralph W. E. Reid to Director, 24 February 1960, Series 52.1, M1–1, RG 51, NA.

74. Memo of conversation, Anderson and Gray, 21 July 1958.

75. Cutler to the President, 1 April 1955, NSC(2), Whitman Administrative Files, DDEL.

76. Reid to Director, 24 February 1960, Series 52.1, M1–1, RG 51, NA.

77. Alfred Dick Sander, *A Staff for the President: The Executive Office, 1921–1952* (Westport, Conn., 1987), pp. 246–247.

78. Report to the President, 1 April 1955, NSC(2), Whitman Administrative Files, DDEL.

79. Henderson, *Managing the Presidency*, p. 79.

80. Prados, *Keepers of the Keys*, p. 72.

81. Smith Interview.

82. Report to the President, 1 April 1955, NSC(2), Whitman Administrative Files, DDEL.

83. NSC Structure and Functions, 26 February 1960, NSC Misc(2), CFEP (Randall), DDEL.

84. Gray, "Role of the National Security Council in the Formulation of National Policy," 10 September 1959, American Political Association, Series 52.6, M1–24/59.1, RG 51, NA.

85. Cutler Report to the President, 1 April 1955, NSC(2), Whitman Administrative Files, DDEL.

86. Ibid.

87. Henderson, *Managing the Presidency*, pp. 73–74.

88. Paul L. Morrison to Cutler, 30 April 1954, Series 52.6, M1–21, GR 51, NA.

89. Fiscal 57 Budgetary Outlook, 10 May 1954, Hughes, R. (3), Whitman Administrative Files, DDEL.

90. Roland Hughes to President, 4 August 1954, Hughes, R. (3), Whitman Administrative Files, DDEL.

91. Ibid.

92. BOB Director to Cutler, 23 November 1954, Series 52.1, M1–1/1, RG 51, NA.

93. Anna K. Nelson, "Before the National Security Adviser: Did the NSC Matter?"

94. Cutler to the President, 1 April 1955, Operations of NSC, Jan 53–Apr 55, NSC(2), Whitman Administrative Files, DDEL.

95. Henderson, *Managing the Presidency*, pp. 84–85.

96. John W. Sloan, "The Management and Decision-Making Style of President Eisenhower," *Presidential Studies Quarterly*, 20 no. 2 (spring 1990): 306.

97. Anderson Oral History, p. 52.

98. Eisenhower to Cutler, 17 March 1953, Presidential Papers 1953 (3), Special Assistant for National Security, DDEL; Participation by Executive Departments in Work of NSC, April 1954, NSC Organization and Functions (2), WHO Clean Up, DDEL.

99. Anna K. Nelson, "Before the National Security Adviser: Did the NSC Matter?"; Dillon Anderson Oral History, DDEL.

100. Cutler to President, "Operations of the NSC," 1 April 1955, January 53–April 55, NSC(2), Whitman Administrative Files, DDEL.

101. Ibid.

102. Ibid.; Gray, "Role of the National Security Council in the Formulation of National Policy."

103. Anderson Oral History, DDEL.

104. Gray Memos of Conversations with Maurice Stans (12 August 1958) and Richard Nixon (28 July 1958), NSC General(1), WHO Clean Up, DDEL.

105. Anderson Oral History, DDEL.

106. Cutler to the President, "Operations of the NSC," 1 April 1955, January 53–April 55, NSC(2), Whitman Administrative Files, DDEL.

107. Ibid.

108. Harr Oral History, DDEL.

109. Elmer Staats interview by author 10 September 1979.

6

The Origin of the Operations Coordinating Board

The "P-Factor" was a popular buzzword in Washington in the early 1950s. It referred to the application of psychological warfare strategy in the Cold War. How well the Truman administration incorporated the P-Factor into its policies became a political issue during the 1952 campaign when Eisenhower questioned its effectiveness during a speech in San Francisco. The candidate claimed that psychological warfare was much more than the use of propaganda to win over men's minds and wills. He thought every significant act of the government should be so timed, so directed at a principal target, and so related to other governmental actions, as to produce the maximum effect. Eisenhower urged that all government agencies be brought together into concerted action under an overall strategy.[1]

During World War II the United States had begun to practice overt psychological warfare when, in 1942, the Office of War Information was set up. Then, in 1943, the JCS assigned covert information and propaganda responsibilities to the Office of Strategic Services (OSS). After the war the responsibility was divided between the State Department, which took over public foreign information, and the CIA, which was charged with developing covert propaganda.[2]

Because of the development of the Cold War an Interdepartmental Coordinating Staff (ICS) was set up in 1947 under the direction of the assistant secretary of state for public affairs with representation from the Departments of State, Army, Navy, Air Force, and the CIA. Its function was to develop psychological objectives for Cold War programs and to coordinate the related activities of the operating agencies. The ICS agreement gave the secretary of state responsibility for peacetime psychological operations during the Cold War but the question of psychological warfare was left open. The policy was refined by the National Security Council in NSC 59/1 which proposed giving the secretary of state responsibility for psychological operations during the early stages of a war and converting the ICS into the Interdepartmental Foreign Information Staff. Truman approved this policy statement in March 1950.[3]

THE PSYCHOLOGICAL STRATEGY BOARD

The Defense Department was not happy with this arrangement. In the fall of 1950 Secretary Louis Johnson proposed the immediate establishment of an "Interim Psychological Warfare Board" in the Executive Office of the President as a step toward establishing an independent agency to perform this function.[4] Because of State Department objections, Truman created an ad hoc committee composed of Deputy Director of the Budget Elmer Staats; the recently resigned executive secretary of the NSC, Sidney Souers; the Director of Central Intelligence, Walter B. Smith, and his deputy, Allen Dulles, to study the problem and recommend a solution. The group suggested that the president set up a mechanism to be called the Psychological Strategy Board.[5]

This recommendation was a compromise between two extreme positions. Most agreed that the United States had not been as effective as it might be in the Cold War struggle because the departments involved in the effort were too busy protecting their own turf. Some thought this situation called for the appointment of a sort of chief of staff for the Cold War who, working directly under the president, would develop a broad strategy and direct the overall national effort. Those who feared this proposal would give a warlike cast to what they hoped would be a peaceful mission, suggested instead a coordinating mechanism high up in the chain of command. The ad hoc committee did not recommend such a chief of staff, but it did advise the president to direct some of the highest officials in the government to provide "more effective planning, coordination and conduct . . . of psychological operations."[6]

In response, a presidential directive creating the PSB was issued on 4 April 1951. The board was composed of the under secretary of state, the deputy secretary of defense, and the director of Central Intelligence with a representative of the JCS as its principal military adviser. Under the board was a presidentially appointed director and a permanent staff. The board was responsible for the "formulation and promulgation . . . of over-all national psychological objectives, policies and programs, and for the coordination and evaluation of the national psychological effort." Periodically it was to report to the NSC on its own efforts and the activities of the government intended "to influence men's minds and wills."[7]

The first director of the PSB was Gordon Gray. He had worked in the Pentagon during the war where he got to know Bobby Cutler. One of Gray's first moves in creating a PSB staff was to recruit Cutler temporarily as his special assistant. Cutler later recalled that the PSB had turned out to be "a mare's nest."[8]

The initial PSB staff was borrowed from state, defense, and the CIA. A major problem in the recruitment of the staff was that there were few people available with any background in psychological strategy and operations. Nor was there any body of thought on what constituted psychological strategy. At one end of the spectrum it was merely "word warfare," while at the other extreme it could cover just about everything. Opponents of the PSB concept thought the world too dynamic a place to ever put down on paper a policy statement that could serve as an adequate guide for governmental action.[9]

Cutler later recalled that while he was with the PSB no one could agree on what "psychological strategy" was. He finally decided that it was simply "the timing, the expression, and the effect of large and small actions by the government itself."[10] (Eisenhower later concluded that psychological warfare "can be anything from the singing of a beautiful hymn up to the most extraordinary kind of physical sabotage."[11]) Both Cutler and Gray agreed that the PSB was an evolutionary step and that the ultimately valid mechanism to interject the P-Factor into governmental policies "is still to be thought out."[12] The lack of definition in the PSB mission made the existing agencies wary that the board might invade their areas of responsibility. To help the agencies work out their conflicts Gray, in November 1951, instituted private luncheon sessions to be held prior to the monthly PSB meetings. Here Gray hoped the principals could talk out their difficulties and hopefully resolve them before the formal PSB meeting. Ironically this device developed into the most effective and long lasting of all the precedents the PSB established.[13]

Shortly after completing his term as the director of the PSB staff Gray concluded that

a strong, well-directed NSC committee could do the PSB job. By that, I mean not a committee of subordinates but a committee with the Secretary of Defense, the Secretary of State and the Director of Central Intelligence as participating members. They would need a strong chairman for PSB matters, who would have a staff similar to the one we set up. I discussed the matter with the President [Truman] without too much reaction from him. The real catch, of course, would be the strong chairman, which would be resisted by the present State Department and perhaps by any State Department.[14]

During its short life span the PSB staff grew to over seventy individuals with a budget of a half million dollars. Gray left his post in January 1952 and was replaced by Ray Allen from the University of Washington. Allen did not work out well because of his lack of government experience. After a short time the returning ambassador from Moscow, Admiral Allen Kirk, replaced him.[15] When Eisenhower was elected, Kirk resigned and was replaced by his deputy, George Morgan, a Foreign Service officer. Morgan agreed to stay on until the new administration could figure out what to do with the PSB.[16] The board held its final meeting on 2 September 1953 in Denver where Eisenhower was then staying.

EISENHOWER AND THE P-FACTOR

Eisenhower's concern with the psychological impact on popular attitudes of the U.S. government's actions grew out of his responsibilities during World War II.[17] After the war he was disappointed with the Truman administration's effectiveness in this area. When he ran for the presidency he decided to address the issue if he was elected. This determination was expressed during the 1952 campaign in a speech (written by Cutler) that the candidate delivered in San Francisco. He said:

Psychological strategy is more than the use of propaganda to win over mens' minds and wills. Every significant act of government should be so timed and so directed at a principal target, and so related to other governmental actions, that it will produce the maximum effect. All agencies and departments must be brought together into concerted action under an over-all scheme of strategy that is unified and coherent. We must realize that as a nation everything we say, everything we do, and everything we fail to say or to do, will have its impact in other lands; it will affect the minds of men and women there. . . . A man of exceptional qualifications must be chosen to handle the national psychological effort; having the full confidence of and direct access to the Chief Executive.[18]

As president, Eisenhower maintained an active interest in psychological strategy and continually pushed his subordinates to improve their performance in this area. It became one of the major differences between Foster Dulles and himself. The secretary of state did not put much faith in the "P-Factor": in fact it was "close to anathema" to him.[19]

Eisenhower thought that because of organizational limitations in the federal government only the president or someone very close to him could be aware of all of the considerations affecting world issues.[20] He tried a variety of organizational schemes, with varying degrees of success, to address this problem. After watching these efforts to improve the country's psychological strategy over a seven-year period, one of his subordinates observed, "You have wrestled continuously with the question of organizing the Executive Branch and the Executive Office to achieve optimum effect in this area—without ever reaching a solution you felt entirely satisfactory."[21]

C. D. JACKSON

Eisenhower's initial approach to the development and coordination of psychological strategy was twofold. Besides reorganizing the PSB, he appointed Charles Douglas Jackson as his special assistant for international affairs to advise him on Cold War matters. Apparently Eisenhower considered Jackson to be the "man of exceptional qualifications" that, during the campaign, he had promised to name to head the "national psychological effort."

The president's confidential secretary remembered Jackson as a "very impulsive person" whose chemistry with John Foster Dulles was "just awful." She could understand why "Dulles naturally resented this younger man coming up from New York. He pretended to know all about foreign affairs where he, John Foster Dulles was supposed to be the boss." Andrew Goodpaster, the president's staff secretary, agreed that Jackson "didn't impose too high standards on himself, but that's what he was for. . . ." That is, he was there to generate new ideas for the president. There is no doubt that the president enjoyed talking to Jackson and that the two men shared a common philosophy.[22]

C. D. had served as deputy chief of psychological warfare on Eisenhower's staff during World War II. As one of Henry Luce's vice presidents, Jackson served as the publisher of *LIFE* magazine, he was an early Eisenhower supporter who soon became the new president's friend and close adviser. During the campaign he served as a speechwriter on the train with the candidate. After the election, Jackson agreed to join the president's staff for a limited period. While a member of the White House staff he was one of the president's primary confidants as well as a speechwriter. He left in 1954 because Time-Life paid more handsomely than the government, but periodically Eisenhower asked Jackson to visit the Oval Office to talk over problems with him and to seek his advice.[23] It seems clear that the antagonism between Dulles and Jackson contributed to the latter's early departure. It was common for Eisenhower to deal with personnel conflicts by eliminating one of the antagonists.

As the presidential assistant for the Cold War, Jackson had wide-ranging responsibilities. His task was to make sure that Cold War strategy was built into national policy by sitting in on meetings of the Cabinet and the NSC where he could educate the policy makers to think in terms of psychological warfare. He was also to make sure that some projects were dreamed up and executed solely for Cold War purposes.[24] Jackson had a staff of eight to ten, primarily drawn from the PSB, to help him develop P-Factor projects that he could then try to interject into various national policies.[25]

THE WILLIAM JACKSON COMMITTEE

Eisenhower, the day after his inauguration, officially established "The President's Committee on International Information Activities" to study the PSB organizational problem and propose a new approach.[26] The committee had begun to assemble unofficially to consider its formidable task weeks before Eisenhower moved into the Oval Office.[27] The chairman of the committee was William H. Jackson, a wartime psychological warfare officer and former CIA official. Among its members were Bobby Cutler and Gordon Gray. The committee gathered its data through in-depth interviews with officials, media experts, publishers and commentators. While the group went about its work, Cutler and Gray began dismantling the PSB.[28]

The Jackson committee soon discovered that restructuring the PSB was but one of the problems it faced. It had been apparent for some time that the failure of the NSC to implement or follow through on its policy recommendations was a major flaw in its organization. The committee decided that it should address this problem in addition, proposing a psychological strategy mechanism.

The role of the NSC in the implementation of presidentially approved NSC policies had been a controversial issue throughout the Truman years. Truman, Souers, and Lay consistently maintained the position that the NSC "does not determine policy or supervise operations . . . nor is it an implementing agency."[29] Lay argued that if the NSC got involved in implementation it

would radically alter the principle under which the Executive Branch operates, namely the various heads of departments and agencies are directly responsible to the President for the conduct of their operations. In effect, the Council as a committee would be interposed between the President and his Cabinet members and other agency heads. This is not the American way of Government.[30]

As a result of this attitude a member of the NSC Senior Staff reported that the NSC itself "has never had any real follow-through machinery and its directives have tended, therefore, to be more in the nature of policy frames or exhortation than actual means of getting something done."[31] When Dodge had looked at Truman's NSC operation he found that the problem of implementation of its policies (and by whom) was a serious one. He reported to Eisenhower: "There are practical obstacles to designating one member of the

Council to coordinate implementation partly through other equal agencies. There has been considerable difficulty and delay in getting action on NSC projects in the Departments to which they are assigned and in other departments of interest."[32]

THE JACKSON COMMITTEE REPORT

The Jackson committee gave the president its recommendations on 30 June 1953. The report gave the psychological strategy problem short shrift. It concluded that the P-factor was an "ill-defined area" which could not be organized separately but had to be "fully wedded to the deeds of the United States."

Accordingly, the Committee recommended the abolition of the Psychological Strategy Board established in 1951, and urged consideration of the establishment of more effective machinery within the structure of the NSC for the coordination and implementation of approved national security policies and programs. Thus, beginning with a charter to study ways of making more vigorous the psychological programs of the Government, the Committee undertook to propose the establishment of a group explicitly charged with the supervision of the execution of approved national security programs. In this manner the Committee believed that the psychological impact of each program could be maximized in the implementation of the program.[33]

The mechanism the committee proposed to carry out this responsibility was actually its third choice. Its preferred solution was to have the president receive his national security advice and deal with both policy and execution through the same collective staff machinery; namely, that of the NSC. Cutler devised an "Operations Coordination Board" which was to be a complete counterpart to the NSC Planning Board that Eisenhower had already approved. The one group was to deal with policy and the other with operations. This idea "was rejected reluctantly after Mr. Cutler had asserted that one person could not possibly supervise both, and that in effect operation would drive out planning or at a minimum would tend to decrease the effectiveness of the planning mechanism."[34]

The other choice the committee obviously preferred to the one it finally recommended was the development of a "Department of Foreign Affairs" to oversee all aspects of national security policy implementation. This was not proposed because the committee recognized the reluctance and probably the inability of the state department to assume this larger role.[35]

Reluctantly the Jackson committee recommended the establishment of an "Operations Coordinating Board" within the NSC structure. This board was "to assign detailed planning responsibilities to departments, to examine the resulting plans for adequacy, consistency with policy and with each other, and then to coordinate and follow up with the execution of such plans, seeking in the process to achieve the maximum advantage for the United States."[36] Achieving "maximum advantage" meant injecting the P-Factor.

The management analysts in the budget bureau were quick to react to the Jackson committee's recommendations. In a draft report they agreed that if the recommendations were accepted they would result in a clearer fixing of responsibility for coordinating the execution of NSC policies but argued that their implementation would create worse problems than they would solve. Echoing the Lay view of the proper role for the NSC, the bureau analysts warned:

The proposal to establish an OCB places a direct challenge upon the authority of the Cabinet Officers of the Government to administer their departments and programs. It is a proposal which has been rejected since the early establishment of the NSC, since it would conflict with our form of government under which the President holds each department head individually responsible for carrying out his policies. Further, because of the proposed composition of the OCB, including on the Board the Under Secretary of State and the Deputy Secretary of Defense, subordinate officers of the two major departments concerned with national security policies would be placed in a position to supervise and coordinate the execution of policies by the departments over which their superior officers are the heads. This is a grave anomaly, destructive of proper accountably to the President.[37]

The official bureau reaction to the Jackson committee proposal was more muted than the above draft. It criticized the committee's failure to focus on its original charge of examining the organizational problems in creating a psychological strategy, while admitting the difficulty of finding "specialized staff concerned with planning for interjecting the so-called 'P-factor' into our national security policies." The bureau then cautioned against including the OCB within the NSC structure because "all previous studies had warned against giving the NSC any role in 'operations' because it would impair the executive authority and responsibility of the President and department heads." The bureau also feared that if the NSC got involved in implementing its policies it would tend to focus on operations rather than on its primary function of formulating policy recommendations for the president.[38]

The bureau then made an alternative proposal to deal with the NSC implementation problem. It suggested that, as chairman of the NSC, the president should ask the council to review existing policies "to remove vagueness on the one hand and unnecessary details on the other." He should also instruct the NSC staff to include specific recommendations rather than mere generalities in the implementation assignments given the agencies. Further, the Planning

Board should make greater use of the progress reports that existing procedure required the agencies charged with implementation to file with the NSC. In terms of organizational actions the bureau told Eisenhower he could avoid including the Operations Coordinating Board within the NSC structure by "requesting" his department heads to set up an OCB on their own. The bureau's proposed "voluntary" OCB would consist of the deputies of the department heads, be chaired by the State Department representative, and be served by a staff made up of personnel from the member departments.[39]

The next month the bureau sent the White House a draft executive order that would establish the kind of voluntary OCB it had recommended. In a memo for the record Arnold Miles privately analyzed the whole problem. Basically he thought the best way "to assure more aggressive execution of Presidential decisions in the area of national security" would be to add personnel to the NSC staff so that its own follow-up activities could be more effectively carried out. The bureau considered the proposed OCB "a second best alternative" because Cutler had opposed expansion of his own staff.[40]

Eisenhower accepted the budget bureau's recommendation when, on 3 September 1953, he signed Executive Order 10483 which established the Operations Coordinating Board. Like all executive orders, it has been drafted by the budget bureau. Eisenhower thus created the OCB under the president's general authority to create interagency committees. Each agency was to fund its part of the OCB's expenses so that the administration would not have to go Congress for authority to create a new agency.[41] The board was not made responsible for discharging the functions recommended for it by the Jackson committee but instead was told to "advise with the agencies concerned" respecting those functions.[42]

The fact that the OCB was not initially established as part of the NSC organizational structure made it inevitable that its role would be misunderstood and confused by many parts of the government. Nor was its name very descriptive of its function. The board's executive officer complained:

The Executive Order status of the OCB, its method of financing, and the uncertainty of its relationship to the NSC have created the attitude in some quarters that it is an experimental and possibly only a temporary arrangement. This has created an attitude detrimental to the effectiveness of the OCB mechanism in some cases and to the success of obtaining the most competent personnel for the OCB Staff.[43]

The membership of the board consisted of the under secretary of state, the deputy secretary of defense, the director of Central Intelligence, the director of the U.S. Information Agency (USIA), the director of the International Cooperation Administration (ICA), and a representative(s) of the president. Eisenhower assigned both C. D. Jackson and Robert Cutler to the board as his representatives. Soon after it began to meet, the board extended standing invitations to the under secretary of the treasury and the chairman of the Atomic Energy Commission to regularly attend its weekly meetings.[44]

The coordinator of the board's activities was its executive officer, Elmer B. Staats. Staats had entered the budget bureau as a career employee in 1939. With a Ph.D. in public administration from the University of Minnesota, he soon became the bureau's highest-ranking nonpolitical appointee. He relinquished his career status in 1950 when he accepted Truman's invitation to become the deputy director of the budget. With the election of Eisenhower, he helped Dodge get acclimated to the bureau and then left the government to accept a position with Marshall Field in Chicago. When the OCB was set up, Staats was recruited to serve as its executive officer.[45] He then remained in the government until he retired, nearly forty years later, as chief of the Government Accounting Office.

By the beginning of 1954 the OCB was in operation. Staats described it as a

means of (a) assuring coordinated implementation of national security policies approved by the President, (b) allocating agency responsibilities, (c) anticipating emerging problems, (d) developing agreed-upon plans of operations, and (e) reporting to the NSC on actions taken. The OCB is basically a cooperative arrangement. . . . Its strength derives in large measure from the fact that the Board is made up of individuals at the agency head or deputy level who are in a position to agree upon actions to be taken by their respective agencies. Actions in the OCB are therefore best expressed in terms of concurrence or agreement rather than in terms of direction or approval.[46]

The reader may note that Staats did not even mention psychological strategy (the initial justification for an OCB) in his description of the board's work.

So the OCB was a cooperative arrangement without any independent funding or authority. It worked primarily because it was made up of individuals high enough in their departments or agencies to have their organizations take action on matters they agreed on. The catalyst that was to transform this amorphous group into a high level coordinating mechanism for economic, psychological and political warfare was the inclusion in its membership of the president's special assistant for the Cold War, C. D. Jackson. His involvement provided several important benefits:

(a) The fixing of responsibility in the Executive Office for leadership in the initiation of psychological measures; (b) the provision of an individual (with staff supplied by the OCB) whose sole responsibility was to look ahead and plan but who was tied into realities through participation in the NSC and other Presidential councils, the Planning Board and the OCB.

The problem was that Jackson left the government a few months after the OCB began operating. This left "an important gap in the Executive Office structure."[47]

Jackson's involvement in the OCB was not an unmixed blessing, however. The state department complained that his staff (composed of eight or ten professionals who had been inherited from the Psychological Strategy Board) were known to take "C.D.'s wild ideas that hadn't been staffed or had been and had been rejected and first thing anybody knew C.D. had written 'Beedle' Smith or was having them circulated as OCB staff papers, much to Staats' embarrassment."[48]

MEETINGS

During the last months of its existence the PSB dispensed with its official meetings but continued to hold the informal weekly luncheon sessions. The OCB met each Wednesday afternoon at the State Department and continued the PSB practice of preceding each of its formal meetings with a luncheon session in the secretary of state's dining room. Many believe that it was in these luncheon meetings that the OCB took the most important actions in expediting the work of the national security apparatus.

The atmosphere of the luncheon meeting was conducive to bureaucratic business. The meetings were limited to just the members of the OCB and its executive officer with no staff backup admitted. According to one of the participants,

not even a waitress was allowed in the room. . . . We'd have sandwiches and milk so that there'd be no need for service, and we would discuss the most sensitive things . . . that is, the hot problems that we all had, or that had more than one Department involved or more than one interest involved. . . . It was a free discussion, people telling each other what was going on, what the problem was, telling each other what we were doing about it within our own agency, trying to come up with some bright ideas as to how it could be better handled and so forth. . . . It was an extremely useful tool because it was so well contained, in terms of security, and yet it was so broad in scope in terms of the diversified representation there. There was almost nothing of importance on the national security side that couldn't be discussed, and discussed by the people who had the operational responsibility.[49]

These luncheon meetings thus served as a forum in which the OCB members consulted informally with each other on a wide spectrum of concerns. They reached agreement on some items while others were referred to interdepartmental committees known as the OCB working groups.[50]

Elmer Staats, the OCB executive officer, agreed that the luncheon meetings were very important. He recalled that the members of the OCB

had some pretty free-wheeling discussions. Particularly in the early days the relationship between CIA and Defense, and State and Defense, were not good at all. Through the process of these luncheon sessions the whole thing loosened up. They were a lot more comfortable. I could see the change that was taking place in this relationship. I could see that a lot of conversation was going forward in between meetings.[51]

The formal meeting that followed the luncheon was guided by a written agenda. In addition to the members of the OCB, their support staff also attended these meetings. That is

a backup for each of the members and the actual OCB staff itself, and we addressed ourselves to the formal part of the agenda, which was basically devoted to arguing about and approving or revising operations plans, and arguing about or accepting or not accepting progress reports. This is where the real infighting of the various agencies took place, and it's where the procedural, sometimes dull but, I thought, always important work was done of having these top people in government sign off, on behalf of their agencies, together, on something that would be called an Operations Plan for the U.S.; or accept together a report about some area, a progress report.[52]

ORGANIZATION

The organization of the OCB consisted of three elements: the board assistants, the working groups, and the OCB staff. Each member agency of the OCB appointed a person who reported directly to the board member representing that agency. Together these individuals were known as the board assistants. The duties of the board assistants were varied:

Collectively they comprise a group to complete final staff work on subjects to be considered by the Board. In general, they are responsible for assuring that subjects for the consideration of the Board are fully and clearly presented, including differing agency views where they exist. They are authorized to act on behalf of their principals and take final action on certain matters at their discretion. Each Assistant gives general guidance to his agency's representatives on OCB working groups.[53]

The board assistants met each Friday morning under the chairmanship of Staats to consider matters before they were brought to the board and to develop an agenda for the formal meetings of the OCB.[54] These meetings, which some considered excessively time consuming, were "1/3 devoted to votes & relationships, 1/3 to fretting about job of 'assuring climate of opinion' [i.e., the P-factor], 1/3 to setting up, monitoring, etc. special task forces for implementation of NSC policies."[55]

Since the OCB was concerned with operations rather than policy, the Bureau of the Budget did not seek to become a full-fledged member. Other reasons the bureau was not anxious to formally join the OCB were: "a) existing limitations on the time of the senior personnel of the Bureau who would be involved and who believed other activities more deserving of priority, and b) reluctance to permit final decisions to be taken in a contest in which the Budget Bureau participates merely as an additional member."[56]

But the bureau was very interested in what the OCB was up to and in influencing its actions. To achieve this, the chief of the bureau's international division sat as an "observer" at meetings of the OCB, and one of the members of that division regularly attended meetings of the Board Assistants as an observer. This level of participation served to keep the bureau informed of developments in the OCB that had a bearing on bureau work. It also provided an opportunity to occasionally influence operational decisions that would not, in the normal course of events, be presented to the bureau. By the time a document reached the board assistants, the representative of the bureau's international division had circulated among the agencies and lined up the votes the way the bureau wanted an issue to be decided. "Perhaps 90% of what the Bureau could hope to accomplish in influencing the formalized papers of the OCB has taken place by the time documents leave the Board Assistants for the OCB itself."[57]

The OCB working groups were interdepartmental committees established on a permanent or semipermanent basis to convert NSC papers into operating programs and prepare progress reports on their implementation.[58] Most of these groups were divided by subject into geographic areas such as the Far East, Near East, Africa, Europe, and Western Hemisphere and were made up of specialists in the various areas. For example,

the Committee on Iceland would be made up of the State desk officer on Iceland, the guy from Defense who happened to have that responsibility, the fellow from USIA who did, ICA, CIA and so forth, and that would be the working group. . . . These fellows would fight out initially, from their different departmental points of view, the document that would come to the OCB. Pretty thorough fight sometimes—long, hard work involved—some of these guys were just fighting entirely for angles.[59]

Each of the working groups developed an outline plan for the NSC action assigned to them that laid out the specific courses of action that each agency was to take to implement the policy and its timing. A management expert from the budget bureau who studied the performance of the working groups felt that "while some don't perform too well and others permit formal OCB status to tie them up in red tape—written terms of reference, progress reports, etc.—on balance they are good and contribute something." According to Staats, the "papers were really less significant than the fact that you had people who met and who had to discuss these things and had to exchange views, exchange ideas. That was the real worth of the thing."[60]

One member of one of the working groups considered the board assistants a superfluous echelon that should be abolished because "they constituted a useless layer which was not personally acquainted with the problems of the working group in the same manner as the operating officials. He felt that at the board assistants' meetings other agencies were exercising political judgments that they should not have nor express."[61]

The OCB had its own permanent staff, which was drawn from CIA, the United States Information Agency, state, and defense.[62] Headed by executive officer Staats, the staff was to eventually grow to include forty people organized into four units: secretariat, psychological warfare information, intelligence liaison, and area. A member of the area staff sat with each of the working groups as the "eyes and ears" of the NSC. However, since the OCB had no decision-making power (as Prados reports), "these people could do little more than pass the word about problems or obstructions while they busied themselves preparing working group agendas and minutes."[63]

SUMMARY

The OCB was initially set up as a powerless interagency committee outside the NSC structure because the budget bureau convinced Eisenhower that the Jackson committee recommendations would violate basic management principals. In spite of these limitations, the OCB significantly improved the implementation of NSC policies.

The management experts of the bureau monitored the work of the OCB and sought to blunt efforts to inject the board into matters that the bureau considered unrelated to its basic mission, and which, they warned, would endanger the capacity of the OCB to perform its primary mission. The bureau was particularly concerned about pressure that developed to give the OCB statutory status and an independent budget. Such an approach conflicts with the basic concept of the OCB—an arrangement under which responsible agency heads join to facilitate and coordinate the execution of their separate responsibilities—and poses the threat of establishment of a "super agency" or "Assistant President for National Security."[64]

The pressure to change the status of the OCB to more closely approximate the recommendations of the Jackson committee continued through the remainder of the Eisenhower administration. As we will see they were eventually largely successful.

NOTES

1. Robert Cutler to Dwight D. Eisenhower, 27 December 1952, Cutler 52–55(5), Whitman Administrative Files, DDEL.

2. James Lay to NSC, 15 March 1955, Psychological Warfare, NSC 127/1, WHO, Special Assistant for National Security, DDEL.

3. Ibid.

4. Ibid.

5. Elmer Staats, interview by Author, 10 September 1979, Washington, D.C.

6. "The Origins of the Psychological Strategy Board," 22 February 1952, Truman PSB 1952(1), Gordon Gray Papers, DDEL.

7. Ibid.

8. John Prados, *Keepers of the Keys: A History of National Security from Truman to Bush* (New York, 1991), p. 77; Robert Cutler, *No Time for Rest* (Boston, 1956), p. 65.

9. Origins of the PSB, 22 February 1952, Gray Papers.

10. Cutler, *No Time for Rest*, p. 65.

11. DDE to John Foster Dulles, 24 October 1953, November 53, Dulles-Herter Series, Whitman Administrative Files, DDEL.

12. Cutler to Gordon Gray, 10 March 1952, PSB Personnel(4), Gray Papers.

13. Prados, *Keepers of the Keys*, pp. 54–55.

14. Gray to Wallace Carroll, 16 April 1952, PSB Personnel(3), Gray Papers, DDEL.

15. Elmer Staats Interview, 10 September 1979.

16. Cutler to DDE, 10 January 1953, Cutler 52–55(5), Whitman Administrative Files, DDEL.

17. Karl G. Harr to the President, 1 September 1959, OCB Organization, WHO, Special Assistant for National Security, DDEL.

18. Cutler to the President, 27 December 1952, Cutler 52–55(5), Whitman Administrative Files, DDEL.

19. Joint Staff Interview, OH-508, DDEL.

20. 11 August 1954, ACW Diary, August 54(3), Whitman Administrative Files, DDEL.

21. Harr to President, 1 September 1959, OCB Organization, WHO, Special Assistant for National Security, DDEL.

22. Joint Staff Interview, OH-508, DDEL.

23. Stephen E. Ambrose, *Eisenhower: The President* (New York, 1984), pp. 203–204.

24. Abbot Washburn to C. D. Jackson, 11 April 1953, 262 OCB, OF 260–D, DDEL.

25. William Finan's OCB Study, 5 October 1954, 52.1, M1–1/2, RG 51, NA.

26. Cutler, *No Time for Rest*, p. 313.

27. Cutler to DDE, 10 January 1953, Cutler 52–55(5), Whitman Administrative Files, DDEL.

28. Prados, *Keepers of the Keys*, p. 64.

29. Alfred Dick Sander, *A Staff for the President: The Executive Office, 1921–1952* (Westport, Conn., 1989), pp. 326–327.

30. James Lay, "Suggestions for Further Strengthening NSC," 19 January, 1953, M1–1\1, Series 52.1, RG 51, NA.

31. W. Y. Elliott to G. F. Stauffacher, 19 November 1952, NSC Organization and Functions(4), WHO, Project Clean Up, DDEL.

32. Dodge to DDE, "National Security Council," 22 December 1952, BOB 1952, OF-72–B, DDEL.

33. BOB Draft, "Implementation of NSC," 7 July 1953, M1–1, Series 52.1, RG 51, NA.

34. GFS [Schwarzwalder], 16 February 1956, M1–22/53.1, Series 52.6, RG 51, NA.

35. Ibid.

36. G. B. Erskine to Deputy Secretary of Defense, 10 June 1954, M1–22/53.1, Series 52.6, RG 51, NA.

37. "Implementation of NSC," 7 July 1953, M1–1, Series 52.1, RG 51, NA.

38. "Implementation of Approved NSC Policy," 10 July 1953, M1–1, Series 52.1, RG 51, NA.

39. Ibid.

40. "Establishment of OCB," 6 August 1953, M1–1/2, Series 52.1, RG 51, NA.

41. Staats Interview.

42. "Proposed Reorganization of OCB," 22 December 1955, OCB Organization, Special Assistant for National Security Affairs, WHO, DDEL.

43. Staats to OCB, 3 January 1955, No. 128 OCB, PACGO, DDEL.

44. OCB Handbook, 14 February 1958, CEA Records, DDEL.

45. Staats Interview.

46. Staats to OCB, 3 January 1955, No. 128 OCB, PACGO, DDEL.

47. Roland Hughes to DDE, 24 November 1954, Hughes, R. (1), Whitman Administrative Files, DDEL.

48. Radius interview, Finan OCB study, M1–1/2, Series 52.1, RG 51, NA.

49. Harr Oral History, DDEL, p. 25

50. Philip G. Henderson, *Managing the Presidency: The Eisenhower Legacy—From Kennedy to Reagen* (Boulder, Colo., 1988), p. 86.

51. Staats Interview.

52. Harr Oral History, p. 26.

53. OCB Handbook, 14 February 1958, Operations Coordinating Board, CEA Records, DDEL.

54. R. M. Macy to Director, 6 May 1958, M1–1/2, Series 52.1, RG 51, NA; Finan to Director, Ibid.

55. Finan's notes of OCB, 17 September 1954, M1–1/2, Series 52.1, RG 51, NA.

56. Ralph Reid to Director, 10 March 1958, M1–1/2, Series 52.1, RG 51, NA.

57. R. M. Macy to Director, 6 May 1958, M1–1/2, Series 52.1, RG 51, NA.

58. Ibid.

59. Harr Oral History, p. 27.

60. Staats Interview.

61. Roy Melbourne to Frederick Dearborn, 1 August 1957, OCB Organization, WHO Special Assistant for National Security, DDEL.

62. Staats Interview.

63. Prados, *Keepers of the Keys*, pp. 74–75.

64. Finan to Director, 18 October 1954, M1–1/2, RG 1, NA.

7

The Evolution of the Operations Coordinating Board

The Operations Coordinating Board was initially established as a "voluntary" interdepartmental committee rather than as an official element in the National Security Council organizational structure. As a result its role was frequently misunderstood by those agencies that did not regularly participate in OCB activities. Further confusion arose because its title was not particularly descriptive of the subject matter of its responsibility. Its stature was not enhanced by the fact that it had no budget of its own. One third of the 1953 budget of $155,000 was contributed by the Department of Defense and the remainder came from the CIA.[1]

This method of financing and the uncertainty about the OCB's relationship to the NSC created the impression among some that its existence was experimental and probably temporary. Among other problems this caused was difficulty in obtaining the most competent staff available.[2] To some degree the passage of time and the successful operations of the board overcame these problems, but there continued to be agitation for a regularized budget and a formal place within the NSC organization. Both of these objectives were eventually attained.

The Jackson Committee on International Information Activities had recommended the establishment of an OCB that would assign detailed planning responsibilities to the departments for the implementation of NSC-approved policies, check these plans for adequacy, and then follow up on their execution. Because the budget bureau opposed this proposal and Eisenhower accepted the bureau view, the OCB, which was created in 1953, was something of an organizational anomaly. All too often the OCB ended up doing its coordination after the fact rather than before. A representative of the Defense Department thought

This condition results from its failure, as an essential, first step in the coordination of National policy, to see to it that a basic interdepartmental program of actions is promulgated which will clearly indicate (1) what is to be done, (2) who is to do it, (3) target date for completion, and (4) criteria for evaluating performance.[3]

The chairman of the OCB from its establishment in 1953 until 1960 was the under secretary of state. Staats thought that making this official the chairman was a good idea because the state department had never accepted the fact that the NSC should meddle in foreign policy, an area they considered their exclusive domain.[4] The department was even less inclined to accept the idea that the OCB should tell it how to implement foreign policy. Holding the chairmanship of the OCB gave the department a sense that it was still in control. Another reason it made sense was that the State Department was usually charged by the OCB with carrying out the policy actions it ordained.

The State Department chairmanship did not represent a problem so long as Walter Beedle Smith was the under secretary. Eisenhower's chief of staff during the war, Smith had been appointed deputy head of the CIA by Truman. As a result of these contacts and experiences, as well as his personality, he was well equipped to do a fine job at the OCB. The problems at the OCB began when he was succeeded by Herbert Hoover, Jr., and later Christian Herter. As Staats recalled, Hoover

had few qualifications. He had done a good job of negotiating the arrangements in Iran, but in terms of comprehending the scope of activities involved in OCB and NSC it was really fairly tragic. It made him suspicious, it made him over cautious, he was uncertain of himself. As an individual he was likeable but he was just not up to it. Beedle Smith told me after he left the government that the worst mistake he made in all the time he was in the government was to recommend Herbert Hoover for that job. When he [Hoover] left Christian Herter took over. He was not a strong person as an individual. He picked up a lot of criticism of the OCB. One unfortunate statement he made was that sometimes when he was sitting in the [OCB] meetings he was wondering why he was there. Later on he more or less corrected his appraisal of [the OCB].[5]

The method of financing the OCB was the same as had been used for the Psychological Strategy Board. Cutler realized that that had been unsatisfactory so he began trying to change the OCB's budgetary status as early as 1953.[6] He was also anxious to formalize its relationship with the NSC. By the fall of 1954 when the staff of the OCB had grown to fifty-six, Cutler joined in efforts to have this staff moved to quarters adjacent to the NSC staff in the Old Executive Office Building.[7] Neither of these efforts was successful at the time, but they indicated continuing unhappiness with the budget bureau-designed OCB organizational arrangements.

Although Cutler regretted that the OCB was not part of the NSC and did not have its own line in the budget, in retrospect Staats did not think these things made that much difference in terms of actual operations. It was clumsy that way, he recalled,

but we worked around it. I for example was on the payroll of the CIA during that time but I could have been on the State Department payroll just as well. It was purely a matter of the agencies putting the money together. We had a permanent staff drawn from CIA, USIA, State and Defense. Of course the task groups were all *ad hoc*. Most of them were headed by State Department people. There were some that clearly should be headed by USIA, there were a few by CIA. Defense chaired some, then of course we pulled in Atomic Energy people and Treasury people and on occasion Agriculture on things like food for peace. I thought it worked out fairly well.[8]

Twenty-five years later Staats thought that the OCB had worked "pretty well," but at the time Cutler (and probably Staats) was unhappy. In an effort to initiate some organizational changes, Cutler in 1954 got Eisenhower to ask the budget bureau to make a study of the OCB and evaluate its operations. William Finan, who headed up the bureau's staff of management experts, undertook it. He interviewed Staats and representatives from defense, state, and the bureau's own man on the OCB Board Assistants. Staats complained of the complications that the OCB's lack of a budget line caused. He told Finan that he could only hire supergrads on the CIA payroll, that the State Department had refused to give a security clearance to an ex-CIA man who had been assigned to their payroll, and that the Defense Department was getting restive with their contribution. Staats suggested that the National Security Act could be easily amended to provide for an OCB budget. Finan disagreed.[9]

After his interviews Finan identified the problems in the OCB as:

1. An increasing pressure to inject the OCB into matters not related to its basic mission, with accompanying pressure to enlarge OCB membership, endangers the OCB capacity to discharge its primary mission.
2. Pressure has developed to give the OCB statutory status and an independent budget. Such an approach conflicts with the basic concept of the OCB—and poses the threat of establishment of a "super-agency" or "Assistant President for National Security Affairs."

3. The vacant position of Special Assistant to the President for Cold War Affairs (C. D. Jackson's old post) has created a distinct gap in the OCB structure.[10]

Since the then existing structure of the OCB was based on Finan's own initial design, it is not surprising that he did not suggest that it be changed. No action resulted from his study other than an increased effort to find a replacement for C. D. Jackson as the president's man on the OCB.

NELSON ROCKEFELLER

During the life of the OCB five men served as special assistants representing President Eisenhower on the board. All of them were faced with the problem of sailing "his craft with enough skill and care to avoid the Scylla of being an intolerable nuisance to the Secretary of State and the Charybdis of being so inoffensive as to be worthless."[11] Certainly one of the reasons C. D. Jackson resigned was that he became an "intolerable nuisance" to John Foster Dulles. But everyone agreed that the departure of Jackson about six months after the OCB began operations had left a real void. By September 1954 there was talk of Jackson's coming down from New York two or three days a week for OCB activities with General Paul Carroll filling in for him in his absence. That plan was dropped when Carroll died suddenly.[12]

In late November the budget bureau urged the president to replace C. D. Jackson as soon as possible. But Jackson was a very unique individual who was not easily replaced. Nelson Rockefeller was the other member of the administration who was noted as a generator of ideas. Eisenhower recalled that the two men "have 100 ideas; maybe one idea out of those hundred is brilliant and can be used and its worthwhile to have them around, and maybe 99 of them are bad."[13] Two of the good ideas were notable. Jackson came up with the "Atoms for Peace" concept while Rockefeller contributed the "Open Skies" proposal.[14]

The relationships these two men had with the Eisenhower were quite different. Jackson became the president's friend and confidant. Rockefeller had no close friends and was famous for paying to surround himself with brilliant thinkers. As a result the president thought Rockefeller got "used to borrowing brains instead of using his own." Eisenhower treated Rockefeller "like one of the smart young boys in the Administration" who played a useful role as an adviser on psychological warfare,[15] but the president did not really like him. As Arthur Burns observed, Rockefeller frequently got into trouble with the president "by proposing too many new ideas and departures, rather too bumptiously for a junior man."[16]

When Jackson left the administration Rockefeller was serving as under secretary at the new Department of Health, Education and Welfare. He was also chairman of the President's Advisory Committee on Government Organization. During the Roosevelt administration Rockefeller had acquired some background in foreign policy while serving as an assistant secretary of state during World War II. Eventually, and probably reluctantly, Eisenhower asked Rockefeller to join his White House staff as Jackson's replacement.

THE PLANNING COORDINATION GROUP

Rockefeller assumed his new job as special assistant and vice chairman of the OCB in late 1954. It was hoped that under his day-to-day supervision the board would improve its effectiveness. Within a few weeks he got the president to approve the establishment of a special committee outside the OCB to coordinate the implementation of NSC policies toward the Soviet satellite countries. Rockefeller chaired the committee which was composed of the Under Secretary of State, the deputy secretary of defense, and the director of Central Intelligence. As appropriate, representatives of the justice department, the Foreign Operations Administration, the U.S. Information Agency, and other interested departments and agencies joined the committee. This committee was established because of a need for high-level, restricted attention to developing sensitive programs. The committee and its small staff were supposed to develop "dynamic, new and imaginative ideas."[17]

On 4 March 1955 this special committee was reconstituted as the Planning Coordination Group within the framework of the OCB. The group was still chaired by Rockefeller and was composed "of a special grouping of OCB members." Its purpose was to infuse into the plans and programs of the agencies "new ideas to diagnose precisely how best to meet the over-all problems of a given country or area, to bring into balance all aspects of a problem and all private organizations and foreign individuals" involved. It was specified that the "Planning Coordination Group would not itself engage in operations or enter into the stream of agency operations."[18]

The Planning Coordination Group (PCG) was created pursuant to a budget bureau recommendation, which grew out of its review of the coordination of economic, psychological, and political warfare and foreign information activities. However, by the end of 1955 the PCG itself recommended that "it be abolished as a separate mechanism, partly because it became clear it would not be able to accomplish its objectives and partly because its existence both detracts from the OCB and blocks a desirable strengthening of the Board."[19]

One of the responsibilities of the Planning Coordination Group was to give policy approval to major covert programs initiated by the CIA under NSC 5412.[20] With the PCG's demise a separate and very secret "5412" Group was constituted. It met before or after the OCB luncheon meetings. With an agenda controlled by Allen Dulles, this group consisted of the CIA chief, Herter, Cutler, and Donald Quarles, (who was then the deputy secretary of defense). Originally it was considered a part of the OCB but then Eisenhower made it a separate group when he designated it as a substitute for the NSC mechanism in certain sensitive areas. It dealt with CIA political operations, which Allen Dulles thought went beyond his current policy guidance.[21] According to Gordon Gray the purpose of the 5412 group was to "scrutinize proposed CIA actions, policies, and programs to make certain they did not get the President or the country in trouble."[22]

THE ROCKEFELLER PAPER

One of the reasons C. D. Jackson came into conflict with John Foster Dulles was that he tried to establish operations in the White House that presented a real or imagined threat to the prerogatives of the secretary of state. Rockefeller pursued the same course even more overtly.[23] He used his position as chairman of the President's Advisory Committee on Government Organization to get its staff to study the OCB organization and make recommendations. Near the end of December 1955 that staff produced its "Proposed Reorganization of the OCB."[24]

The PACGO staff reviewed the findings that the William Jackson committee had arrived at in 1953 and agreed that it had correctly

a. rejected a federal structure under the Secretary of State,

b. emphasized the importance of the military,

c. approved the appointment of a special assistant for national security affairs, and

d. recognized the lack of a clear dividing line between peace and war.

But the PACGO staff thought the Jackson committee had made an error by not recommending that the OCB be chaired by an official comparable to the Bobby Cutler NSC position—i.e., a coordinator who is responsible directly to the president and who is organizationally situated above and apart from the agencies being coordinated. Instead, the OCB that was created was chaired by "a departmental executive whose primary duties are among the most exacting in government." As a result the state department "is in effect directing itself whenever the OCB gives it advice."[25]

Before he took the PACGO staff's recommendations to the other members of PACGO, Rockefeller asked the budget bureau to comment on them. Based on the bureau's suggestion, he agreed to reduce and simplify the proposals to two basic points: (1) The president should make the OCB responsible for executing the tasks that the Jackson committee had envisioned for it; and (2) The president should appoint a Special Assistant for National Security Affairs to chair the OCB.[26]

On 27 December 1955 Rockefeller sent to the president a report entitled "Coordination of Foreign, Political, Military, Economic, Informational and Covert Operations." The report concluded that the foreign operations of the United States were not being effectively coordinated, but that the situation could be remedied by giving the OCB command authority with an independent staff and by making the president's special assistant (Rockefeller) chairman of the OCB. William Jackson was critical with this reworking of his original recommendations. He said that this proposal meant that Rockefeller wanted the president to "delegate to his Special Assistant Presidential powers over the Executive Branch so far as foreign operations are within the scope of the OCB."[27] Jackson did not think this was "feasible except perhaps as part of a very drastic change in the whole setup of the Presidency. Even in the event of such a drastic change, the scheme would be very difficult for the established bureaucracy to swallow and would require the continuing and unswerving support of the President."[28] Eisenhower never acted on Rockefeller's proposal.

Rockefeller left the administration shortly after submitting his report, but not necessarily because of it. There were four people in the administration with whom he could not get along. He called them "the four H's." They were Herbert Hoover, Jr., the undersecretary of state whom Rockefeller was attempting to dislodge as chairman of the OCB; Roland Hughes, the director of the budget bureau; the president's good friend George Humphrey, the secretary of the treasury; and John B. Hollister, director of the International Cooperation Administration. These personnel conflicts were probably an important factor in Rockefeller's departure because Eisenhower did not like dissension on his team.[29] On 16 January the president confided to his diary:

Bill Jackson is coming down to join the staff, assuming that his wife agrees to the move. If he comes, he will take the place of Nelson Rockefeller, and I feel at last that I have gotten in that post a man of exactly the temperament, knowledge, and experience that I have been seeking. I expect him to do a bang up job.[30]

On 1 March 1956 William H. Jackson, the original architect of the OCB, became Eisenhower's special assistant for psychological warfare, replacing Rockefeller.[31]

Jackson made a conscious effort to avoid being, or appearing to be, a threat to the prerogatives of the secretary of state.[32] He stayed in this position during most of 1956. After Dillon Anderson left his post as special assistant for national security affairs he filled that job as well. In fact he thought the two positions should be combined.[33] He told Milton Eisenhower,

It is highly important for the work of the NSC, the Planning Board, and OCB to be closely integrated, and he feels that can best be done by having a Special Assistant to the President (operating under the general guidance of The Assistant to the President [Adams]) serve as chairman of the Planning Board and chairman of the OCB. The Special Assistant should have two deputies, one of whom would be vice-chairman of the Planning Board and one of whom would be vice-chairman of the OCB.

By this time it was known that Cutler would be back at his old job in a few weeks and it was rumored that Vice President Nixon might serve as chairman of the OCB.[34]

CUTLER RETURNS

As he prepared to return to the White House, Cutler submitted a new list of recommendations to make the NSC mechanism more effective. He again urged that an executive order be issued to bring the OCB within the NSC structure and that it be financed through the NSC budget. He also renewed his call to have the OCB staff office space juxtaposed with that of the NSC staff. He endorsed Rockefeller's and Jackson's recommendations that the president's special assistant replace the undersecretary of state as the chairman of the OCB.[35]

Cutler was formally appointed to his second tour as special assistant to the president for national security affairs on 7 January 1957. Because he had since departed the administration, Culter also inherited William Jackson's role as the president's representative on the OCB and the board's vice chairman. To insure that he was fully advised on all the activities and problems of the federal government, his appointment letter invited him "to attend meetings of the Cabinet, Council on Foreign Economic Policy, and other relevant groups."[36]

By mid-January the rumor that Vice President Nixon would be named to replace the undersecretary of state as the chairman of the OCB had become enough of a reality to cause Cutler to warn the president against the move. His objection was threefold. First, he stressed that the function of the chairman was coordinative, not directive. If someone with the prestige of a vice president became chairman the role would tend to become directive, and "no directive body should intervene in the line of authority running from the President to

his responsible ministers, unless the President intends to make a radical departure in the top organization of the Executive Branch." Cutler was also concerned that the involvement of the vice president in the affairs of the OCB
would attract media attention to the board's work. Finally Cutler told Eisenhower that John Foster Dulles would consider the move a "personal slap" at
him.[37]

The same day that Cutler sent his memo to Eisenhower the secretary of state
registered his own strong objections to the president.

I believe that the relations of the Secretary and the Under Secretary of State to the President in regard to foreign affairs are and should be more intimate than those of the Vice
President. If the time comes when the Vice President more authoritatively expresses
the President's view on these matters than the Secretary of State, then a revolution will
indeed have been effected in our form of Government.

Eisenhower managed to duck this issue until after Dulles's death a few years
later.[38]

REORGANIZATION OF THE OCB

One result of Cutler's return was the adoption of his long sought recommendation that the OCB be included within the structure and funding of the
NSC. The then existing OCB had been established as a voluntary interdepartmental committee by Executive Order 10483 of 3 September 1953 with a staff
drawn from the member departments. Executive Order 10700 of 25 February
1957 placed the OCB organizationally within the structure of the National Security Council as of 1 July 1957. Although the responsibilities and functions of
the OCB were not changed, its staff was now "within the staff of the" NSC so
they would be paid from funds appropriated for the council. The problem of
the board's chairmanship was finessed by specifying that he would be "designated by the President from among its members."[39]

FREDERICK DEARBORN

Because of the departure of William Jackson (who thought one person
could do both jobs), the position of Special Assistant for Security Operations
was vacant when Cutler returned to the White House. Cutler did not agree
with the one-man approach, but Eisenhower asked him to fill in by appointing
him vice chairman of OCB. As a result for several months Cutler was working
sixty-five hours a week while he desperately sought someone to replace him in
the OCB position.[40]

The person he found was Frederick M. Dearborn, who, like Cutler, was a Boston lawyer who had been active in Republican state politics. Cutler assured the president that Dearborn was "well-known to Secretary and Mrs. Humphrey" and promised that he (in contrast with Rockefeller) would work "very harmoniously with Herter." In fact, Dearborn had been special counsel to the governor of Massachusetts while Herter was the governor. He had also worked with Gordon Gray in the past.[41] Eisenhower accepted the recommendation, appointing Dearborn special assistant for security operations coordination on 27 May 1957.[42]

The appointment of Dearborn, who lacked the public stature or position of any of his three predecessors (the two Jacksons and Rockefeller), marked an effort to accommodate the state department concerns about the OCB. He was not an independent operator. Dearborn's influence was limited to how much the other members of the OCB thought he represented the thinking and desires of the president.[43] However he did not have much of an opportunity to demonstrate the effectiveness of this approach because he died suddenly in February 1958.[44]

KARL G. HARR

Shortly after Dearborn's death, Cutler got Eisenhower to appoint Karl G. Harr to replace him as vice chairman of the OCB and as the presidential representative on the board. Harr held the position for the remainder of the Eisenhower administration. He, like Dearborn, was not well known, but he was experienced in national security matters because of his service as assistant secretary of defense for international affairs. He had replaced Gordon Gray in this position and served as the Defense Department representative on the Planning Board. He was thus well versed in NSC and OCB matters before he joined the White House staff as a presidential assistant. Harr never developed the personal relationship with the president that his predecessors, C. D. Jackson, Rockefeller, and William Jackson, had enjoyed. Even though he had the same rank as Cutler and Gray, he tended to be subordinate to them.

By the time Harr became vice chairman of the OCB it had been in existence for six years. In governmental terms it had become "institutionalized" in the sense that the departments and agencies involved in its operations understood, and accepted, its purposes and functions as well as its limitations. One result of this was that agency activities recognized as having an impact on overseas operations were now routinely submitted to the OCB machinery.[45] As vice chairman, Harr was "really the one charged with sparking the whole thing" because the chairman, the under secretary of state, had many other duties "which were much more demanding on his time." Harr was also the line supervisor of the OCB executive officer.[46]

With the creation of the OCB and its growth into a relatively effective organization, the NSC, for the first time, had an institutionalized reality check on the feasibility of the policies it developed. Each policy had to be reduced to suggested actions by a working group composed of individuals who were knowledgeable about the geographic area or specialty involved in the policy. These suggestions were then considered and massaged by the board assistants before being forwarded to the OCB for final approval. At each level there were usually fights, papers generated, and finally compromises. After the OCB approved the document there was a paper against which to measure the implementation of a policy. For example, if it involved Iran, the ambassador, the desk officer at the State Department, and the responsible officers in defense, the ISA, the CIA, commerce, etc. had something to work against and hold others and themselves responsible for. According to Harr the document would serve as the basic operations plan

and every six months the OCB structure would have to produce a progress report on how well that operations plan was proving out, whether it was being implemented, whether it was still valid, whether it was feasible, whether the situation had changed enough so that you should have a new one. . . . This was I think, the real effectiveness of the overall NSC structure, that it integrated all of these things, from the first initial formulation of policy, coordination, up through approval at the top level, down through an implementing structure that had built into it a procedure that would require accounting from time to time.[47]

It is not likely that an operation as flawed as the Bay of Pigs could have survived this process. Unfortunately the OCB no longer existed when that plan was approved.

The person in Harr's position had a key role in this process. The last ten or fifteen minutes of the typical NSC meeting were devoted to his OCB progress reports in which the NSC would learn how well their policies were being implemented and whether they appeared to be still viable.[48] This closure of the loop was fundamental to the NSC procedure but it could easily degenerate into a bureaucratic routine. Eisenhower sought to minimize the possibility of wasting the time of his high-level executives by warning Harr "that the burden of proof is on the OCB to demonstrate that any report should be made to the Council when no policy review is indicated."[49]

Harr was also the link to the Planning Board where he served as the OCB representative. There his most significant function was to push the Planning Board to state its objectives, policy recommendations, and courses of action in clear and unambiguous terms so that, if they were accepted by the NSC, the OCB would understand the directive it was given to implement.[50]

The relations between Eisenhower and Harr were apparently never close. In April 1959 Harr asked the president if he could see him "to discuss fundamental reassessment of the OCB." In September he addressed a long, rather plaintive, memo to Eisenhower in which he said

Where I personally feel the most serious lack is in the link I am supposed to provide between you and the departments and agencies engaged in national security and psychological impact operations. I think it is my fault that you are not kept more completely aware of the current nature of our activities designed to achieve psychological impact. I confess also that there is insufficient direct interchange between us for me to feel completely confident that I am pursuing the course you wish to see followed within the Executive Branch to further our psychological impact objectives. As far as I am concerned remedying of these two deficiencies would offer the most useful and practical means of enhancing our over-all national efforts, through the OCB and otherwise, to fully exploit our assets in this area.[51]

In late 1958 Elmer Staats returned to the budget bureau as the deputy director under Maurice Stans. It was the same position that Staats had held during the last years of the Truman administration and was to continue to hold during the Kennedy administration. To replace him as executive officer of the OCB, Eisenhower named Bromley K. Smith. Smith had been the senior member of the Policy Coordinating Special Staff of the NSC since Cutler recruited him from the State Department in September 1953. At state he had held various positions including the Policy Planning Staff and alternate representative on the NSC Planning Board. Earlier he had been a Foreign Service officer and a reporter.[52] He was to serve as executive secretary of the NSC during the Kennedy and Johnson administrations.

GRAY BECOMES OCB CHAIRMAN

John Foster Dulles resigned in April 1959 and was replaced by Christian Herter. With Herter's promotion Livingston Merchant became chairman of the OCB. He was soon succeeded by the veteran diplomat Robert Murphy.[53] When Murphy retired in late 1959 Gray tried to get Under Secretary C. Douglas Dillon to assume the OCB chairmanship but Dillon repeatedly refused to do so. As the special assistant for national security affairs Gray, as well as Harr, were members of the OCB. Both men believed strongly in the efficacy of the board and were devoted to its continuance. Since the executive order under which the OCB now operated provided that the president could name the chairman from among the members, Gray got Eisenhower to appoint him to the post in January 1960.[54]

Perhaps one reason Gray became chairman of the OCB at this point was that the administration was entering into its final year. Nevertheless, his appointment marked the culmination of Cutler's and Rockefeller's efforts to place the White House firmly in charge of OCB operations. The organization of 1960 was a far cry from the voluntary coordinating mechanism that had been created in 1953.

In summarizing the work of the OCB for the president, Gray felt that the board made

a double contribution: one a tangible product that can be evaluated from its written record; the other a contribution which is less tangible and little known except to those who have actively participated in the work of the Board. This latter extremely valuable contribution is the gain in effectiveness deriving from the fact of the Board's existence. The Board has facilitated smoother teamwork among members of your Administration who have worked together in the Board and under its auspices. More over, the easy availability of the Board for interdepartmental consultation and the systematic scrutiny by the Board of overseas operational planning and results constitute strong deterrents to uncoordinated actions or unnecessary interdepartmental conflicts.[55]

The "less tangible" benefits referred to the results of the informal OCB luncheon meetings.

In the late 1960s Gray and Cutler compared notes on their experiences in the Eisenhower administration. By then Gray no longer believed that the OCB should have continued in exactly the form it had reached by the end of the administration. In retrospect he thought "it had become too much of a paper mill and overgrown." However he still saw the practice of the weekly luncheon as "vital." He was also sure that the chairmanship of the OCB should be devolved on the special assistant for national security affairs to insure that the board would be president-oriented rather than state department oriented.[56]

President Eisenhower himself thought that the OCB "functioned fairly well," but he did not think its was the best solution to the need for daily coordination of the far-flung foreign policy operations of the country. Instead, he felt that the executive branch needed an assistant president for foreign affairs or "First Secretary" as he eventually called him. He believed that such an official with a small staff would have been more effective than the OCB committee approach.

If such a plan were adopted the individual needed would, of course, have to be knowledgeable in international affairs, capable as a leader, and intimately familiar with all activities of the relevant departments and agencies so as to achieve the maximum of willing and effective cooperation. He would become, in a practical sense, a Deputy Chairman of the National Security Council. During the intervals between the President's meetings with the Council such an assistant would be, day-by-day, engaged in the task of making sure that agencies having any connection with foreign problems were all working together to carry out the President's decisions.[57]

The year of Gray's chairmanship was closer to this model than the earlier organizational schemes employed by the OCB. John Prados found that "with his follow-up and scheduling powers, his broad contact with the President, his initiative in the NSC, . . . Gray became *de facto* national security adviser though he still lacked the job title."[58]

KENNEDY AND THE OCB

There is no doubt that Eisenhower hoped that his successor would keep the OCB in existence. It was one of the reasons he had the OCB reorganized late in his administration. He told Gray to leave things in his area in "apple pie order" for Kennedy. Gray recalled that he really "broke my pick" to do so. McGeorge Bundy, Kennedy's national security adviser, was briefed on the OCB process by Gray but it was a hurried affair because Bundy's appointment was quite late in the transition period and everyone was trying to brief him at the same time.[59]

Elmer Staats, who was a part of the Kennedy administration, recalls that

the new administration came in with the idea that they were going to try to informalize the White House, informalize the Executive Office, go back to the Roosevelt traditions as they called it. So the one thing they seized on was the NSC. The Planning Board was to be dropped and the OCB was to be dropped, meantime they were going to continue some kind of undersecretaries group. I persuaded them to continue the luncheon discussions for a while, but Bundy chaired those meetings and they just were not the same kind of product at all.

Staats is convinced that the Bay of Pigs disaster would not have occurred if the OCB had not been abolished.[60]

Bromley Smith, who also continued under Kennedy as the executive secretary of the NSC, thought the OCB "a beautiful operation." He felt guilty because he was not able to convince the new administration to keep it. Smith urged Bundy to allow the OCB to continue to function but later realized that he should have been pleading with Walt Rostow who was the one who wrote the memo recommending that it be abolished. Later Harvard professor Richard Neustadt, who was advising Kennedy on organizing his administration, wrote a memo admitting it had been a mistake to end the OCB. It was partially a political decision that was aimed at Eisenhower but ended up causing problems for Kennedy.[61]

In any event, Kennedy lost little time in abolishing the OCB. On 19 February 1961 he issued a statement to accompany Executive Order 10920 that revoked Eisenhower's action in establishing the board. Kennedy explained that the secretary of state would assume much of the responsibility of the OCB's work. The White House and "Mr. [Edward R.] Murrow of USIA" would do the psychological warfare portion of the board's concerns.[62]

The closest the Democrats came to reestablishing an OCB came in 1967 when the Johnson administration created the Senior Interdepartmental Group (SIG). Like the OCB it was composed of the highest officials of the government below the Cabinet level. Like the early OCB it was chaired by the under secretary of state and included the deputy secretaries of defense, treasury, and the CIA as well as the chairman of the JCS. Its role was to review the options presented to the NSC and to follow up on the decisions the council reached. Like the OCB the SIG oversaw a battery of interdepartmental working groups focused on the various geographic areas. It was largely ineffective because the NSC rarely met during the Johnson years and most of the decisions were made during the Tuesday lunches that were outside the SIG structure.[63]

But the need for a coordinating organization like the OCB continues to exist in the NSC system. When General Colin Powell was charged with rescuing the NSC in the wake of the Iran-Contra affair during the Reagan administration, one of the first actions he took was to establish a Policy Review Group. Like Eisenhower's OCB, this group was made up of subcabinet officials from State, Defense, the JCS and the CIA. Its job was to coordinate the actions of the departments and agencies in carrying out the policies developed through the NSC.[64]

NOTES

1. Elmer Staats to OCB, 3 January 1955, No. 128 OCB, PACGO, DDEL; 1956 Budget Recommendations, Table 7, Budget 55–56, Whitman Administrative Files, DDEL.

2. Staats, ibid.

3. G. B. Erskine to Deputy Secretary of Defense, 10 June 1954, M1–22/53.1, Series 52.6, RG 51, NA.

4. Staats Interview, 10 September 1979.

5. Ibid.

6. Robert Cutler to Wilton Persons, 12 November 1953, Project Clean Up, NSC Organization and Functions, DDEL.

7. Cutler to Sherman Adams, 26 October 1954, 262 OCB, OF 260–D, NA.

8. Staats Interview, 10 September 1979.

9. William Finan Notes on OCB, 17 September 1954, M1–1/2, Series 52.1, RG 51, NA.

10. Finan to Director, 18 October 1954, M1–1/2, Series 52.1, RG 51, NA.

11. Karl G. Harr to the President, 1 September 1959, OCB Organization, WHO, Special Assistant for National Security, DDEL.

12. Finan's Notes on OCB, 17 September 1954, M1–1/2, Series 52.1, RG 51, NA.

13. Joint Staff Interview, OH-508, DDEL; Robert J. Donovan, *Confidential Secretary: Ann Whitman's 20 Years with Eisenhower and Rockefeller* (New York, 1988), p. 165.

14. Joint Staff Interview, OH-508, DDEL.

15. Donovan, *Confidential Secretary*, p. 165.

16. Tom Wicker, *One of Us: Richard Nixon and the American Dream* (New York, 1991), p. 222.

17. Roland Hughes to the President, 3 March 1955, M1–1, Series 52.1, RG 51, NA.

18. Ibid.; Functions and Organization of the OCB, undated, No. 128 OCB, PACGO, DDEL.

19. "Proposed Reorganization of OCB," 22 December 1955, OCB Organization, WHO, Special Assistant for National Security, DDEL.

20. Hughes to the President, 3 March 1955, M1–1, Series 52.1, RG 51, NA.

21. R. M. Macy to the Director, 6 May 1958, M1–1/2, Series 52.1, RG 51, NA.

22. Stephen E. Ambrose, *Eisenhower: The President* (New York, 1984), p. 506.

23. Harr to the President, 1 September 1959, OCB Organization, WHO, Special Assistant for National Security, DDEL.

24. Proposed Reorganization of OCB, 22 December 1955, OCB Organization, WHO, Special Assistant for National Security, DDEL.

25. Ibid.

26. Nelson Rockefeller to Roland Hughes, 22 December 1955, M1–22/53.1, Series 52.6, RG 51, NA.

27. William H. Jackson to Sherman Adams, 2 April 1956, W.H. Jackson(1) October 54–March 56, WHO, Staff Secretary, DDEL.

28. Comments of Rockefeller's Paper, 2 April 1956, OCB Organization, WHO, Special Assistant for National Security, DDEL.

29. Joint Staff Interview, OH-508, DDEL.

30. Robert H. Ferrell, ed., *The Eisenhower Diaries* (New York, 1981), 16 January 1956 pp. 308–309.

31. Finan to Director, Draft, 5 March 1956, M1–22/53.1, Series 52.6, RG 51, NA.

32. Harr to the President, 1 September 1959, OCB Organization, WHO, Special Assistant for National Security, DDEL.

33. Cutler to the President, "Interim Report on Organization of the NSC Mechanism," 20 March 1957, NSC Organization and Functions(8), WHO, Clean Up, DDEL.

34. Milton Eisenhower to Kimball, 11 December 1956, No. 128 OCB, PACGO, DDEL.

35. Recommendations, 24 November 1956, Cutler 56–57(3), Whitman Administrative Files, DDEL.

36. Eisenhower to Cutler, 7 January 1957, NSC Organization and Functions(8), WHO, Clean Up, DDEL.

37. Cutler, "Reorganization of Operations Coordinating Board," 14 January 1957, OCB Integration Into the NSC, WHO, Project Clean Up, DDEL.

38. Anna K. Nelson, "The Top of Policy Hill: President Eisenhower and the National Security Council." *Diplomatic History* 7 (fall 1983): 314.

39. OCB Handbook, 14 February 1958, OCB, CEA Records, DDEL.

40. Cutler to the President, 20 March 1957, Cutler Vol. I(1), WHO, Staff Secretary, DDEL.

41. Ibid.

42. Eisenhower to Dearborn, 27 May 1957, NSC Misc(7), CFEP, DDEL.

43. Harr to the President, 1 September 1959, OCB Organization, WHO, Special Assistant for National Security, DDEL.

44. Harr Oral History, DDEL.

45. Harr to the President, 1 September 1959, OCB Organization, WHO, Special Assistant for National Security, DDEL.

46. Harr Oral History, DDEL.

47. Harr Oral History, DDEL.

48. Ibid.

49. Gordon Gray to Harr, 10 June 1959, OCB Organization, WHO, Special Assistant for National Security, DDEL.

50. Harr to Staats, 28 March 1958, OCB Organization, WHO, Special Assistant for National Security, DDEL.

51. Harr to the President, 1 September 1959, OCB Organization, WHO, Special Assistant for National Security, DDEL.

52. Press Release, 19 December 1958, OCB 474, WHO, Staff Secretary, DDEL.

53. Harr Oral History, DDEL.

54. Gray to the President, 13 January 1961, Gray NSC(1), Whitman Administrative Files, DDEL.

55. Ibid.

56. Gray to Cutler, 15 November 1968, Anderson-Cutler(1), Gordon Gray Papers, DDEL.

57. Dwight D. Eisenhower, *The White House Years: Waging Peace, 1956–1961* (Garden City, 1965), pp. 634–635.

58. John Prados, *Keepers of the Keys: A History of the National Security Council from Truman to Bush* (New York, 1991), pp. 78–79.

59. Joint Staff Interview, OH-508, DDEL.

60. Staats Interview, 10 September 1979, Washington, D.C.

61. Smith Interview, 6 September 1979, Washington, D.C.

62. Henry M. Jackson, ed., *The National Security Council: Jackson Subcommittee Papers on Policy-Making at the Presidential Level* (New York, 1965), pp. 302–303.

63. Henry Kissinger, *The White House Years* (Boston, 1979), p. 42.

64. Colin L. Powell, *My American Journey* (New York, 1995), p. 337.

<u>8</u>

The Bureau of the Budget

By 1953 the central purpose of the Bureau of the Budget was to get and maintain a reliable working knowledge of the programs, practices, and problems of the agencies of the federal government. Based on this knowledge the bureau employees sought to fix, within reasonable limits, the budgets of the respective agencies. They also provided technical assistance to the agencies in certain specialized fields such as statistics, organization, and management. Another important feature of the bureau's work was the review and coordination of legislative proposals of concern to the executive branch. In performing these functions it was not the bureau's role to assume direct responsibility or a supervisory relationship over the operations of the agencies. That is, the program analysis, examination, and review the bureau did had the character of staff work. Basically its job was to supply advice and assistance to the president and the agencies.[1] In its day-to-day work the bureau served as an institutional nerve center for the president.[2]

Most of the work of the bureau was done by budget examiners who were assigned to five operating divisions that were organized according to the functional areas of the government. The names of these divisions were Commerce and Finance, International, Labor and Welfare, Military, and Resources and Civil Works. Each department and agency in the executive branch was assigned to one of these divisions. Budget examiners in these divisions reviewed and analyzed the programs of each of the departments and agencies and developed recommendations for the next year's budget. This work required continuous study throughout the year of all phases of the agencies' activities, particularly as they related to budget and legislative requirements and to problems of management and organization.[3]

In doing this work many in the bureau pictured themselves as David versus Goliath. One division chief saw the process like this:

In every area of the Bureau, we find little clusters of young men, in units of two or three, who must set themselves against the battalions of bureaucracy in the operating agencies. The agency staffs are large, diversified, highly-paid, and affiliated with pressure groups. They have the resources, the professional skills, and the time to generate a mass of new proposals, to reduce those proposals to reams of justification, add drafts of legislation, and to argue. The Bureau's limited staff must wade through all this to find clues as to the real meaning of the proposals, their necessity, their consistency with policy, the implications for costs and alternate ways for getting the same desired result. In doing this, the Bureau staff can give only such time as can be spared from necessary work on budget review, apportionments, congressional requests for reports, and other business. The net of it is that the Bureau sets itself a prodigious objective, and assumes that there are no limits to the demands that can be made on its small resources.[4]

Each spring the bureau, with the Council of Economic Advisers and the Treasury Department, developed economic assumptions for the fiscal year that was to begin fifteen months hence. Based on these assumptions the agencies then prepared their preliminary estimates of the funds they would require during the coming fiscal year. After discussions with the agencies, the bureau developed a total estimate of the probable federal expenditure level. The bureau then made its assumptions about the condition of the country's economy during the next fiscal year and compared these with the Treasury Department's estimates of revenue. All these estimates were then discussed with the president, the Cabinet, and the NSC. From these meetings policies were developed to guide the departments and agencies in the preparation of their detailed budget submissions. These submissions were then reviewed and analyzed by budget examiners who had an intimate knowledge of the individual agencies. The examiners discussed their findings with the agencies and made their recommendations. These served as the basis for the annual director's review.[5] Roger Jones described this next process:

The director's review is when the budget divisions, the substantive divisions, come in with their recommendations for what you do to the submissions that have been made by the agencies, and you arrive at a position which the director then recommends to the President. In many cases the President's delegated the authority on the little stuff, and you just tell the agencies what allowances they've got and then they have to go back and settle it with our examiners.

The agencies still had the right to appeal the bureau's decisions directly to the president, but Eisenhower let the departments and agencies know that he did not welcome these appeals so there were not many of them during his administration.[6]

In addition to the five divisions there were also five staff offices organized to parallel the bureau's functions. These were Budget Review, Accounting, Legislative Reference, Management and Organization, and Statistical Standards. Budget Review was responsible for the complex job of planning, scheduling, and controlling the preparation of the budget. This included working on definitions and concepts and general budgetary policies and assumptions as well as preparing material for submission to the president and the Cabinet. Accounting provided staff assistance to the entire executive branch in improving its accounting and financial management. Statistical Standards, whose independent origins went back to 1908, had been incorporated into the bureau in 1939 but always led a semiautonomous existence. It had long had government-wide responsibility for eliminating duplication in the collection of information, seeing that the methods used in preparing statistical information were adequate, and minimizing the reporting burdens on the public.[7]

From the beginning of the budget bureau in 1921 it had played an important role in the legislative process. That year all agencies were ordered to clear all their legislative reports and proposals that could involve future appropriations with the bureau to see if these were "consistent with the president's financial program." In the 1930s the proliferation of depression-generated proposals for expanding the functions of the federal government prompted Roosevelt to require the agencies to also clear their legislative policy proposals with the bureau. Then, in 1939, the bureau was made the president's agent on enrolled bills. By the time of the Eisenhower administration the bureau's legislative role had been expanded further to include an increasing number of direct requests from congressional committees for bureau reports. Significantly, during the Truman administration the bureau also began coordinating the president's legislative program. The techniques of planning the broad outlines of the president's program as well as the details of many of its major components were developed still further during the Eisenhower years. These myriad functions were the responsibility of the Office of Legislative Reference.[8] Roger Jones headed the office during Eisenhower's first term.

A Division of Administrative Management had been set up in the bureau in 1939 to do government-wide studies and agency surveys and to provide advice to the president on wartime organization. During the war and immediately thereafter, the group focused on helping the agencies help themselves to improve their management techniques. In April 1952 the bureau went through a

significant reorganization, and most of the organization and management personnel were dispersed to the operating divisions to work along with the examiners in providing assistance directly to the agencies. This move primarily
affected the Division of Administrative Management. It was renamed the Office of Management and Organization (OMO), and the personnel that remained were left to work on "must items" of immediate presidential concern
and to provide staff support for PACGO. The office was headed by William Finan.[9]

The broad purposes of the 1952 reorganization of the bureau were intended
to achieve

(a) a better grouping of functions and a stronger supervisory structure to secure continuing consideration within the Bureau of the interrelation of budgetary, fiscal, management, and legislative problems with respect to major areas of the Government's
programs; (b) a deployment of the Bureau's staff of specialists to obtain more effective
use of its limited manpower resources; and (c) a strengthening of the Bureau's working
relationships with the agencies of the executive branch, with which the Bureau deals on
a continuing basis.

The general lines of the reorganization resulted from ideas long discussed
within the bureau and from suggestions made by the first Hoover Commission.[10]

Finan and many of the onetime members of the OMO staff were never
happy with the 1952 reorganization that stripped away most of his staff. Those
who remained in the Office of Management and Organization continued to
show a propensity to involve themselves in the portion of this area that was
now the responsibility of the various divisions. The division chiefs, however,
tended to favor the results of the reorganization. One of them, R. M. Macy, believed the new organization fundamentally sound and a distinct improvement
over the one it replaced. Regarding OMO he felt that

on 80 or 90 percent of the organizational matters that we have dealt with, the organizational and legislative issues have been so intertwined with the budgetary problems that
I don't see how the organizational issues could be separately dealt with effectively by another part of the Bureau. I think the end result would not only suffer but more people
would be required to accomplish the same result.[11]

Another division chief, William D. Carey, had a similar view:

In the 1952 reorganization of the Bureau, the divisions were given limited administrative management responsibilities, but not much staff with which to carry them out.
The role of OMO was to be confined to government-wide management projects. For a

year, I had an alumna of OMO as my management adviser, but at the year's end she and I agreed that the most such an individual could do was to point up the management problems facing our parish, and ride herd on the examiners to get moving. I decided that I would do the latter myself, and on this amicable basis we piped her back to shore duty with OMO. There is a general impression that the divisions do not and will not undertake management work. I disagree.[12]

This did not mean that Carey did not see a role for the Office of Management and Organization. He believed that many of the agencies "simply lack the vision and the aggressiveness to install continuing management audit services. The Bureau should have a full-time staff in OMO to guide the agencies in making management audits."[13]

Many considered the reorganized bureau to be at the height of it effectiveness. Its staff was nonpartisan, professional, and highly skilled. One of its non-career alumni believed that the existence of the budget bureau was why the presidency was still operable. "If you didn't have that professional staff . . . who between them know what's going on everywhere in government, I don't know how the President could make an intelligent decision."[14]

THE 1952 TRANSITION

Although the Bureau of the Budget had been created in 1921 under a Republican administration, it was then a far different organization than the one that greeted President Eisenhower in 1953. In 1939 the bureau became the dominant unit within the Executive Office of the President. Through most of the next fourteen years it was the president's most effective tool for managing the executive branch. But the presidents during those years had been Democrats! There was a real question as to whether the bureau could adapt its thinking and give its loyalty to a Republican president and whether that president would believe them if they did.

In 1948 Truman had insisted that the budget bureau prepare for the transition to a new administration. Although he was sure that he would be reelected, many people were not, and he believed strongly in the institutional role of the bureau in providing continuity for the presidency. This had never been done before, and the first time the bureau did not do a very thorough job of it.[15]

Certain that a new chief executive would be selected and more aware of its role as the institutional memory of the presidency, the bureau was determined to do better in 1952 and as the election approached, began to produce materials designed to instruct the incoming chief executive in the nature and the work of the Executive Office of the President. One long document the bureau prepared read like a high school civics book. For example, in regard to the Cabinet it said:

The presidency in the American system of government bears executive responsibility. The President cannot divest himself of this responsibility by seeking the advice of his department and agency heads individually or collectively. The President must retain his flexibility of action, no matter what system of relationships he creates among his personal advisors and department heads.[16]

The purpose of the paper was apparently to introduce the new president to the philosophy behind the Executive Office of the President and to articulate some principals he should follow in organizing it. The advice may have been good, but there is no evidence that it reached Eisenhower's desk. It is interesting primarily as an exposition of how the bureau viewed the EOP in 1952.

In October the staff held meetings to prepare a bureau position on the structure and functions of the Executive Office. Those attending developed a list of organizational matters they believed the new president would need to address. At the head of the list was the Psychological Strategy Board that, as we have seen, Eisenhower converted into the OCB.[17] They also prepared background material on how the Council of Economic Advisers had gotten to be such a problem and recommended jettisoning the three-man nature of the organization. The bureau also had definite ideas about how the White House staff should operate. The new president should be advised that the Brownlow theory about administrative assistants seeking anonymity was sound advice. Recommendations included merging the functions of the liaison personnel officer and the appointments secretary, abolishing the post of minority groups assistant, and examining the institutional responsibilities of the executive clerk.[18] While it is true that Eisenhower did not assign one of his administrative assistants exclusively to minority affairs, his White House staff was largely of his own design.

Once it was known that Eisenhower was to be the new president the bureau examined his campaign speeches for clues as to his organizational policies. It was not a comfort to them that he had referred to the budget bureau as well as the NSC in these remarks. They were hopeful that, since appropriations for the EOP had been progressively reduced over the past five years, the new president might wish to make the method of financing his personal staff a matter of issue. It was also hoped that he would seek greater statutory flexibility from the new Republican Congress in the functions and organization of the EOP.[19]

JOSEPH DODGE

Both Eisenhower and the budget bureau were fortunate that Joseph Dodge was his first director of the budget. At the time even bureau career people knew that the budget was out of control.[20] Dodge's challenge was to deal with this problem while retaining the bureau's professionals and overcoming the new administration's political suspicions of the bureaucrats. Dodge was respected by both Truman and Eisenhower: no mean achievement! Dodge had considerable government experience including service with MacArthur in Japan. He knew how to get things done in Washington.[21]

At the time of his appointment Dodge was a Detroit banker. He was named budget director-designate a few days after the election, and in a few more days he was in Washington attending bureau sessions on Truman's last budget. As he recalled, "Originally I accepted this assignment on a short term basis and principally to help meet the emergency connected with the new Administration's intended prompt revision of the 1954 Truman Budget. At the time I agreed to not less than six months and my leave from the bank was for a period of not more than one year."[22]

On Truman's orders nothing about the budget was hidden from him. He sat in on all the deliberations that were occurring between the bureau officials and the various departments and agencies.

This gave Dodge invaluable information about current fiscal matters while bolstering his confidence in the professionalism of the career officers, with whom he developed an excellent relationship. The Bureau staff took pride in the fact that two months after Truman's budget was submitted to Congress they substantially revised it in accordance with instructions from Eisenhower and Dodge. In the process, any remaining political suspicions of the Budget Bureau were allayed and Dodge retained its professionals.[23]

In order to maintain morale in the bureau and smooth the transition Dodge also arranged with Sherman Adams to retain the services, for a time, of Frederick Lawton and Elmer Staats, Truman's last budget director and his deputy.[24]

Dodge's predecessors, Harold Smith and James Webb, tried to avoid Cabinet meetings because they sought a special relationship with the president and did not want to be considered one of the crowd. Smith argued that "if I go to cabinet meetings then I am going to be a party to these discussions and even though I don't say anything the fact that I don't say something I would be to some degree committed." Staats did not agree with Smith's logic. As he rationalized later, "There is no point in trying to be all that pure." [25]

Dodge apparently agreed with Staats so, when Eisenhower offered him Cabinet status, he readily accepted. One of his reasons for attending Cabinet meetings was that he knew that was where Eisenhower liked to make decisions. Dodge wanted to be there to insure that the bureau was part of the decision-making process.

To many in the bureau the attendance of their director at meetings of the cabinet fulfilled "their prayer and wish." In their opinion it was the only way in which the bureau could assume its proper role in the federal hierarchy. but the new eminence arrived overnight, and the bureau was really not ready to accept its additional responsibility. "The workload generated by the change in status and the Director's requirements grew while the personnel was not increased commensurately."[26] The size of the bureau declined 20 percent between 1950 and 1959, even though its overall magnitude of concern steadily expanded.[27] The bureau's decline from its peak strength in 1946 was even more striking. In 1956 Roger Jones complained that "We are working too hard and too intensely for the long pull. We take on every new job without any assessment of whether we have adequate resources to perform it. The result has been that the job is now managing us, rather than the reverse."[28]

As director of the budget, Dodge had a clear concept of his role. For example, early in his tenure he declined appointment to the Commission on Intergovernmental Relations because "for the Director to be responsible for official advice to the President, he should maintain an independent position."[29]

While he was director, Dodge regularly had his share of personnel problems because the other departments raided the staff of his highly regarded bureau. He frequently had to try to recruit organization and methods examiners and budget examiners at the intermediate and higher grades because it was "becoming more and more difficult to maintain the existing standard of quality, and almost impossible to improve it."[30]

Although Dodge was generally well respected by other Republicans, he had great difficulty getting some of them to believe in the professionalism of the bureaucrats in the budget bureau. As a result, he was under immediate pressure to appoint deserving Republicans to supervisory positions in the bureau so they could watch the career civil servants he had inherited from the Truman administration. The problem was to make some additional political appointments in the bureau while protecting the professionalism of the career employees. Dodge sought to achieve this by getting Congress to authorize new "assistant director" positions that could be filled by party appointees.

The original concept was that these officials were to act in a line capacity and were to serve three basic purposes, (1) to provide a projection of the administration's "team" objectives into Bureau orientation, and (2) to relieve pressure on career staff by Cabinet and subcabinet officers, and (3) relieve the Director of pressures originating from these officers.

This ploy reflected Dodge's conviction that the bureau's mission could best be accomplished by the career civil service but he acknowledged the necessity of providing a "buffer zone" during what, he considered, a critical transition phase. As time went on these "statutory" assistant directors were relegated to acting in a staff capacity to the director. The assistant directors could only act for the director in areas referred to them by him.[31]

In May 1953 Congress, at Dodge's request, changed the title of his regular assistant director to "Deputy Director" and authorized the appointment of two general "Assistant Directors" in lieu of an executive assistant director and a special assistant to the director. (The following year a third assistant director was authorized.) One of the new positions was filled by Paul Morrison, late a finance professor at Northwestern, who had an MBA and a Ph.D. and was a certified public accountant.[32] The second appointment went to Donald R. Belcher. He had recently retired as treasurer of AT&T and was working as a consultant to the House Appropriations Committee.[33] The following year Congress authorized a third assistant director. This was filled by Ralph Reid who was merely promoted from assistant to the director and continued his regular assignment of representing the bureau on the NSC Planning Board and concerning himself broadly with national security matters.

The assistant directors were difficult to assimilate into the organization. A task force appointed by the director in 1959 to look at problems in the bureau found that the

role of the noncareer Assistant Directors badly needs clarification. Not only is there uncertainty as to their role but they sometimes create problems by taking a position or acquiescing in a position taken by others without benefit of consultation with staff. The virtual unanimity of criticism not only emphasizes the need for clarification of their roles but also raises the question of whether they are really needed at all.[34]

The duties of the assistant directors were eventually spelled out as follows: "Although the usual relationship of the Assistant Directors to the offices and divisions of the Bureau is staff rather than line, the Director keeps open the possibility of assigning line responsibilities to the Assistant Directors in well-defined areas from time to time." Assistant Director John Beckett gave staff guidance to OMO and accounting.[35] While he was an assistant director Robert Merriam served as a political adviser to the director and served as the administration's spokesman on Capitol Hill. Merriam served briefly as deputy director before joining the White House staff in 1958.[36]

With the budget out of control and Republicans believing that the free spending record of the Democrats had to be reversed, Dodge could not exempt his budget bureau from his drive to lower the federal budget. He did not believe the bureau had too many people, but reductions had to be made to set an example. Dodge finally decided that the least damaging action he could take was to eliminate the budget bureau's field service. Staats urged him not to take hasty action because, he believed, rather than eliminate the field service, it should be strengthened. Dodge waited another six months to abolish the offices, and then did so reluctantly. This economy move resulted in a saving of over $200,000.[37]

Elmer Staats considered Dodge an able, broad-gauged person. When asked how he would pick a budget director if he had that responsibility, Staats, who worked for many of them, said "I'd be looking primarily for a person who can work easily with the president. That's the primary consideration. If you don't have the president's confidence, if you don't have his ear, the word gets around fast and you can't be effective."[38] Dodge passed this test for he was very close to Eisenhower. Shanley thought Dodge one of the finest men he had ever known. "He was the type of man that was very good for the Bureau, and defended the Bureau, worked for them and guarded them, and I think, gave them a good deal of policy."[39]

After a year on the job Dodge felt he had to return to his bank in Detroit. He also believed that many of the actions he had taken to get the budget under control had made him unpopular. He believed "there would be advantages for the President in having a change in this post." He told Adams that the prestige Eisenhower had conferred on him as director of the budget should make it easier to obtain a suitable replacement.[40] After Dodge left the bureau Eisenhower continued to call on him for various assignments. Dodge was one of the "Seven Wise Men" that the president brought in periodically to meet with the NSC.[41] As we have seen Eisenhower also asked Dodge to come back later in 1954 to study the problem of coordinating foreign economic policy. It was Dodge who recommended the establishment of the CFEP and then headed the council as a member of the White House staff for a time.[42]

ROLAND HUGHES AND PERCIVAL BRUNDAGE

When he resigned as budget director after only about a year, Dodge cautioned that his successor "should be expected to serve a long term. This, I am convinced, is essential to the President's best interests. There should be no parade of relatively short term Budget Directors. The work requires more knowledge of government than anyone without prior experience can acquire in a short time."[43] The advice was not followed and there was a "parade" of directors who served for an average of two years each. With the departure of Dodge,

Eisenhower also began the practice of promoting the deputy director to director that continued throughout the remainder of the administration.

Dodge's deputy was Roland Hughes who was appointed in April 1953. At
that time he was a vice president of the National City Bank of New York where
he specialized in taxation, fiscal, and related subjects. He had worked with
members of the Republican 80th Congress and was well known to its leaders,
Senators Taft, Styles Bridges and Irving Ives, as well as the current chairman of
the House Ways and Means Committee, John Taber.[44] Eisenhower named him
director shortly after Dodge's departure in April 1954.

Hughes's relatively short two-year tenure as director of the bureau was not a
happy time for anyone. His background as an accountant had apparently not
prepared him to lead the many-faceted budget bureau. Staats considered him a
"disaster" because "He did not have the comprehension of what the problems
were or what the programs were."[45] Shortly before Hughes departed, one of his
division chiefs said that the budget bureau needed

a new sense of direction. By this I mean it needs a redefinition of its objectives in the
broadest terms. It needs to know what the Director thinks is important for the Bureau
to do, to what aspects of the total Bureau job the Director attaches the greatest significance, and his concept of relative agency and Bureau responsibilities in the areas where
the Bureau functions. This could provide supervisors in the Bureau with a fresh frame
of reference approved by the top management within which they could guide Bureau
operations.[46]

In January 1956 Hughes went to see Eisenhower to tell him he had decided
to resign. The president accepted the resignation reluctantly because, as he recorded in his diary,

I will miss Hughes, who has been a very hardworking and efficient public servant.
Strangely enough, he does not give the normal reason for wanting to leave. He merely
states that ever since coming down here in 1953 he has not missed a day of duty, and he
is tired to the bone. Since in the budget post it is impossible to take an extended leave,
he sees no alternative but to resign. Moreover, he has a very bad eye, which demands
continuous treatment, and he says he has had to neglect it.[47]

Eisenhower's comments indicate he was out of touch with the personnel in the
budget bureau who, of course, did not consider Hughes an "efficient public
servant."

On 2 April 1956 Hughes was replaced by his deputy, Percival F. Brundage,
whom Eisenhower considered "an extremely able man." One reason he appointed him was to "prevent any major break in policy or method" from the
Hughes years.[48] Staats, on the other hand, regarded Brundage, who had been

head of the Price, Waterhouse accounting firm, as "a fairly narrow-gauged rail-road."[49]

Shortly after Brundage took over he was given the results of a survey of the bureau's operations conducted by Percy Rappaport. The survey had been done to consider whether changes should be made that would improve the bureau's existing organization, practices, and procedures. Rappaport's report consisted of twenty-nine recommendations. One of them called for finding better ways to convey to the staff "the Director's point of view, in terms of policy guidance, work priority, and specific instructions."[50] Brundage's response was rather innocuous.[51] He continued as director for two more years, departing on 17 March 1958.

In 1960 Professor Richard E. Neustadt gave a paper at the annual meeting of the American Political Science Association entitled "Reorganizing the Presidency." In it he said that the budget bureau during the Eisenhower years, after the departure of Dodge, "suffered from a quaint White House conception of its functions, symbolized by CPA's in the Directorship. With at least two of Eisenhower's Budget Directors, limits of personality compounded damage done by limits of profession and experience."[52] Clearly the two directors he referred to were Hughes and Brundage. Neustadt had served in the budget bureau while he was writing his dissertation and then moved over to Truman's White House staff. Since he later served as one of the architects of Kennedy's executive office, he was not a totally objective observer, but many agreed with his evaluation of the performance of Hughes and Brundage.

Robert Merriam, who worked in the bureau during this period and whose father had been a member of the Brownlow committee, considered Hughes and Brundage unhappy choices who were "absolutely politically unsophisticated and insensitive." He thought that Eisenhower's selection of accountants as budget director showed that he saw the bureau strictly as a financial control device and demonstrated that he did not understand the role of the budget director.[53] Eisenhower had first encountered the budget bureau when he served on General Douglas MacArthur's staff during the 1930s. In those days the bureau role *was* limited to financial control. Perhaps he never lost this view of the bureau's function.

MAURICE H. STANS

The last of the CPAs to serve as budget director under Eisenhower was Maurice H. Stans, who followed the usual path by serving for a year as the deputy to his predecessor. But Stans was different because he arrived at the bureau after serving four years in the management of the Post Office Department, so he already knew his way around the federal government. Merriam, who served briefly as Stans's deputy, thought he had a much broader perspective than Hughes or Brundage.[54] A senior bureau official thought the appointment of Stans was "like opening up all the curtains in the building and letting the sun shine in. There was confidence, there was leadership, everything turned around. . . . I used to think that if Kennedy found a strong Budget Bureau when he arrived it was because of what Stans did to put it back on its feet after four awful years."[55] Stans went on to become Richard Nixon's commerce secretary and fund raiser.

Two careerists followed Merriam as Stans's deputy. In 1959 Roger Jones, after serving as deputy director for six months, was appointed chairman of the Civil Service Commission by Eisenhower.[56] He was succeeded by Elmer Staats who moved over from the OCB. Amazingly, Staats had the unique opportunity of being named deputy director of the budget bureau (a political appointment) under four successive presidents: Truman, Eisenhower, Kennedy, and Johnson.[57] Congress chose him to head the General Accounting Office in 1965.

In 1959 the bureau engaged in a major self-study of its operations. The study, initiated on 2 February, was undertaken by a group with an aggregate of 246 years of experience in the bureau. To meet its deadline of 1 May the group frequently had to work from 7:00 A.M. to midnight.[58] Although in retrospect, and in comparison with Hughes and Brundage, Stans was considered a competent budget director, one of the major findings of the self-study was that "practically every official in the Bureau did not think it was being effectively managed, particularly in the flow of communications and the control of work priorities." Another finding was "that the roles of the three assistant directors are not clearly understood by them, by the Office and Division Chiefs, nor by the Director."[59]

While one of Stans's division chiefs agreed that usually the role of the assistant directors was "anomalous and confusing," he told Stans that

the worst thing we could do would be to cut the assistant directors off from the operating areas. This would leave them orbiting decoratively but uselessly in a no-man's land. They could not contribute to the day's battles, and whatever authority they possessed would be canceled out by their lack of practical knowledge, which is acquired by getting one's hands dirty.

He assured Stans that "regardless of how the boxes look on the chart, each new Director will run the establishment the way he chooses, and the troops will adjust to his habits."[60]

Stans ordered OMO to carry out those recommendations of the study group that involved:

(a) broad management problems cutting across a number of agencies, (b) problems which the divisions are not equipped to handle, (c) leadership in developing management improvement efforts in all the agencies, and (d) counsel and assistance to divisions in their work of identifying and resolving management needs in agencies assigned to them.

He promised to seek the additional manpower resources that carrying out these reforms required. However, he told the study group that he had decided "not to change the organization of his own office, including that of the assistant directors."[61]

More than a year earlier Stans had realized that the bureau was in some difficulty because of lack of confidence in Hughes and Brundage and that the president was disappointed in its performance. At a White House meeting he suggested some ways that the bureau could be strengthened to handle matters better. These included: (1) appointing an executive assistant to the director to route and handle papers; (2) collecting in one place all the ideas on how money could be saved; (3) taking the assistant directors out of the line and making them staff; and (4) getting a project list from every office as to organizational steps that could be taken to improve bureau management. He hoped that if the White House could develop more confidence in the bureau it in turn would tackle jobs more aggressively.[62] These, of course, were not earth-shaking ideas but they indicated the kind of dissatisfaction that led to the 1959 self-study.

There is no doubt that Eisenhower was dissatisfied with the performance of his budget bureau. In his presidential memoirs he described his understanding of the role of the bureau. It was to see to "the development and execution, under presidential supervision, of the detailed expenditure programs for the coming year, to certain matters of government organization, to review of departmental legislative proposals before they reach the president's desk, and the supervision of some of the statistical services." He added cryptically, "Obviously there is much more to business management than this."[63] As we will see in the next chapter he sought to obtain these broader services by reorganization rather than encouraging the bureau to perform the additional functions.

The problems that surfaced in the bureau by the end of the Eisenhower years had several causes. One was the fact that the president tended to view the budget bureau essentially as a fiscal control agent rather than the many-faceted organization it had become during the early Truman period. Another was a decline in manpower resources that, in turn, was partly due to Eisenhower's focus on reducing the budget. In order to enforce this stringency, the bureau felt it had to set an example by reducing its own staff. Richard Neustadt observed that, as a result, there was

a widening gap in the presidential staff resources left by the Budget Bureau's failure to live up to the high hopes of two decades ago. For fifteen years the Bureau has been suffering a cumulative drain of talent, energy, elan. . . . And for three years the Bureau has been suffering, besides, from the strain of conducting economy drives too strong for the stomach even of its own professional staff.[64]

NOTES

1. Percy Rappaport to Director, 16 April 1956, Series 52.2, B1–13, RG 51, NA.

2. BOB Study Group Major Findings, 1959, Series 52.2, B1–13/2, RG 51, NA.

3. Percival Brundage lecture to War College, 9 December 1957, Series 52.2, B1–3/1, RG 51, NA.

4. William D. Carey to Rappaport, 9 February 1956, Series 52.2, B1–13/1 RG 51, NA.

5. Ibid.

6. Roger Jones Oral History, DDEL.

7. Brundage lecture to the War College, 9 December 1957, Series 52.2, B1–3/1, RG 51, NA.

8. Legislative Coordination, 31 March 1959, Series 52.2, B1–13/2, RG 51, NA.

9. OMO Discussion Notes, 20 February 1959, Series 52.2, B1–13/2, RG 51, NA.

10. "The Bureau of the Budget: Its Background," Series 52.2, B2–1, RG 51, NA.

11. R. M. Macy to Rappaport, 6 February 1956, Series 52.2, B1–13/1, RG 51, NA.

12. William D. Carey to Rappaport, 9 February 1956, Series 52.2, B1–13/1, RG 51, NA.

13. Ibid.

14. Robert Merriam Oral History, DDEL.

15. Jones Oral History, DDEL.

16. Appendix C, 1952, Series 52.6, E2–50/52.1, RG 51, NA.

17. Appendix C, PSB, Series 52.6, E2–50/52.1, RG 51, NA.

18. Edward B. Strait to Files, 30 October 1952, ibid.

19. "Federal Organization and Management Problems," 14 November 1952, Series 52.6, E2–24/52.1, RG 51, NA.

20. Macy to Rappaport, 6 February 1956, Series 52.2, B1–13/1, RG 51, NA.

21. Carl M. Brauer, *Presidential Transitions: Eisenhower through Reagan* (New York, 1986), p. 17.

22. Joseph Dodge to Sherman Adams, 18 January 1954, DDE Diary, January 54(2), DDE Diary Series, DDEL.

23. Brauer, *Presidential Transitions*, p. 17.

24. Dodge to Adams, 22 December 1952, BOB 1952, OF-72–B, DDEL.

25. Elmer Staats Interview, 10 September 1979.

26. Sam R. Broadbent to Director, 15 June 1959, Series 52.2, B1–13/2, RG 51, NA.

27. BOB Study Group Major Findings, ibid.

28. Jones to Rappaport, 9 February 1956, Series 52.2, B1–13/1, RG 51, NA.

29. Dodge to Adams, 26 May 1953, BOB May 53, OF 72–B, DDEL.

30. Dodge to Young, 17 February 1854, BOB February 54, ibid.

31. Office of the Director, Series 52.2, B1–13/2, RG 51, NA.

32. White House Press Release, 1 May 1953, BOB May 53, OF 72–B, DDEL.

33. White House Press Release, 15 June 1953, BOB June 53, ibid.

34. OMO Discussion Notes, 20 February 1959, Series 52.2, B1–13/2, RG 51, NA.

35. Office Memorandum No. 60–35, 31 March 1960, Series 52.2, B2–1, RG 51, NA.

36. Merriam Oral History, DDEL.

37. Internal Organization and Management, 30 April 1953, Series 52.2, B2–1, RG 51, NA; Maurice Stans to Gale McGee, 26 July 1960, Series 52.2, B1–1, RG 51, NA.

38. Staats Interview, 10 September 1979.

39. Barnard Shanley Oral History, DDEL.

40. Dodge to Adams, 18 January 1954, DDE Diary January 54(2), DDE Diary Series, DDEL.

41. Dillon Anderson Oral History, DDEL.

42. See chapter 1, pp. 30–31, this work.

43. Dodge to Adams, 18 January 1954.

44. Dodge to DDE, 7 April 1953, BOB August 53, OF 72–B, DDEL.

45. Staats Interview, 10 September 1979.

46. William F. McCandless to Rappaport, 2 March 1956, Series 52.2, B1–13/1, RG 51, NA.

47. Robert H. Ferrell, ed., *The Eisenhower Diaries* (New York, 1981), pp. 308–309.

48. Ibid.

49. Staats Interview, 10 September 1979.

50. Rappaport to Brundage, 16 April 1956, Series 52.2, B1–13/1, RG 51, NA.

51. Director to Rappaport, 25 April 1956, ibid.

52. Strait to Arthur Flemming, 30 September 1960, PACGO(1), Merriam Records, DDEL.

53. Merriam Oral History, DDEL.

54. Ibid.

55. Quoted in Larry Berman, *The Office of Management and Budget and the Presidency, 1921–1979* (Princeton, 1979), p. 55.

56. Jones Oral History, DDEL.

57. Staats Interview, 10 September 1979.

58. Larry Berman, "The Office of Management and Budget That Almost Wasn't," *Political Science Quarterly* 92 (1977): 288.

59. BOB Study Group Major Findings, Series 52.2, B1–13/1, RG 51, NA.

60. W. D. Carey to Director, 21 May 1959, Series 52.2, B1–13/2, RG 51, NA.

61. Director to Study Group, 29 September 1959, ibid.

62. White House Meeting, 21 April 1958, Rockefeller Committee (5), WHO, Staff Secretary, DDEL.

63. Dwight D. Eisenhower, *The White House Years: Waging Peace, 1956–1961* (Garden City, N.Y., 1965), p. 635.

64. Edward B. Strait to Arthur Flemming, 30 September 1960, PAGO (1), Merriam Records, DDEL.

9

Failed Plans

The idea that the president should have a second vice president for administration to help him govern the country began to be an issue in 1955 when ex-President Herbert Hoover casually threw out the suggestion. Senator John F. Kennedy, ever on the alert for an opportunity to embarrass the Republicans, decided to have the subcommittee he headed hold hearings on Hoover's proposal. To establish his party's position, the senator asked Harry Truman to comment on Hoover's proposal. Truman liked Hoover, but he was a Democrat first. He responded:

I have always been of the opinion that the Chief Executive of this great Government of ours is the responsible head of the Government and that it is not possible for him to delegate any of the functions of his office as they are set out in the Constitution. . . . The suggestions made about an executive vice president would require, in my opinion, an amendment to the Constitution of the United States. I hope that your committee will go into this situation very thoroughly, and I want to say to you that if I had the final say on the subject, the powers and functions of the Presidency would in no way be limited beyond the restrictions set out in the Constitution.[1]

Kennedy also asked the administration for its views. Robert Merriam, who was then an assistant director of the Bureau of the Budget, was sent down to Capitol Hill to state the administration's position. Because of Hoover's status as an elder statesman of the party, Merriam had the problem of opposing the idea without saying so. He may not have been convincing, but the next witness, John Steelman, once the dean of Truman's White House staff, delivered the message clearly for him.[2]

President Eisenhower began to consider the possibility of two additional vice presidents during the spring of 1956. In a very general discussion he asked Sherman Adams to think about the possibility of "having two people, one for the domestic field, the other for foreign" to assist him. However he worried that their mere existence would lessen the president's control, and he clearly wanted to be able to get rid of them if he wanted to, but on balance he thought it would be a distinct improvement. Eisenhower indicated that he would want to have Foster Dulles as vice president for foreign affairs and name Adams to coordinate the administrative area. Adams said he thought it was a fine idea "provided they are under your control."[3]

When Eisenhower's ideas about two additional vice presidents became widely known in later years, many thought he was simply uninvolved in his job and wanted to delegate more of his work. Actually Eisenhower did not particularly want the arrangement for himself but thought it would be useful for future presidents. At this point, late in his first term, his hope was "to have the plan all ready, then bring it out about the third year of the second term (if elected)."[4]

After Eisenhower was reelected in 1956 he proceeded with this idea by asking PACGO to develop a proposal to provide for the two new assistant presidents. In the early stages of the discussion the name usually given the coordinator of foreign affairs was "First Secretary of the Cabinet." Hoover's suggestion of a title like "Administrative Vice President" was used to designate the person who would coordinate domestic matters.

The initial effort to look at the problems that might arise if the president's ideas were implemented was made by Don K. Price who was a well-known expert on presidential staff assistance. He was eventually appointed to replace Rockefeller on PACGO, but in 1957 he was still working as a consultant to the committee. Price was a onetime budget bureau employee who had served as Hoover's primary aide during the ex-president's study of the federal government. He was soon to become the longtime dean of Harvard's Graduate School of Public Administration which, in the next decade, became the Kennedy school. He agreed that international affairs and general administration were two subjects of special importance in the organization of the president's office because both cut across departmental lines and in both the president's special authority is recognized in the Constitution. Price recommended that basic information about the functions be developed before any plan was proposed.[5]

In his next effort Price developed questions in the form of an academic exercise on the proposed titles of the new positions.

(a) Would the rank and authority implied by such a title require a statute to establish it? If so, would the creation of such a position with its own statutory powers, apart from the constitutional authority of the Presidency, invite the Congress to set it up in explicit and rigid detail, and then seek to influence or control it? (b) Would objection be made (in case of a V.P. title) to duplicating a Constitutional title by a statutory one? (c) With either V.P. or "First Secretary" formula, would the implications of imitating the parliamentary system lead to criticism on grounds that this would reduce the Presidency to status of a constitutional monarch. . . . (d) Is it possible to set up and maintain offices with their own statutory power (as distinct from the power that is exercised as an offshoot of the President himself) above the level of the heads of the major Executive Departments, in view of the close ties between each Department and particular Congressional committees?

Price also raised questions about which agencies should report to the administrative vice president and whether his authority should be delegated by the president or conferred by statute. Although the material that Price prepared was not designed to argue for or against the president's proposal, Price recognized that it "reveals my prejudices without saying any more."[6] The fundamental nature of these questions demonstrated the complexity of the problem that Eisenhower had asked PACGO to solve.

Price's disenchantment with replacing the budget bureau with an administrative vice president was particularly obvious. One big advantage to keeping the budget bureau intact, in his view, was that its director did not have to face senatorial confirmation. Price feared that that waiver would not be continued in a law written to establish a new organization. He also believed that "a strong career stem is possible only in a large and important agency and the various administrative staff functions are all mutually reinforcing and can be more effectively administered together."[7]

THE FIRST SECRETARY

Milton Eisenhower apparently came up with the idea of a super secretary of state quite early and had shared his thoughts with Dwight. In August 1954 the president had a conference with C. D. Jackson, Sherman Adams, and Pete Carroll to try to find some way to replace Jackson, who had resigned. In a wide-ranging discussion they considered the problem of matching the communists in the world struggle. The president said

that the U.S. has always been lacking in an organism here in Washington to pull together, except only in the person of the President or someone very close to him all of the
considerations affecting world issues which are handled in several compartmentalized
departments of our government. He said that his brother had a solution—the State
Department ought to be raised to the dignity of a super-Cabinet, we ought to have
world economic, diplomatic affairs, political affairs and information affairs, and Secretary of State ought to have people under him of the rank of Secretary—then he would
have time to devote himself to thought, he could get a better grasp of what the thinking
of Kansas and the thinking of Iran would be. You are always riding a two horse team
that is not always pulling together. I believe that one good person is more valuable than
a large staff, has more authority.[8]

By January 1958 Eisenhower had outlined in a letter to C. D. Jackson his
concept of the First Secretary's duties. He "would coordinate the international
activities of all Departments; would not have the responsibility of Committee
testimony on the Hill; and would have time to 'think.' " He would also be designated by the president to attend international conferences in his place. When
Eisenhower saw Rockefeller on the 16th, he gave him permission to tell Dulles
about his plan to make him the first secretary. By the end of the month the
president had talked to Senator William Knowland, the minority leader, about
how much legislation would be required to establish the new position. Eisenhower also thought that Rockefeller or Jackson might write an article on the
idea to see what the public's reaction to it might be.[9]

Although initially cool to the idea of becoming the first secretary, Dulles, by
April, was agreeable to the plan and urging Eisenhower to sound out some
senators on the idea. Eisenhower was not ready to do this, however, and Sherman Adams also thought that it was premature. The chief of staff told PACGO
to get busy spelling out the details of the proposal and have it ready for the
president to review around 15 November in connection with the development
of a 1959 reorganization plan. Adams said that would allow consultation with
congressional leaders to take place between 15 November and 15 December.
Then, if their reaction was favorable, the president could include a reference to
the First Secretary idea in his State of the Union message.[10]

PACGO did not quite make this deadline, but on 6 December 1958, the
committee did send the president a formal proposal of why and how the position of "First Secretary of the Government" should be established and what his
duties and relationships would be. The document purported to be the work of
Foster Dulles, Maurice Stans, and PACGO. Their studies "made clear that
present Executive Branch organization is no longer adequate to support the
President in carrying the increasingly more complicated and heavy burden of

national security and foreign policy direction, forward planning and coordination."[11]

The organizational change they proposed was to establish by statute the new position in the Executive Office of the President of first secretary "with status and salary above that provided for heads of Executive Departments." This official's job would be to assist the president "in his over-all direction of national security and international affairs, and their integration with domestic policies and programs." To do this the National Security Act would need to be amended to enable the first secretary to become the executive chairman of the NSC. The president would then make him responsible for the coordination of the NSC Planning Board, the OCB, the Council on Foreign Economic Policy, the National Advisory Council on International Monetary and Financial Problems, and the Trade Policy Committee. It was further recommended that the first secretary "be provided such additional highly qualified staff as he may require."[12]

Most of the first secretary's duties were completely dependent on the president's discretion and thus subject to change by him at any time. PACGO worried about the necessity of going to Congress to get the position of executive chairman of the NSC established but there was no way around it because the council had been established by statute. They were concerned that Congress would be tempted to spell out the executive chairman's duties or call on him for testimony before its committees. PACGO urged the president to request Congress to leave the first secretary's role to be entirely defined by the chief executive.[13]

The document expressed the hope that the first secretary would have enough status so that the president could name him to represent the nation at international meetings of prime ministers and other heads of government. To assuage the feelings of the Cabinet the document emphasized that the new position "would not impinge upon or reduce the individual responsibilities of the Secretary of State, the Secretary of the Treasury, the Secretary of Defense and other heads of heads of departments and agencies with respect to whom he would assist the President in a coordinating capacity."[14]

THE OFFICE OF EXECUTIVE MANAGEMENT

The development of documents to establish the other deputy president followed a much more tortuous and contentious path marked by vicious infighting between some career people in the budget bureau and PACGO's staff. It was thus a contest between organizational management professionals.

As we have seen, the president asked PACGO to develop some proposals for the two new vice presidents soon after the 1956 election. Chairman Rockefeller responded on 10 January 1957 with a memo that sketched out for Eisenhower PACGO's idea for a new Office of Administration in the Executive Office. It would include functions such as budget, personnel management, legislative reference, organization and management, property management and reporting, and statistical management. Other possibilities for inclusion were government-wide planning for public works then being done in the White House by General Bragdon and perhaps an inspector general function. This list included all of the functions then being performed by the budget bureau plus a few more drawn from the White House and some not then being done anywhere. The memo concluded with an offer to study these options further if "this general idea impresses you as being worthy of early consideration."[15]

PACGO met with the president on that day and again on 26 March about ways to strengthen the general management of administrative matters in the executive branch. At the March meeting "the approach which seemed to be most promising was establishment of the position of Administrative Vice President to supervise this important study of administrative agencies and to serve in effect as the business manager of the government." In July PACGO suggested as a first step in a series of actions "the appointment of a Presidential assistant responsible for coordination among the offices of the Executive Office of the President of such planning and management activities as are assigned to him from time to time by the President or the Assistant to the President [Adams]."[16] By the next month PACGO had decided that the General Services Administration was too big to be transferred to the Executive Office but recommended that its head should report to the new presidential assistant it had recommended "with respect to policy matters requiring White House consideration or decision."[17]

Percival Brundage, the director of the budget, reacted negatively to this idea and said that in its present form it was not even suitable for discussion with the president.

Its proposals would increase still further the number of officials and units in the Executive Office—it would add (1) a new Presidential assistant for management; (2) a Bureau of Inspections, and (3) an Office of Planning, without any compensating reductions or consolidations elsewhere. I agree with the need to make provision for the inspection function and to improve arrangements for long-range planning. I do not believe, however, that we should continue an approach which has had the effect over the past 10 years or so of making of the Executive Office a collection of numerous separate offices and organizations posing ever-increasing problems of coordination and making it more and more difficult for the Executive Office to live up to the objective of "completed staff work" for the President. . . . With specific regard to the fields where the President needs assistance of a professional or administrative (as distinguished from a personal or political) character, I would urge that responsibilities be placed upon the institutionalized units of the Executive Office to the maximum extent possible, rather than upon individual staff members of the White House Office.[18]

That is: give the work to William Finan's Office of Management and Organization in the budget office and stop assigning the bureau's work to White House staffers. This memo was almost certainly drafted for Brundage by Finan.

In spite of Brundage's objection, PACGO, on 13 August, told Eisenhower he should appoint a new "Presidential Assistant for Management" rather than an "Administrative Vice President." The committee feared that the latter title would require legislation and considerably delay the establishment of the new position. Further, "any statutory prescription as to the duties might involve undesirable inflexibility and inadvertently might even result in some encroachment on Presidential powers." The duties PACGO would assign to this new cabinet-level presidential assistant included "long-range planning and such management functions as budget, personnel management, inspections, and the like as are delegated to him by the President." While the committee said that the opportunity for the heads of Executive Office units to confer with the president would not be lessened, it believed that the authority the new official would have to make decisions would make the personal involvement of the president unnecessary.[19]

A further recommendation in this memo was "that in view of the lack of adequate White House and Executive Office facilities for long-range planning," an Office of Planning be established in the Executive Office to work with the new presidential assistant. This office could "provide an organizational base for special planning staffs and study groups which you may establish from time to time." It was to this office that PACGO would assign the public works and aviation facilities planning then being done in the White House.[20]

To try to soften budget bureau opposition, Arthur Kimball, the head of PACGO's staff, told Finan that, while the committee had approved the above recommendations, it wanted to discuss the proposal with the budget director before proceeding further. To prepare the director for this discussion, which was to take place on 10 September, Finan gave him his analysis of the PACGO plan. He ridiculed PACGO's concept of a planning office. "Experts needed for planning studies," he said, "must come from the fields being studied, not from a group of 'expert planners.' We know of no professional group from which 'expert planners' could be recruited." And he insisted that an inspector general should not be subordinate to another officer but needs to have direct access to the president.[21]

Rather than propose amendments to PACGO's proposal, Finan suggested that Brundage tell them that their objections could be better realized by the following four steps:

1. Give Adams a new staff assistant to help him with agency management problems.
2. Set up an inspection staff along the lines recommended by both PACGO and the bureau.
3. Talk to Burns and Saulnier about using the Council of Economic Advisers as an Executive Office planning agency.
4. Strengthen the budget director's "already substantial capacity" in administrative management.[22]

When Brundage went to PACGO's meeting on 10 September he told them that his budget bureau was already trying to perform most of the management functions envisaged in the committee's proposal, "but due principally to the lack of funds and the congressional cutback in our budgetary requests, we have not been able to expand our activities as far as we and the President had planned." He thought the recommendation for another presidential assistant was the opposite direction from the real need, which was for consolidation. Brundage admitted that he was not at all satisfied with the bureau, the White House staff, and many parts of the government "but I do think we need an awful lot of study before we start out on a large reorganization."[23]

PACGO was not persuaded by this argument, so on 10 October it discussed its proposal with Eisenhower. As a first step PACGO suggested that the president appoint an "Assistant or Deputy Assistant to the President for Management" to work under the general coordination of Sherman Adams. His job would be to coordinate and stimulate long-range planning and management functions (budget, personnel, inspections, etc.) without assuming the operational direction of the EOP agencies involved. As a second step this official would (1) upgrade the bureau's management functions, (2) convert Siciliano's operation into a Bureau of Personnel Management (perhaps in 1958), (3) set up a bureau of inspections in the EOP, and (4) set up an Office of Planning in the EOP. PACGO concluded the discussion with the president by telling him of the budget director's opposition to the proposal.[24]

Brundage responded to this move by trying to involve Adams in the controversy and quoting from the executive order that had established the bureau in 1939 that he said clearly made it the president's staff in the field of management. He claimed that PACGO's recommendation would require

(1) a basic change in the long standing concept of Executive Office organization, (2) numerous amendments to existing laws, particularly those relating to the Budget Bureau, (3) the creation of a large new staff in the Executive Office with an accompanying reduction in the size of the Budget Bureau, and (4) amendments to numerous Executive Orders.[25]

Adams sent PACGO a copy of the Brundage memo on 25 November. Chairman Rockefeller, speaking for the committee, angrily retorted that their recommendation for a presidential assistant for management was an effort to compromise with the bureau. "You may recall that" what PACGO really wanted was a new Office of Administration and Management in the Executive Office that would absorb the bureau, Siciliano's and Bragdon's White House operations, and add a new inspector general function. Rockefeller claimed that the committee had been deterred from recommending this originally because it would require a reorganization plan and other legislation, but it now felt the climate was favorable to the full proposal. "If your estimate of the outlook for the next session of Congress coincides with ours," he said, "we would favor omitting the interim step which we proposed previously and instead would propose transmittal of a reorganization plan early next year to accomplish without delay the basic legislative changes which are needed." Rockefeller asked Adams for the authority to work with the bureau to draft the necessary reorganization plan and executive orders.[26]

Attached to this memo was an organization chart for the proposed "Office of Administration and Management." It was headed by a secretary with Cabinet rank and composed of the following units: Budget, Personnel, Planning Coordination, Legislative Reference, Management and Organization (to include and inspector general function), and Statistical and Reports Control.[27] A following memo spelled out a reorganization plan that would transfer the budget bureau to the new office along with all the authority now vested in the director of the budget. It would also transfer Siciliano's group to the new organization along with "such other White House and Executive Office administrative and management offices, personnel and facilities, as the President may determine from time to time."[28]

On 3 January Arthur Flemming discussed this memo with the president. Eisenhower accepted the proposal and ordered the preparation of a reorganization plan along the lines of the PACGO recommendation. The only change he wanted was to call the new organization the "Office of Administration and Budget." Adams then passed the PACGO memo to Brundage with a request that the bureau have the reorganization plan ready for transmission to Congress by 15 January. Brundage agreed to have a draft reorganization plan ready for an 8 January meeting with PACGO.[29]

Instead, Brundage came back on 8 January with a "rough" draft changing Executive Order 8248 that had set forth the functions of the budget bureau and the White House Office in 1939 together with a proposed executive order establishing an Office of Inspection. He said he had not responded to PACGO's proposed Department of Administration for two reasons. First,

the Director of the Bureau of the Budget is of Cabinet level but not a Member of the Cabinet, and as such has somewhat greater, as well as lesser responsibilities and position in the administration. As a member of the Cabinet, it would be more difficult for him to entertain appeals from decisions of the Budget staff and to have such appeals carried to you and to the President which would, of course, destroy the value of the changes you are proposing. Second, I would not favor having the appointment of the Budget Director confirmed by the Senate. This would remove the very important advantage of his being responsible directly to the President without outside obligations to anyone.[30]

Brundage thus refused an order from the president and failed to deliver a promised document because he did not agree with the premise behind PACGO's plan. It was an obvious case of the budget bureau stonewalling a proposal it found distasteful.

The memo was Brundage's final word in the controversy. He was succeeded by his deputy, Maurice Stans, on 18 March. Stans decided to accept the PACGO proposal. He did so because he thought it could enlarge and strengthen the budget bureau without interfering with the director's relationship with the president. He also liked the idea of including within the upgraded organization the personnel and organization functions then being performed within the White House. So far as the name was concerned he did not have strong feelings, but he thought the word management should be in its title. Whatever the reorganization, he was determined to resist the interposition of anyone between the head of the new organization and the president. PACGO agree that Stans would be the first director of the new organization. Although the budget director was now on board, William Finan continued to resist the idea with all his considerable skills.[31]

The PACGO proposal was now retitled "Office of the Executive Assistant to the President for Administration" and scheduled for discussion with the Cabinet on 18 April, and with the legislative leaders on 22 April. Anticipating no major problems arising from these meetings, Eisenhower planned to send a draft bill to Congress by the end of the month.[32] The game of cat and mouse began. The bureau career people, who still opposed the plan, got Stans to have Adams withdraw it from the Cabinet's agenda. When PACGO protested, Stans said that while he still favored the plan, he felt it would be better strategy "to go ahead and establish the new Executive Assistant position by executive order, withholding until next January any legislative proposal."[33]

Early in May Stans and his deputy Robert Merriam met with PACGO and worked out yet another draft bill to create an Office of Executive Management headed by a director. Following their agreement Finan was told to prepare three documents: a letter to the president to be signed jointly by PACGO and Stans, a draft bill, and a message to Congress requesting action on the bill. With these documents in hand, they planned to ask Adams to have the proposal discussed by the Cabinet and the congressional leaders.[34]

On 12 May there was a meeting between PACGO and Adams together with some of his White House staff who would be involved in the reorganization. Rockefeller told the group that Stans had come up with a plan to create an Office of Executive Management (OEM) that PACGO had adopted because it was similar to the one the committee had developed the previous December. The new organization would have five staff offices: state-federal relations, inspection and compliance, presidential reports, program coordination, and PACGO itself. The operating offices were to be Budget Administration, Legislative Reference, Organization and Management, and Personnel Management. The General Services Administration would report to the director of OEM but not be a part of the organization.[35] A few weeks after this meeting Finan had finished preparing the joint letter and had produced three versions of the draft bill. Rockefeller observed that a public relations effort on behalf of the bill was now badly needed.[36]

The OEM proposal was scheduled to be discussed by the Cabinet on 13 June, but again it was withdrawn from the agenda.[37] Stans and White House assistants Siciliano and Kestnbaum continued tinkering with the details of the proposal over the next two weeks and agreed to an interim shifting of resources between the White House and the bureau. Adams approved of these moves with the proviso that they were not in conflict with the proposed reorganization of the Executive Office.[38]

During the summer, while Sherman Adams fought demands for his resignation as White House chief of staff, Milton Eisenhower worked out a further modification of OEM. A member of PACGO's staff, Jerry Kieffer, then discussed these changes with William Finan and reported back to Dr. Eisenhower.

Bill [Finan] persists in the inconsistency so often practiced by the Budget staff; namely, that the Budget Bureau which is supposed to be a principal staff arm of the President really is not a part of his staff but exists separately and apart from him (thus safe from political retribution and restaffing after a change of Administration.) The facts are that we are creating the Office of Director for Executive Management at a level above present budget, management, personnel, etc. functions and we fully intend that the new Director should be able to handle White House level problems and Presidential delegations.

Kieffer felt that, although the problem of executive privilege that Finan raised about the new position was a real one, if Congress were to press the OEM director for documents or testimony, he could plead executive privilege at the president's direction just as any White House officer might.[39]

Sherman Adams was finally forced to resign in September while Rockefeller was elected governor of New York in November. Arthur Flemming was designated to replace Rockefeller as chairman of PACGO. Before Rockefeller resigned as chairman, he and the committee met with the president to consider the latest version of the OEM paper. It was a thorough presentation complete with organization charts. Eisenhower gave it his blessing even though Rockefeller cautioned him that "Budget Director Stans and Mr. Robert Merriam have asked that I make clear that they have a few reservations or questions with respect to the specific details." Before the presentation these officials had warned PACGO that there might be a legal problem in trying to abolish the bureau by the same reorganization plan that would transfer its functions to OEM.[40]

By year's end the *Washington Post* carried a report that an Office of Executive Management was to be established "under an official who would be a sort of Assistant President." When asked if this was true James Hagerty, Eisenhower's press secretary, admitted that the idea had been under study for some time but insisted that no final decision had been reached. Of course the president had already approved the plan several times, but these could be interpreted as tentative endorsements pending discussions with the cabinet and legislative leaders. When Hagerty was asked about the demise of the budget bureau he replied, "They haven't got that far."[41]

The OEM proposal had been placed on the agenda for the cabinet meeting of 12 December and was again withdrawn.[42] Finally, on 23 January 1959, Arthur Flemming, the acting chairman of PACGO gave the cabinet a full presentation of the plan to create an Office of Executive Management. When the original meeting was scheduled, the Cabinet members were given a copy of the proposal. One section of the paper that focused on the need for the OEM was prepared by Kimball. The balance was carefully drafted by Finan to keep it flexible "at points where I anticipate some slight modifications of the plan may be required for technical reasons and to gloss over some items on which, so far as I know, no final decision has been reached."[43]

One of the still disputed areas had to do with who would name the heads of the various activities within OEM. PACGO thought they should be presidential appointees while the reorganization message drafted by Finan gave that power to the director of OEM. Robert Merriam, who had moved over from deputy director of the bureau to the White House staff and had edited the whole document, agreed with the PACGO position but he did not change the draft because he did not want to call attention to the disagreement. PACGO thought this a betrayal of Siciliano who had been told that he would not lose prestige in the reorganization. The committee also feared that the commerce secretary, Lewis Strauss, might raise a question about the distinction between the staffs in the White House and the OEM. They thought it "much ado about nothing since all of these personnel work in the staff facilities of the Presidency." Finally the PACGO staff, from a public relations standpoint, believed "every effort should be made to avoid any connotation that this reorganization is intended to permit the President to slough off or relegate to some other official the management functions of the President. The danger of allowing this interpretation is very great."[44]

The Cabinet was told of the steps that were planned to establish OEM. In late January an executive order was to be issued which would: (a) establish OEM (except the functions then performed by the budget bureau); (b) transfer from the White House staff functions such as personnel management (Siciliano) and public works planning (Bragdon); (c) assign to OEM program coordination responsibilities; and (d) designate the budget director to serve also as Director for Executive Management. At about the same time a reorganization plan would be sent to Congress that would transfer to OEM the budget bureau's functions, director, funds, and personnel. After the reorganization plan went into effect, the plan called for legislation to be drafted which would provide: (a) Cabinet salary for the OEM director, (b) under secretary salary for his deputy, and (c) five statutory officials at the assistant secretary salary level (replacing three budget assistant directors).[45]

The Cabinet was also advised that Flemming planned to take up the OEM proposal with the legislative leaders on 27 January and that both the reorganization plan and its transmittal letter would be referred to the members of the Cabinet for comment before they were laid before the attorney general. One of the Cabinet members told Flemming that he and two or three of his colleagues were concerned that the proposed director of executive management might be interposed between them and the president.[46]

In the Oval Office after the Cabinet meeting, the agriculture secretary told the president that he was concerned that the budget director might become isolated from the president as a result of the OEM idea. The postmaster general told Eisenhower that he wanted the OEM duties to be more clearly defined. Eisenhower said they could not be spelled out in more detail, but he agreed to circulate the proposal to one more meeting of the Cabinet before sending it to Congress. By this time the first secretary plan had reached the stage where the State Department had discussed with PACGO drafts of the legislation that would be required to implement it. At this Oval Office meeting the president also decided that the First Secretary plan should be presented to the Cabinet.[47]

In a separate session following the Cabinet meeting, Finan and Roger Jones of the bureau met with Flemming and Price from PACGO. Flemming told the group that he thought the seven statutory officials planned for OEM should be filled by presidential appointment. Finan replied that he thought he had convinced Stans they should be filled by the director for executive management and that he believed he would be able to convince Flemming of that point of view. Flemming asked that the reorganization plan be as brief as possible and that the accompanying presidential message as well as Stans's testimony emphasize the modest character of the reorganization involved. Finan and Jones agreed.[48]

Arthur Flemming and Don Price thought it very important that the seven statutory officials of the proposed OEM be exempt from Senate confirmation. This was why it was planned to set these positions up by separate legislation since exempt positions could not be created via the reorganization plan procedure. Arthur Kimball, who headed the PACGO staff, tried to convince Milton Eisenhower (and through him the president) that this process was flawed.

Perhaps I an unduly pessimistic, but in reviewing the long history of this project [OEM], I am becoming more and more doubtful that the actions now contemplated will accomplish the major improvement in the organization of the President's staff facilities for business management which has been the goal of our committee. Frankly I fear we are being out-maneuvered by the Budget staff. They have been unsuccessful in their many attempts to block this project. However, because of procedural problems, they seem to be about to succeed in watering it down to where it will amount to little more than renaming the Budget Bureau. This may be the result if we continue to insist that OEM officials be exempt from Senate confirmation. . . . It is planned to rely on subsequent legislation to establish the new, high-level positions. However, you can guess the probability of success if legislation of this type is submitted about next May when the budget hassle may be at its peak on the Hill. On the other hand, if we accept Senate confirmation of the key OEM officials, the entire Committee proposal can be attempted at once by means of a reorganization plan. At Cabinet last Friday, your brother appeared unconcerned whether or not Senate confirmation is required. It is possible he is not fully aware of the basic values which hinge on this question of Senate confirmation.[49]

THE PLANS FAIL

Up until January 1959, the plan that President Eisenhower had in 1956 of preparing a proposal for two high-level assistants, "one for the domestic field, the other for foreign . . . all ready, then bring it out about the third year of the second term,"[50] seemed to be right on schedule. But he had anticipated that Sherman Adams would be his man for the domestic field and John Foster Dulles would take care of the foreign. Now Adams was gone, and in February Dulles took leave to enter the hospital. He died in May. These developments, together with the resistance of the budget bureau staff and questions raised by Cabinet members seemed to give Eisenhower pause. Ten months were to pass before he was to resurrect his plans.

The summer was a time for discussion and second thoughts. In respect to PACGO priorities Don Price suggested that the first secretary proposal and OEM be at the top of the list. He thought that the foreign affairs area was sure to be stirred up by the hearings Senator Henry Jackson had begun that focused on the NSC. In the OEM area he believed that

we may find it important to get as clear an agreement as possible on the theory of the President's Executive Office and staff machinery, especially with respect to (a) the delegation to it of actual decision-making power, and (b) its relationship to the Congress and the press. . . . What I fear about the "First Secretary" proposal is that you cannot simultaneously give a man full decision-making authority above the Cabinet level, and still pretend that he is merely a staff adviser to the President who should be granted by the Congress a status of immunity from direct accountability to Congressional committees. . . . I am eager for the President to have staff to whom he can delegate just as much as can be properly delegated without exposing that staff to the statutory and Congressional restrictions that would make it no longer staff at all, but another operating agency to be coordinated with the rest.[51]

Eisenhower again gave his attention to the reorganization proposals in November 1959. In a discussion with Robert Merriam, he said he was anxious to proceed with both the business manager and first secretary papers. He "reaffirmed his intention to discuss these two concepts with the Cabinet shortly after his return from the December trip. He indicated he would not make a final decision on sending these two proposals forward until after the cabinet meeting."[52] Merriam, serving as a political adviser, cautioned that since it was Rockefeller's committee that came up with the idea that the first secretary would head up the National Security Council, the pundits would say that this was an example of the New York governor trying to downgrade Nixon, his rival for the 1960 GOP nomination. Eisenhower replied, "I don't give a damn, I want to do it." Merriam did not like the first secretary idea, nor did the budget bureau, and most members of the White House staff thought it unworkable, but the president wanted it so Merriam polished it up as best he could.[53]

The plans were then sent to Herbert Brownell for a legal opinion. Brownell said that they appeared to be constitutional "but he had thought these proposals were to be recommended by the President after the November election." He believed that the proposal would "be criticized in Congress and elsewhere as an effort on the part of the Administration to gain power for Mr. Nixon—the Administration assuming that Mr. Nixon will be the next President." Nor did Brownell "think the Congress would enact the proposal at this session under any circumstances—because of the uncertainty as to who will be the next President." He said he would want to speak to the president before anything was sent to Congress.[54]

During January 1960 a draft message to Congress on the OEM proposal was prepared. PACGO decided that, even if the president decided to withhold the first secretary proposal until near the end of the administration, the OEM recommendation should go to this session of Congress. The committee considered three alternative draft bills for OEM, one of which would give up, for strategic reasons, presidential flexibility in organizing the office. Don Price and Arthur Kimball thought that if this were necessary they questioned whether it was worth sending the plan forward at all.[55]

In spite of these concerns, by the next month a draft message to Congress had been prepared that included both proposals. The draft first stated Eisenhower's rationale:

Having but one more year to serve the people of the United States as President, my concern runs to those who must in the future bear the responsibilities which go with this office. I believe that the overwhelming need is to make the Executive Office organization fully responsive to Presidential needs. I ask the cooperation of the Congress in the taking of steps promptly which will enable me to hand over to my successor the Office of the President in the strongest possible condition.

The message then presented the arguments for both the first secretary and OEM recommendations. For these reasons the president was asking for legislation

which will authorize the President to (a) transfer functions among the various units of the Executive Office of the President; (b) change the names of units and titles within the Executive Office; (c) make changes in the membership of statutory committees in the Executive Office; and (d) within the limits of existing law and available appropriations, establish new units and new offices in the Executive Office and fix the compensation of the statutory officers.

Given those powers, the draft then described how Eisenhower would use them to create the first secretary position and the Office of Executive Management.[56]

This was as close as Eisenhower came to recommending the proposals to Congress. On 21 March 1960 the *Wall Street Journal* reported that the president had decided against "sending Congress two major reorganization plans designed to lighten the overwhelming work burden of the Presidency." The *Journal* gave two reasons for the president's decision. One was that several Cabinet members and other high officials, "fearing their own authority might be weakened by the proposals, carried on a campaign against them behind the scenes and delayed agreement on the plans." Secondly, Eisenhower decided that, because of the delay, sending the proposals to Congress now might bring about a partisan, preelection debate that would obscure the true merits of the plans. He also doubted whether the Democratic Congress would approve the changes at this time.

So instead of submitting them to Congress, he'll spread his recommendations before the public after the November 8 balloting. He'll say that this is what he would have proposed in 1953 if he had known then as much about the Presidential workload as he knows in 1960. And Mr. Eisenhower will express the hope that his advocacy of the changes will help any future President who might want to make similar changes.[57]

During the summer Don Price put down his mature thoughts about the First Secretary concept and how it had developed in PACGO.

The original idea we were discussing several years ago called for a new officer whose attendance at meetings of prime ministers would be justified by the fact that on any agreement he might make he could deliver the goods, because he could give orders to the Secretary of Defense, Secretary of Agriculture, et al. The proposal is now radically different; the First Secretary is to have no line authority whatsoever, but is to be merely a staff officer, with the line responsibilities of the Department heads carefully safeguarded from his authority. This may be more realistic, in one sense; in another, it makes it much harder to justify giving him treatment internationally as a Prime Minister, and at home higher salary and rank than Department heads. There is, of course, an absolute logical dilemma here, if this new office is to be set up with great fanfare, whether or not by law, and whether or not with formal line authority, everything the man does will be tested to see whether he does, or does not, have authority to issue orders. The Department heads will be obliged, by their pride and the pressure of their subordinates, to make every issue a test case. If they win, the First Secretary will no more belong at a Prime Ministers' meeting than would Gordon Gray today; if they lose, the effect on the positions of the President and the Secretary of State will be unpredictable. This is why I favored a discreet and gradual build up of the Secretary of State into the desired position, leaving the ultimate issue ambiguous.[58]

Meanwhile Elmer Staats, back at his old post of deputy budget director, expressed deep reservations about the projected form of the OEM. He was particularly concerned about that part of the existing plan for the new office that separated management and organization from legislative reference. Staats's solution was to overhaul the whole Executive Office of the President. A key part of his plan was an Office of Administration that would include budgeting, organization and management, and legislative reference. He would also create an Office of Economic Policy to which he would assign the Council of Economic Advisers and the bureau's statistical standards unit. Three other offices in Staats's dream EOP would be devoted to Personnel Policy, Science Policy and National Security Affairs. Generally the budget bureau was relaxed about the OEM issue at this point because it was confident that PACGO was working on a "legacy" document for the next administration rather than a plan that would be implemented sometime during the remainder of the Eisenhower administration.[59]

During the spring and summer of 1960 many then serving and former members of the Eisenhower administration testified before Senator Henry M. Jackson's Subcommittee on National Policy Machinery. Governor Rockefeller used the occasion of his appearance on 1 July to recommend that Congress adopt the PACGO proposals. He urged the creation of the post of first secretary of the government to assist the president in the foreign affairs and national security area. He also recommended the creation of the Office of Executive Management to which would be transferred all of the functions of the budget bureau and some functions from the White House Office such as personnel management and public works planning. The next month Senator Jacob Javits (R-N.Y.) introduced S. 3911 to establish the first secretary position and the Government Operations Committee requested agency reaction to it.[60]

In September Professor Richard Neustadt gave a paper entitled "Reorganizing the Presidency" at the American Political Science Association's annual meeting. In it he was highly critical of the Rockefeller recommendations to establish a first secretary and an Office of Executive Management. This was in the midst of the presidential campaign of 1960, and Neustadt by implication was disparaging of Eisenhower's organizational arrangements in general. He said they would not work for Nixon or Kennedy who both seemed to be "aware that even if they wanted to they could not get away with playing Eisenhower in the White House. This is a role reserved for heroes, barred to politicians, in the present state of the Union and of politics."[61]

After Rockefeller made his recommendations, Milton Eisenhower seemed to be the only one in the administration still at work on the two proposals for high-level presidential assistants. He drafted a proposed presidential message

to be delivered in January 1961. He would have his brother say that he had accepted these ideas over a year ago but he had waited until now to propose them
because he considered them nonpolitical and he did not want them interjected
into the campaign. Milton's version of the first secretary would be an official
who would be a member of the NSC and direct the Planning Board, OCB, and
the Council on Foreign Economic Policy. These units would be brought together in an Office of National Security Affairs. This first secretary's duties
would *not* be prescribed by statute.[62] Long after the end of the Eisenhower administration, Milton Eisenhower thought the president should have two top
assistants.

Milton Eisenhower continued to develop his ideas. By 1980 his mature plan
was for an "Executive Vice President for Foreign Affairs" and an "Executive
Vice President for Domestic Affairs" provided that

both these Executive Vice Presidents should be appointed by the President subject to
Senate confirmation, serve at the pleasure of the President, and not be in the line of
Presidential succession. We would, in essence, have two prime ministers, one for foreign affairs and one for domestic affairs. Their powers could best be defined by Constitutional amendment.[63]

In his memoirs President Eisenhower described the OEM and first secretary
plans. He recalled that he had first begun discussing these ideas in 1955 and
"quickly learned that to obtain the adoption of the plan a great deal of educa-
tional work would have to be done, beginning with the Cabinet itself." He
did not go into detail on "all the baffling obstacles, legislative and otherwise,"
that prevented him from submitting these plans to Congress but he still believed, "firmly, that they could be helpful to the President." But having said
that, he realized that the organization and procedures around the president,
"save where they are rigidly fixed by law, should conform to each President's experience, desires, and methods of work."[64] This does not seem to explain why,
at one point, he seemed ready to ask Congress to establish these positions "by
law."

It is difficult to know how strongly Eisenhower really felt about the two
proposals. Andrew Goodpaster was as close to Eisenhower as anyone during
this period. He recalled that PACGO tried many approaches. The president
would think that their ideas were "great, but there would always be some question about relationships and they were reformulated and reformulated and it
never quite hardened into something." Eisenhower apparently did not believe
that the concepts were "salable" so he would always have another question.
Goodpaster thought that "that was his way" of dealing with the problem. On

the other hand, Ann Whitman, Eisenhower's private secretary, "never thought he was really serious about" the proposals.[65]

NOTES

1. Harry Truman to John Kennedy, January 1956?, No. 68, PACGO, DDEL.
2. Robert Merriam Oral History, DDEL.
3. ACW Diary, 19 March 1956, March 56 (2), Whitman Diary, DDEL.
4. Ibid.
5. "Don Price Tentative EOP Notes," 6 April 1957, Series 52.6, E2–50/57.2, RG 51, NA.
6. Don K. Price to Donna M., 21 April 1957, No. 69, PACGO, DDEL.
7. Ibid.
8. Conference Notes, 11 August 1954, August 54(3), Whitman Diary, DDEL.
9. Diary entries for 16 and 30 January 1958, January 58 (2), Whitman Diary, DDEL.
10. Arthur Kimball to PACGO, 23 June 1958, Rockefeller Committee (5), WHO, Staff Secretary, DDEL.
11. PACGO to the President, 6 December 1958, PACGO (2), Whitman Administrative Files, DDEL.
12. Ibid.
13. Ibid.
14. Ibid.
15. Nelson Rockefeller to President, 10 January 1957, Series 52.6, E2–50/57.2, RG 51, NA.
16. Arthur Flemming to the President, 2 July 1957, ibid.
17. Rockefeller to the President, 13 August 1957, No. 69, PACGO, DDEL.
18. Percival Brundage to Flemming, 25 July 1957, ibid.
19. Rockefeller to the President, 13 August 1957, ibid.
20. Ibid.
21. William Finan to Director, 6 September 1957, Series 52.6, E2–50/57.2, RG 51, NA.
22. Ibid.
23. Brundage to PACGO, 10 September 1957, No. 69, PACGO, DDEL.
24. Discussion Outline, 10 October, No. 69, PACGO, DDEL.
25. Brundage to Sherman Adams, 18 November 1957, Rockefeller Committee (3), WHO, Staff Secretary, DDEL.
26. Rockefeller to Adams, 24 December 1957, Series 52.6, E2–50/57.2, RG 51, NA.
27. Ibid.
28. Rockefeller to Adams, 3 January 1959, No. 69, PACGO, DDEL.
29. Kimball Memo for the Record, 3 January 1958, No. 69, PACGO, DDEL.
30. Brundage to Adams, 8 January 1958, No. 70, PACGO, DDEL.

31. Larry Berman, "The Office of Management and Budget That Almost Wasn't," *Political Science Quarterly* 92 (1977): 286.

32. Kimball to Rockefeller, 15 April 1958, No. 70, PACGO, DDEL.

33. Kimball to PACGO, 22 April 1958, ibid.

34. Maurice Stans to Roger Jones, 8 May 1958, Series 52.6, E2–50/57.2, RG 51, NA.

35. Kimball, Memo for the Record, 12 May 1958, ibid.

36. Notes from PACGO Meeting, 24 May 1958, ibid.

37. Kimball to Andrew Goodpaster, 13 June 1958, Rockefeller Committee(5), WHO, Staff Secretary, DDEL.

38. Staff Notes, 23 and 25 June 1958, Series 52.2, B2–5, RG 51, NA.

39. Jerry Kieffer to Milton Eisenhower, 1 October 1958, No. 71(2), PACGO, DDEL.

40. Rockefeller to the President, 6 December 1958, ibid.

41. Reorganization, 30 December 1958, No. 71(1), PACGO, DDEL.

42. Memo for Arthur Summerfield, 11 December 1958, ibid.

43. Finan to Jones, 22 January 1959, Series 52.6, E2–50/57.2, RG 51, NA.

44. Kieffer to the Secretary of PACGO, 22 January 1959, No. 71(1), PACGO, DDEL.

45. "Steps in Establishing OEM," EOP Organization-Management Act, WHO, Cabinet Secretary, DDEL.

46. Finan to Director, 23 January 1959, Series 52.6, E2–50/57.2, RG 51, NA.

47. Handwritten note, 1/23/59, No. 71(1), PACGO, DDEL; Kimball to Goodpaster, 13 January 1959, Rockefeller Committee (5), WHO, Staff Secretary, DDEL.

48. Finan to Director, 23 January 1959, Series 52.6, E2–50/57.2, RG 51, NA.

49. Kimball to Milton Eisenhower, 28 January 1959, No. 71(1), PACGO, DDEL.

50. ACW Diary, 19 March 1956, Mar 56(2), Whitman Diary, DDEL.

51. Price to Kimball, 15 August 1959, Administration No. 3, PACGO, DDEL.

52. Merriam Memo for the Record, 21 November 1959, Executive Office, Organization-Management Act, WHO, Cabinet Secretariat, DDEL.

53. Merriam Oral History, DDEL.

54. Roemer McPhee to Wilton Persons, 18 January 1960, 344 OEM, OF 342, NA.

55. Kimball to PACGO, 25 January 1960, PACGO, No. 72(1), DDEL.

56. Draft Message to Congress, 9 February 1960, No. 72(1), PACGO, DDEL.

57. *Wall Street Journal*, 21 March 1960, Series 52.6, E2–50/57.2, RG 51, NA.

58. Price to Flemming and Milton Eisenhower, 21 July 1960, PACGO(3), Merriam Records, DDEL.

59. William D. Carey to Tom Morris, 28 July 1960, Series 52.6, E2–50/57.2, RG 51, NA.

60. PACGO Memo, "Presidential Level Organization," 25 October 1960, Series 52.6, E2–50/57.2, RG 51, NA.

61. Edward B. Strait to Flemming, 30 September 1960, PACGO(1), Merriam Records, DDEL.

62. Kimball to Stans and Merriam, 5 July 1960, PACGO(2), ibid.

63. Bradley D. Nash, *Organizing and Staffing the Presidency* (New York, 1980), p. ix.

64. Dwight D. Eisenhower, *The White House Years: Waging Peace, 1956–1961* (Garden City, N.Y., 1965), pp. 635–638.

65. Joint Oral Interview, OH-508, DDEL.

Under Attack

Henry "Scoop" Jackson acquired his nickname while working as a newspaper boy. As an adult, he progressed from prosecutor to congressman by the age of twenty-eight. After twelve years as a representative he was elected to the upper house where, as an outspoken advocate of air power, he was sometimes called the senator from Boeing. Jackson focused his attention on defense policy and soon developed a reputation as an expert in the field. He frequently raised issues in foreign affairs as well as in defense. There was no doubt that he disagreed with the Eisenhower administration on many points in both areas.[1]

To promote his views and focus on his areas of disagreement with the administration, Jackson gave a speech at the National War College on 16 April 1959. In the speech, which was entitled "How Shall We Forge a Strategy for Survival?" he catalogued what he considered the deficiencies of the current policy. Although he conceded that Congress was aware only of "bits and pieces" of what was in NSC policy papers, he was convinced that Eisenhower's NSC mechanism "has not produced, and cannot produce as now operated, a coherent and purposeful national program which sets forth what the United States has to do to survive."[2]

THE JACKSON SUBCOMMITTEE

After this broadside directed at the administration's NSC mechanism, Jackson, in early June, introduced Senate Resolution 115 that proposed the establishment of a Senate subcommittee to investigate "The Formulation, Coordination, and Execution of an Integrated National Policy." This action prompted presidential assistants Gordon Gray and Karl Harr to prepare a memo suggesting what the administration's policy ought to be toward Jackson's move. They recommended that efforts be made to defeat the resolution, but since that was not likely to be successful, the executive branch should be prepared to cooperate, in a limited way, with the committee. The administration should be willing to provide full disclosure to Congress on the composition, organization, and procedures of the NSC, the Planning Board, and the OCB but should refuse to testify on substantive matters before those bodies. This position, they urged, should be made clear in advance. In regard to the OCB specifically, the memo recommended that Congress be told that it "was created by Executive Order; that it is a consultative body" which does not direct operations but achieves its coordinating and implementing function "by having as its members, officers at the Under Secretary level who have full authority to act in and for their respective departments."[3]

When Eisenhower learned of Jackson's effort to investigate the NSC he was furious because he thought it was really directed at him personally.[4] He called it an "unconscionable scramble for publicity." When he and Jerry Persons considered Gray's memo they decided that Persons would try to line up enough votes to stop the Senate from adopting Jackson's resolution. He planned to see Senators Styles Bridges and Richard Russell in this effort.[5] Bridges was then the dean of the Senate Republicans and Russell was chairman of the Armed Services Committee. Bobby Cutler was called in to help. He wrote a point-by-point refutation of the Jackson speech to the War College that, in May 1960, became the basis of his testimony when he appeared before the subcommittee.[6]

The president personally joined in the effort to prevent the passage of S. 115 by asking Majority Leader Lyndon Johnson to withhold further action on the resolution. To support his request, Eisenhower argued that foreign policy was traditionally a responsibility of the chief executive, and since the NSC was strictly advisory to him, Congress should not be involved in how he operated it. He claimed that if Jackson's subcommittee was set up it would inhibit future presidents from using the council and tend to constrict its deliberations. He wrote that he made this plea "only to highlight my conviction that this machinery was of great value in assisting a President in reaching decisions on the Nation's security policies."[7]

Despite the fact that Eisenhower was able to secure the support of both the chairmen of the influential foreign relations and armed services committees, the Senate approved S. 115. Senator Jackson was then named the chairman of the newly established Subcommittee on National Policy Machinery of the

Committee on Government Operations.[8] Bryce Harlow immediately worked out guidelines for the subcommittee's hearings with Jackson based on Gray's recommendations. The chairman promised his hearings would "be a study, not an investigation." He said he would protect security information and focus on "matters involving purposes, composition, organization and procedures."[9] The testimony of present and former officials who served on the NSC was to be taken first in executive session and not released to the press unless it was agreeable to both the subcommittee and the White House. One NSC official quipped that the Jackson study would thus be akin to *Hamlet* without the Prince of Denmark.[10]

The members of the subcommittee besides Jackson were Edmund Muskie (D-Me.), Hubert Humphrey (D-Minn.), Karl Mundt (R-S.D.), and Jacob Javits. The subcommittee had a small professional staff and some Jackson aides that included the future Speaker of the House, Thomas Foley. Richard Neustadt served as a special consultant.[11]

As the time neared for hearings to begin, Gordon Gray's great concern was that they would reveal the existence of the 5412 Group. This was the device that Eisenhower had set up within the NSC mechanism to oversee covert intelligence operations. Gray's strategy was to flood the subcommittee's staff with exhaustive details on the procedural routines of the NSC, the Planning Board, and the OCB to keep them busy. He had Lay, Robert Johnson, and Bromley Smith prepare a sixty-three page "Organizational History of the National Security Council" that was given to the subcommittee's staff on 30 June 1960. Gray himself prepared a paper on the NSC that he delivered at the annual meeting of the American Political Science Association in September 1960.[12]

The administration was clearly on the defensive as the subcommittee began to raise questions about the NSC procedures. In January 1960 it issued an interim report that raised the charge that "papers are still so compromised and general as not to furnish clear-cut guidance for action."[13] The budget bureau's Planning Board member responded:

Under the present Administration the NSC process has been explicitly designed to assure that divergent views, where they exist, are presented to the President and that resultant guidance is relevant and forthright. More than half the policy statements which are sent to the Council from the Planning Board contain split views, largely on important issues on which one or more of the NSC agencies have indicated a strong divergence of opinion.

At his press conference on 17 February 1960, the president said that he wanted every member of the NSC to be "just as free to express his opinion as a man can be" because "sharply defined issues are best debated if alternative courses of action are presented for discussion."[14]

THE HEARINGS

The subcommittee spent the remainder of 1959 assembling a staff, organizing the study and writing on interim report on the problem. Its public hearings, which began on 23 February 1960, inaugurated the first full-scale review of the NSC since the passage of the National Security Act in 1947. These hearings, which lasted until midsummer, were followed by a series of reports issued in late fall and over the course of the 1960–1961 winter. The reports covering such topics as the two vice presidents proposal, the NSC, and the secretary of state.[15] By the time his administration ended, Eisenhower realized that his NSC structure was "bound to be reviewed and reevaluated." And he was disillusioned. He told Gray that despite their best efforts "our people have not received an accurate and valid appreciation of the National Security Council's effectiveness."[16]

In the summer of 1961 the hearings resumed with testimony from Stans and Kennedy's first budget director, David Bell. They were followed by Don Price who addressed the problems of the Executive Office of the President. That fall there was a staff report on the Bureau of the Budget and a concluding statement by Jackson.[17] In 1962 the group was reconstituted as the Subcommittee on National Security Staffing, again under Jackson's chairmanship. It continued to exist under another name on into the Nixon administration.[18]

Those who testified frequently had their own agendas. We have seen that Rockefeller used the occasion to introduce the proposals PACGO had developed for the first secretary and the Office of Executive Management. Bobby Cutler's long statement described and defended the NSC-Planning Board-OCB edifice he had built. Stalwarts of the Truman administration—George Kennan, Paul Nitze, and Robert Lovett—were uniformly critical of the NSC process.[19]

The Jackson subcommittee was just one part of the Democratic attack on the NSC. Richard Neustadt accused it of producing "the lowest common denominators of agreement" rather than allowing the quarrels, including the issues and details, to be brought before the president. Dean Acheson described Eisenhower's NSC procedures as "agreement by exhaustion." The critics did such a good job of condemning the system that its reputation was blackened for twenty years until the documents in the Eisenhower Library showed how wrong they were. By then it was too late, for the criticism encouraged Kennedy to dismantle the system.[20] The Bay of Pigs was one of the results.

CONCLUSIONS

Eisenhower was the first presidential candidate to make an issue over how the Executive Office was organized and managed. It was a tactic that may have increased his margin of victory in 1952, and the lesson was not lost on the Democrats. In 1960 they used the Jackson subcommittee to focus public attention on how well (or poorly) Eisenhower had done with his Executive Office. He had come into office with a reputation as a skilled executive who had led the nation to victory. Since Nixon was perceived by many as a representative of the Eisenhower team, it would help the Democrats if they could tarnish the general's image as a manager. They were quite successful at this, and as often happens they began to believe their own party line. This was one of the reasons that Senator Jackson could claim that the staff reports his subcommittee issued served as planning documents for the organization of the Kennedy administration and even into the Johnson administration.[21] The experience was quite painful to Eisenhower because he believed he *was* an excellent manager who had overseen many significant improvements in the Executive Office. Although he abhorred the tactic, he could not complain too much because he had first introduced the issue of the organization of the presidency into politics.

Robert Lovett was a Wall Street investment banker and registered Republican who had been elevated to high office by Democrats. During the Truman administration he served as under secretary of state, deputy secretary of defense and finally, near the end, secretary of defense. He was the first to testify during the Jackson subcommittee public hearings, which began on 23 February 1960. Lovett demonstrated that his loyalty to Harry Truman and his own public image was greater than to his party affiliation. In the public hearing he responded to written questions about the organization and operation of the State and Defense Departments. By implication he seemed to criticize Eisenhower's efforts to reduce the defense budget when he said "that we are doing something short of our best." His strongest barb was directed at the budget bureau where "you frequently find authority without responsibility."[22]

In executive session Lovett was queried about the NSC. He was under secretary of state when the council was first organized so he was aware that initially it was an outgrowth of James Forrestal's effort to sabotage the unification of the war and navy departments. When that failed and Forrestal himself became the new secretary of defense, he attempted to use the NSC to take over direction of foreign affairs from the president. Truman, aware of Forrestal's intentions, resisted by attending few NSC meetings prior to the Korean War and designating the secretary of state as the presiding officer in his absence.[23] Despite these troubled origins, Lovett pictured the Truman NSC as an efficient mechanism whose

basic purpose was to provide a kind of Court of Domestic and Foreign Relations before which, with the President presiding, both departments could present their views, debate the points, be subjected to cross-examination, and so on. The purpose was to insure that he got first-hand a chance to evaluate an alternative course of action disclosed by the dissenting views, and that all implications in either course of action were explored before he was asked to take the heavy responsibility of the final decision.[24]

Contrast this with (Lovett's boss) George Marshall's description of Truman at NSC meetings: "The President came in, sat down, went out. He was not a leader, a force at the table to bring out discussion."[25] According to Elmer Staats, Truman "was not used to sitting down with a deliberative body and systematically going around the table for debate and statements of position."[26]

Lovett's reference to giving the president a first-hand choice to hear dissenting views gave oblique support to the charge that Eisenhower's Planning Board compromised issues before they reached the NSC so that the president merely ratified the consensus view.[27] We have seen, not only that this charge was false, but that the NSC of which Lovett was a part was characterized as an "organization which permitted log-rolling" so that Truman frequently got the "lowest common denominator of advice from the participating agencies."[28]

Eisenhower and his national security assistants tried to insure that the NSC mechanism provided the executive branch with comprehensive foreign policy guidance by considering, debating, and developing policy on a wide range of issues. Lovett believed that the fewer issues brought before the NSC the better. He claimed that as originally envisaged the NSC was intended to devote "whatever number of hours were necessary in order to exhaust a subject and not just exhaust the listeners." Both Lovett and Eisenhower agreed that too many people attended NSC meetings but Truman was no more successful than Eisenhower in discouraging that development.[29]

In conclusion it seems fair to say that Eisenhower took an Executive Office of the President that was largely in a shambles at the end of the Truman administration and turned it into a functioning organization. In 1953 the Council of Economic Advisers was on the road to elimination. Eisenhower reorganized it, listened to its advice, and used it with good effect. Early in his administration the National Security Resources Board was combined with the Office of Defense Mobilization and the mission of the new organization was redirected. Several years later it was combined with civil defense and served as the basis for today's Federal Emergency Management Agency. Of course Eisenhower also constructed an elaborate National Security mechanism that functioned well for him and, through the OCB, provided an effective mechanism to monitor the implementation of NSC policies. Withal he was able to keep the NSC from developing into the rogue institution it became under Reagan. Eisenhower's only EOP failure was in not utilizing the Bureau of the Budget to its fullest potential but even here he flirted with establishing, with the Office of Executive Management, an organization of some promise.

NOTES

1. John Prados, *Keepers of the Keys: A History of the National Security Council from Truman to Bush* (New York, 1991), p. 92.

2. Philip C. Henderson, *Managing the Presidency: The Eisenhower Legacy—From Kennedy to Reagan* (Boulder, Colo., 1963), pp. 124–125.

3. Gordon Gray to Wilton Persons, 11 June 1959, NSC, Merriam Records, DDEL.

4. Prados, *Keepers of the Keys*, p. 92.

5. Memo for the President, 12 June 59, Staff Notes June 1–15, 1959 (1), DDE Diary Series, DDEL.

6. Anna K. Nelson, "The Top of Policy Hill: President Eisenhower and the National Security Council." *Diplomatic History* 7 (Fall 1983): 320–321.

7. Dwight D.Eisenhower to Lyndon Johnson, 25 June 1959, Staff Notes 16–30 June 1959, DDE Diary Series, DDEL.

8. Anna K. Nelson, "National Security I: Inventing a Process (1945–1960)," in Hugh Heclo and Lester Salamon, eds., *The Illusion of Presidential Government* (Boulder, Colo., 1981), p. 253; Henderson, *Managing the President*, pp. 124–25.

9. Henry M. Jackson to DDE, 9 July 1959, 1959–1960(1), OF 72-F, NA.

10. Prados, *Keepers of the Keys*, p. 92; Nelson, "National Security I," p. 254.

11. Ibid.

12. Ibid.; Nelson, "Top of Policy Hill," p. 321.

13. Henry M. Jackson, ed., *The National Security Council: Jackson Subcommittee Papers on Policy-Making at the Presidential Level* (New York, 1966), p. 8.

14. Ralph Reid to Director of Budget, 24 February 1960, Series 52.1, M1-1, RG 51, NA.

15. Jackson, ed., *The National Security Council*, passim.

16. DDE draft letter, "Dear Gordon," Gray NSC(1), Whitman Administrative Files, DDEL.

17. Jackson, *The National Security Council*, passim.

18. Prados, *Keepers of the Keys*, pp. 94–95.

19. Nelson, "Top of Policy Hill, " pp. 320–321.

20. John P. Burke, *The Institutional Presidency* (Baltimore, 1992), p. 60.

21. Jackson, *The National Security Council*, p. xiii.

22. Ibid.

23. Alfred Dick Sander, *A Staff for the President: The Executive Office, 1921–1952* (Westport, Conn., 1980), pp. 210–244.

24. Jackson, *The National Security Council*, p. 94.

25. NSC Study, 19 February 1953, NSC Organization and Functions(3), WHO Clean Up, DDEL.

26. Francis Heller, *The Truman White House: The Administration of the Presidency, 1945–53* (Lawrence, Kans., 1980), p. 233.

27. Jackson, *The National Security Council*, p. 94.

28. Edward B. Strait to Files, 30 October 1952, Series 52,6, E2-50/52.1, RG 51, NA.

29. Jackson, *The National Security Council*, p. 95.

Bibliography

MANUSCRIPT COLLECTIONS

Arthur F. Burns Papers. Dwight D. Eisenhower Library, Abilene, Kansas.
Gordon Gray Papers. Dwight D. Eisenhower Library.
Neil J. Jacoby Papers. Dwight D. Eisenhower Library.
Harold D. Smith Papers, Harry S Truman Library, Independence, Missouri.

ORAL HISTORIES

Sherman Adams, Dwight D. Eisenhower Library.
Dillon Anderson, Dwight D. Eisenhower Library.
Karl Brandt, Columbia University Library, New York, New York.
Percival F. Brundage, Dwight D. Eisenhower Library.
Arthur F. Burns, Dwight D. Eisenhower Library.
Milton Eisenhower, Dwight D. Eisenhower Library.
Arthur S. Flemming, Dwight D. Eisenhower Library.
Andrew J. Goodpaster, Dwight D. Eisenhower Library.
Gordon Gray, Dwight D. Eisenhower Library.
Karl G. Harr, Jr., Dwight D. Eisenhower Library.
Gabriel Hauge, Columbia University Library, New York, New York.
Neil Jacoby, Dwight D. Eisenhower Library.
Joint Interview, Goodpaster, Whitman, Saulnier, Staats, Burns, Gray, Dwight D.
        Eisenhower Library.
Roger W. Jones, Dwight D. Eisenhower Library.

Arthur Kimball, Dwight D. Eisenhower Library.
Edwin Nourse, Harry S Truman Library.
Ralph W. E. Reid, Dwight D. Eisenhower Library.
Walter Salant, Harry S Truman Library.
Raymond J. Saulnier, Dwight D. Eisenhower Library.
Bernard M. Shanley, Dwight D. Eisenhower Library.

UNITED STATES GOVERNMENT PAPERS

Council of Economic Advisers Records, Dwight D. Eisenhower Library.
Council for Foreign Economic Policy, Randall Subseries, Dwight D. Eisenhower Library.
Dwight D. Eisenhower Papers, DDE Diary Series, Dwight D. Eisenhower Library.
Dwight D. Eisenhower Papers, Whitman Administrative Series, Dwight D. Eisenhower Library.
Dwight D. Eisenhower Papers, Ann Whitman Diary Series, Dwight D. Eisenhower Library.
Dwight D. Eisenhower Papers, Whitman Name Series, Dwight D. Eisenhower Library.
Dwight D. Eisenhower Records, Central Files, Official Files, Dwight D. Eisenhower Library.
Robert Merriam Records, Dwight D. Einsehower Library.
Gerald D. Morgan, Records, Dwight D. Eisenhower Library.
President's Advisory Committee on Government Organization, Dwight D. Eisenhower Library.
Records of the Bureau of the Budget, Record Group 51, National Archives.
White House Office, Cabinet Secretariat Records, Dwight D. Eisenhower Library.
White House Office, Executive Branch Liaison Records, Dwight D. Eisenhower Library.
White House Office, Office of the Special Assistant for National Security Affairs Records, Dwight D. Eisenhower Library.
White House Office, Office of the Staff Secretary Records, Dwight D. Eisenhower Library.
White House Office, Project "Clean Up" Records, Dwight D. Eisenhower Library.
White House Office, Staff Research Group Records, Dwight D. Eisenhower Library.

INTERVIEWS AND CORRESPONDENCE WITH AUTHOR

Don Paarlberg
Bromley K. Smith
Elmer B. Staats
Tom Wicker

BOOKS AND DISSERTATIONS

Ambrose, Stephen E. *Eisenhower: The President.* New York: Simon and Schuster, 1984.

Anderson, Patrick. *The Presidents' Men.* Garden City, N.Y.: Anchor Books, 1969.

Anderson, Wayne William. "President Eisenhower's White House Staff: Its Organization and Operation." Ph.D. diss., Georgetown University, 1974.

Berman, Larry. *The Office of Management and Budget and the Presidency, 1921–1979.* Princeton: Princeton University Press, 1979.

Bock, Joseph G. *The White House Staff and the National Security Assistant: Friendship and Friction at the Water's Edge.* Westport, Conn.: Greenwood Press, 1987.

Brauer, Carl M. *Presidential Transitions: Eisenhower through Reagan.* New York: Oxford University Press, 1986.

Burke, John P. *The Institutional Presidency.* Baltimore: Johns Hopkins University Press, 1992.

Cutler, Robert. *No Time for Rest.* Boston: Little, Brown, 1956.

Donovan, Robert J. *Confidential Secretary: Ann Whitman's 20 Years with Eisenhower and Rockefeller.* New York: E. P. Dutton, 1988.

Eisenhower, Dwight D. *The White House Years: Mandate for Change, 1953–56.* Garden City, N.Y.: Doubleday & Company, 1963.

———. *The White House Years: Waging Peace, 1956–1961.* Garden City, N.Y.: Doubleday & Company, 1965.

Ferrell, Robert H. ed. *The Eisenhower Diaries.* New York: W. W. Norton & Co., 1981.

Fesler, James. *The President Needs Help.* Lanham, Md.: University Press of America, 1988.

Flash, Edward. S., Jr. *Economic Advice and Presidential Leadership: The Council of Economic Advisers.* New York: Columbia University Press, 1965.

Greenstein, Fred I. *The Hidden Hand Presidency: Eisenhower as Leader.* New York: Basic Books, 1982.

Haldeman, H. R. *The Haldeman Diaries: Inside the Nixon White House.* New York: G. P. Putnam's Sons, 1994.

Heclo, Hugh, and Lester M. Salamon, eds. *The Illusion of Presidential Government.* Boulder, Colo.: Westview Press, 1981.

Heller, Francis, ed. *The Truman White House: The Administration of the Presidency, 1945–53.* Lawrence: Regents Press of Kansas, 1980.

Henderson, Philip G. *Managing the Presidency: The Eisenhower Legacy—From Kennedy to Reagan.* Boulder, Colo.: Westview Press, 1988.

Henry, Laurin L. *Presidential Transitions.* Washington, D.C.: The Brookings Institution, 1960.

Hess, Stephen. *Organizing the Presidency.* Washington, D.C.: The Brookings Institution, 1988.

Hoover, Herbert C. *General Management of the Executive Branch.* Part 2, *The Executive Office of the President.* Washington, D.C.: U.S. Government Printing Office, 1949.

Hoxie, R. Gordon, ed. *The White House: Organization and Operations.* New York: Center for the Study of the Presidency, 1971.

Jackson, Henry M., ed. *The National Security Council: Jackson Subcommittee Papers on Policy-Making at the Presidential Level.* New York: Frederick A. Praeger, 1965.

Johnson, Richard Tanner, *Managing the White House.* New York: Harper and Row, 1974.

Kissinger, Henry. *The White House Years.* Boston: Little, Brown and Company, 1979.

Nash, Bradley D. *Organizing and Staffing the Presidency.* New York: Center for the Study of the Presidency, 1980.

Neustadt, Richard E. *Presidential Power: The Politics of Leadership.* New York: John Wiley & Sons, 1960.

Pfiffner, James P. *The Strategic Presidency: Hitting the Ground Running.* Lawrence: University Press of Kansas, 1996.

Polenberg, Richard. *Reorganizing Roosevelt's Government: The Controversy Over Executive Reorganization, 1936–1939.* Cambridge: Harvard University Press, 1966.

Powell, Colin L. *My American Journey.* New York: Random House, 1995.

Prados, John. *Keepers of the Keys: A History of the National Security Council from Truman to Bush.* New York: Morrow, 1991.

Sander, Alfred Dick. *A Staff for the President: The Executive Office, 1921–1952.* Westport, Conn.: Greenwood Press, 1989.

Thompson, Kenneth W., ed. *Portraits of American Presidents.* Vol. 3, *The Eisenhower Presidency.* Lanham, Md.: University Press of America, 1984.

———. *The Virginia Papers and the Presidency: The White Burkett Miller Center Forums, 1979.* Washington: University Press of America, 1980.

Wicker, Tom. *One of Us: Richard Nixon and the American Dream.* New York: Random House, 1991.

ARTICLES AND PAPERS

Berman, Larry. "The Office of Management and Budget That Almost Wasn't." *Political Science Quarterly* 92 (1977).

Nelson, Anna K. "Before the National Security Adviser: Bid the NSC Matter?" SHAFR Conference, Washington D.C., 10 June 1988.

———. "The Top of the Policy Hill: President Eisenhower and the National Security Council." *Diplomatic History* 7 (fall 1983): 318–319.

Saulnier, Raymond J. "On Advising the President." *Presidential Studies Quarterly* 15, no. 3 (summer 1985).

Seligman, Lester G. "Presidential Leadership: The Inner Circle and Institutionalization." *The Journal of Politics* 18, no. 3 (August 1956).

Sloan, John W. "The Management and Decision-Making Style of President Eisenhower." *Presidential Studies Quarterly* 20, no. 2 (spring 1990).

Index

About the Author

ALFRED DICK SANDER is Professor Emeritus of History from Purdue University. A former analyst at the National Security Agency, he has served as department head and chief academic officer at Purdue, Calumet Campus. Among his earlier publications is *A Staff for the President: The Executive Office, 1921–1952* (Greenwood, 1989).